S0-FBB-969

Non-Monastic Buddhist in Pāli-Discourse

Religionswissenschaft

Herausgegeben Horst Bürkle, Manfred Hutter,
Johannes Laube (†) und Hans-Joachim Klimkeit (†)

Band 20

PL ACADEMIC RESEARCH

Sompornnuch Tansrisook

Non-Monastic Buddhist in Pāli-Discourse

Religious Experience and Religiosity in Relation to the Monastic Order

PL ACADEMIC RESEARCH

Bibliographic Information published by the Deutsche Nationalbibliothek
The Deutsche Nationalbibliothek lists this publication in the Deutsche Nationalbibliografie; detailed bibliographic data is available in the internet at http://dnb.d-nb.de.

Zugl.: Bonn, Univ., Diss., 2014

Library of Congress Cataloging-in-Publication Data
Sompornnuch Tansrisook, 1982-
Non-monastic Buddhist in Pali-discourse : religious experience and religiosity in relation to the monastic order / Sompornnuch Tansrisook.
pages cm – (Religionswissenschaft, ISSN 0931-122X ; Band 20)
Includes bibliographical references and index.
ISBN 978-3-631-65716-4 – ISBN (invalid) 978-3-653-05007-3 (ebook)
1. Buddhist laymen–Religious life. 2. Tipitaka. Suttapitaka. Dighanikaya–Criticism, interpretation, etc. 3. Tipitaka. Suttapitaka. Majjhimanikaya–Criticism, interpretation, etc. I. Title.
BQ5425.S66 2014
294.3'823–dc23

2014037898

D 5
ISSN 0931-122X
ISBN 978-3-631-65716-4 (Print)
E-ISBN 978-3-653-05007-3 (E-Book)
DOI 10.3726/ 978-3-653-05007-3
© Peter Lang GmbH
Internationaler Verlag der Wissenschaften
Frankfurt am Main 2014
All rights reserved.
PL Academic Research is an Imprint of Peter Lang GmbH.

Peter Lang – Frankfurt am Main · Bern · Bruxelles · New York · Oxford · Warszawa · Wien

All parts of this publication are protected by copyright. Any utilisation outside the strict limits of the copyright law, without the permission of the publisher, is forbidden and liable to prosecution. This applies in particular to reproductions, translations, microfilming, and storage and processing in electronic retrieval systems.

This publication has been peer reviewed.

www.peterlang.com

Table of Contents

Table of Figures IX

Preface XI

Chapter I: Introduction 1

1.1 Background of the Study 2
1.2 Purpose of the Study 12
1.3 Methodology 13
1.3.1 Philological Study of Pāli Discourse 14
1.3.2 Orality of the Pāli Text 15
1.3.3 Theory of Religious Experience 25
1.4 Definition of Key Terms 33
1.4.1 Laity; Non-Monastic Follower – *upāsaka/upāsikā* 33
1.4.2 Monk; Monastic Follower – *bhikkhu/bhikkhunī* 37
1.4.3 Monastic Order - *Saṅgha* 40
1.5 Other Regulations in the Study 42
1.5.1 Orthography 42
1.5.2 Reference to Pāli Canon 42
1.5.3 Reference to Stock Phrase 42
1.6 Outline of the Study 44

Chapter II: Discourse as Imagery of Buddha's Mission 47

2.1 Remarks on Pāli Discourse as Oral Literature 47
2.2 Overview of Discourse Structure 54
2.2.1 Reference to the Way the Sermon Received 55
2.2.2 Introductory Story 58
2.2.3 Message of the Discourse 63
2.2.4 Conclusion of Discourse 65
2.2.5 Conclusion 68
2.3 Expressions at the Conclusion of Discourse 70
2.3.1 Stock Phrase Denoting Hearer's Satisfaction 72
2.3.2 Stock Phrase Denoting Formal Declaration of Belief in Buddha 76
2.3.3 Stock Phrase Denoting a Spiritual Attainment 81
2.3.4 Conclusion 86
2.4 Summary 87

Chapter III: Development of Belief and Religious Experience in Pāli Discourse 89

3.1 At First Hearing the Buddha's Reputation and Seeing Him in Person 89
3.1.1 Buddha 90
3.1.1.1 Buddha's Spiritual Qualities 90
3.1.1.2 Signs of Great Man in Buddha 92
3.1.2 Monastic Follower as Representative of Buddha 96
3.1.3 Conclusion 97
3.2 After Hearing the Sermon 99
3.2.1 Compliment 99
3.2.1.1 Compliment on Ability to Debate 100
3.2.1.2 Compliment on the Meaning of the Teaching 102
3.2.1.3 Compliment on the Monastic Order 104
3.2.2 Apology 106
3.2.3 Conclusion 109
3.3 At the End: Levels of Belief in Buddhism in Reaction to Sermon 110
3.3.1 First Level: Dhammacakkhu Mentioned 111
3.3.2 Second Level: Understanding Described and Belief Declared 115
3.3.3 Third Level: Belief in the Buddha Undeclared 117
3.3.4 Fourth Level: No Expression of Belief 119
3.3.5 Case Studies of the Four Levels of Belief in Comparison 121
3.3.5.1 First Level 121
3.3.5.2 Second Level 122
3.3.5.3 Third Level 123
3.3.5.4 Fourth Level 124
3.3.6 Conclusion 125
3.4 First discussion 127
3.4.1 At First Hearing Reputation and Seeing in Person 130
3.4.2 At Hearing the Sermon 133
3.4.2.1 Development of Knowledge 134
3.4.2.2 Evaluation of Dhamma and Buddha 136
3.5 Summary 141

Chapter IV: Lay Religiosity in Relation to the Monastic Order 145

4.1 Conversion 145
4.1.1 Conversion as the Following Act of Evaluation 147
4.1.2 Conversion into Non-Monastic Follower 150
4.2 Expression of Reverence to Buddha 153
4.2.1 Verbal Expression 154
4.2.1.1 Upāli 155
4.2.1.2 King Pasenadi 159
4.2.2 Non-Verbal Expression 162
4.3 Religious Devotions 166
4.3.1 Donation 168
4.3.2 Religious Education 172
4.4 Second Discussion 177
4.4.1 The Three Jewels 178
4.4.1.1 Buddha 179
4.4.1.2 Dhamma 181
4.4.1.3 Sangha 182
4.4.2 Development of Wisdom on the Spiritual Path 187
4.5 Summary 191

Chapter V: Conclusion 195

5.1 Result of the Study 196
5.1.1 Lay Follower and Religious Experience 196
5.1.1.1 Result of Philological Study 197
5.1.1.2 Interpretation of the Meaning 198
5.1.2 Lay Follower as the Composite of Sangha 199
5.2 Suggestion 207
5.2.1 Methods in Studying Scripture 207
5.2.2 Inclusivism in Buddhism 209

Appendix I: Progressive Talk and Sermon for an Understanding of Doctrine 213

Appendix II: Progressive Talk and Sermon Leading to Reactions to Buddha 219

Appendix III: Code Number of Stock Phrases 223

Appendix IV: Religiosity of Non-Monastic
Follower in Pāli Discourse 225

Bibliography 227

1 Primary Sources 227
2 Secondary Sources 229

Indices 241

1 Pāli-Texts 241
2 Names of Scholars 241
3 Proper Names in Pāli-Discourse 242
4 Subject Index 243

Deutsche Zusammenfassung 245

1 Fragestellung, Methode und Gegenstand der Arbeit 245
2 Ergebnisse der Arbeit 247
  2.1 Ergebnis der philologischen Studie zu dem Pāli-Diskurs 247
  2.2 Entwicklung des Glaubens und Erfahrung 250
  2.3 Religiosität nach der Erfahrung in Bezug auf die
  Gemeinschaft 252

Table of Figures

Figure 1: Taves's Categorization of Religious Experience 27
Figure 2: Taves's Model of Religious Experience "Simple Ascription" 28
Figure 3: Taves's Model of Religious Experience "Composite Ascription" 28
Figure 4: Formation of Ascriptions in Making of Religion 29
Figure 5: Outline of Pāli Discourse in Dīgha-nikāya and Majjhima-nikāya 55
Figure 6: Table Showing Conclusion of Discourses in DN and MN 71
Figure 7: Sermon as the Thing Deemed Special 73
Figure 8: Model of Experience Deemed Religious in Declaration of the Belief 80
Figure 9: Belief in the First Level: Kūṭadanta - Brahmāyu 121
Figure 10: Belief in the Second Level: Soṇadaṇḍa - Jīvaka Kōmārabhacca 122
Figure 11: Belief in the Third Level: Bhagavagotta, Jāliya- Maṇḍiya 123
Figure 12: Belief in the Fourth Level: Sandaka - Nigrodha 124
Figure 13: Buddha Deemed Special in Hearsay 130
Figure 14: Development of Knowledge Traced from Stock Phrase Type I, II 136
Figure 15: Process of Belief in the Nikāya discourse 137
Figure 16: From Understanding of Dhamma to the Conversion 179
Figure 17: Acknowledgment and Non-acknowledgment after sermon 180
Figure 18: Understanding of Dhamma in Relation to the Three Jewels 181
Figure 19: From Hearing Sermon to Religiosity in Relation to the Order 183
Figure 20: Spiritual Path with and without Ānupubbikathā in Comparison 187
Figure 21: Learning and Practicing Dhamma after Conversion until Liberation 190
Figure 22: Taves's Theory and its Application to Pāli Discourse 196

Preface

This book is the publication of a doctoral dissertation in comparative religion (Vergleichende Religionswissenschaft), submitted to the Faculty of Philosophy, Rheinische Friedrich-Wilhelms-University at Bonn, Germany, in December 2013.

The book deals with the concept of upāsaka/upāsikā or the so-called "laity" in the Dīgha- and Majjhima-nikāya of Pāli canon. The question of the study is simple: what is the followership of the lay Buddhist according to the scripture? Responding to the question, different answers have been provided based on method, perspective, orientation, and even belief of the researchers. Nevertheless, the results are not satisfying because they do not offer the sense ("Sinn," in German), the meaning which constructs the followership, the direction of devotions leading to the spiritual goal. As the lay followers are the major composite of Buddhist community as well as the major population of Buddhist society, the basic concept is necessary to acquire for the foundation of studying and researching the people, their behaviour, their activity and organizations in relation to one another and other religious communities in a country, where Buddhism plays a role in the people.

The source of the study is Pāli canon, the religious scripture of so-called Theravada Buddhism, consisting of teaching and explanation composed, collected, and transmitted in the long tradition of Southern Buddhism, which centers are in Sri Lanka and mainland Southeast Asia. By the choice, not only because the scripture is rather an original and complete account of the Buddha's tradition, but also the tradition is rendered to the people until nowadays. The traditional concepts, socialized in the society of the old time, is survived to the modern society and state and significantly influential to the social and cultural dimension of the society and, still, to the thought of the major population. The basic concept of the Buddhist followership is therefore useful to understand the people in the present context in comparison to the ideal in the scripture, in order to see the tendency of existence, adaptation, and change in lifestyle that implies some factors behind. As researcher in Buddhism from Thailand, the author expects that the knowledge about the Buddhist followership of the lay people contribute to the basic understanding of the Thai and their society in some extent.

In working on the scripture, the author applies two thoughts to achieve the concepts communicated in the Nikāya discourses, which have been neglected in the European tradition of Buddhist philology. First, the author applies the knowledge about oral literature to understand the discourses when they are learned by heart and recited to hearers during the oral transmission. In this way, the discourses composed with mnemonic aids or stock phrases in certain patterns are read for the telling imagery of religiosity, not for sermon text, which people nowadays reckon to be the important message. Second, the author focuses on the cultivated relationship between the "religious" and the people who are contacting the religious as described in the discourse that inspires the trust and loyality in the religion, which is the deep foundation of the Buddhist followership. In this perspective, a theory of religious experience is applied to understand the relationship and its development in the individuals expressed in their behaviour and religiosity. In doing this, the author, feeling free in applying methods, considers the lettering of Pāli scripture an account of a Buddhist tradition conveying some information about the Buddha, his teaching, his followers, their activity within the community, their attitude about themselves and the others. In short, the work is thus engaged in deconstructing the text and understanding religiosity and community of the people systematically for the sense or the meaning behind the organization.

Consequently, there is no intention to touch upon other valid conclusions about history of Early Buddhism, which has been continually drawn from researching scriptures of various traditions since the nineteenth century, although the author remains sceptical about the thought and the method in dealing with the orality in the early scriptures, i.e., Suttavibhaṅga and Khandhaka of Vinaya as well as Nikāya discourse, and the historicity of the told stories. The author rather concentrates on the stories as the device for socialization, providing individuals in the tradition with the essential ideas to social and cultural continuity. Apart from the philosophical teaching, the forms of religiosity, the homage to the Three Jewels, the role of homiletics in winning the acceptance and followership, etc. are also learned and practiced by the people in the tradition. Nevertheless, the transformation of the literary tradition from oral to written, which happened to Pāli tradition in Ceylon during the first century, must more or less result in the understanding of the meanings transmitted in the alphabetical form. Commentarians, who were born to the written tradition, played a very important role in the traditional notion that the stock phrases should be the mnemonic aids that preserve the original words of the Buddha exclusively. The word Pali or Paḷi, which refers to the collection of Buddha's words, is understood as "row," the discipline preserving the teaching. In this perspective, it deserves an investigation of how the understanding of the scripture and the meaning in the originally oral scripture is affected as apparent in commentary literatures.

The author is grateful to Anandamahidol Foundation for the financial support of living and working on this topic in the country, in the research university, where students can enjoy freedom of thought and express the thought in their academic work. The author is also grateful to the supervisor, Prof. Dr. Dr. Manfred Hutter, Department of Comparative Religion, for the chance of working in the department, in which the author has learned a lot about studying religions for the creativity in researching Buddhist tradition, as well as, Prof. Dr. Konrad Klaus, Department of Indology, as the second reviewer for admitting the study in spite of not agreeing with some methodological approaches. At the end, the author appreciates the friendship from friends and acquaintances during living in Federal Republic of Germany: among others, Michael Schröders, Deborah Karl-Brandt, Saengdham Kuanard, Kunlaphak Kongsuvannakul, and the author's sister, Arunee Tansrisook.

Bonn 17.07.2014

Of those who have faith at its best,
Who comprehend best dhamma,
Of those who have faith in the Buddha,
Gift-worthy, unsurpassed:
Of those who have faith in dhamma,
Passionless, calming, blissful:
Of those who have faith in the Order,
The field of merit supreme:
Of those who give gifts of their best
The merit doth increase,
Best is their life and beauty,
Fame, good report, bliss, strength.
The sage who gives of his best,
In best of dhammas calmed
Deva-become or human,
Winning the best rejoiceth.

The Book of the Gradual Sayings Vol. II, pp. 39–40

Chapter I: Introduction

Upāsaka/upāsikā or "laity" is known as the person who worships Buddha, follows his teaching, and actively carries out religious activities in relation to Sangha, the monastic order found by the Buddha. As householder, not ordained for the full-time devotion to the spirituality, he forms the majority within the 'community' of Buddha's followers. He is the counterpart of the monastic follower in the community, playing subordinate roles, particularly the supporter.[1] His ideal and virtue as generally pursued aim at a good rebirth, happiness and luck, considered inferior to that of the monastic people, who follow the Buddha's path leading to Nibbāna.[2] In this way, he is considered as Buddha's follower "not in the proper sense."[3] This is the reflection from the notion that Buddhism is a *monastic religion* which exclusively encourages the renunciation for the foster of the liberation.[4] Recently, phenomena of the lay follower after the age of colonialism have shown another tendency: more Buddhist householders nowadays have played a leading role in movements, instruction, and interpretation of doctrine within their community. Not to neglect in favor of field studies on current situations, the study of the phenomena should call for a revision of the upāsaka/upāsikā as represented in the canon for the understanding about the followership in light of insider's perspective.[5]

---

1 Conze, Buddhism, p. 70.

2 Lamotte, History of Indian Buddhism, p. 67.

3 Conze, Buddhism, p. 53: "They (the monk) are the only Buddhists in proper sense of the word."

4 Gombrich, Theravada Buddhism, p. 24: "For Buddhists, religion is what is relevant to this quest for salvation, and nothing else."; Kieffer-Pülz, Die buddhistische Gemeinde, pp. 281–282: "The word 'Buddhist community,' which despite sometimes includes monk, nun, novices, and laity, specifically denotes merely the community of monk and nun."; Tworuschka, "Mönchtum," p. 147.: "Aus Indien stammenende Religionen, z.B. Buddhismus und Jainismus, sind typische Mönchsreligionen, da hier die Heilsgewinnung an das Mönchtum gebunden ist."

5 Wijayaratna, Buddhist Monastic Life, p. 164. Wijayaratna has the opinion that many scholars consider Buddhism an essentially monastic religion because the position of laity has not been sufficiently studied.

The author intends to use the word *non-monastic follower* or *lay follower* in place of *laity*, which is generally used in English or its derivative in a European language, to represent the word *upāsaka/upāsikā* in Pāli language. First, to distinguish the two kinds of Buddha's followers mentioned in the scripture, i.e. between those inside monastic order and those outside the monastic order. Second, to presuppose that the non-monastic follower is "Buddhist," Buddha's follower, *in some way*, although they do not join the order mentioned as the path to the Buddhist goal or Nibbāna. Hence, it is necessary to explore *the way* that makes the people the followership as established in the scripture. Third, the usage of the word avoids the connotation from the sense of the English word *laity* or its European derivatives from Christian culture that reinforces the image of the folks in the high religion attending and supporting the religious activities held by the religious specialist in a community. The followership in Pāli discourse might be unique in some way, and thus, should be handled without influences from other factors.

1.1 Background of the Study

Scholars tried to investigate the concept of *upāsaka/upāsikā* "non-monastic follower," from relation with Buddha and his order and religious goal in Pāli canon. The first scholar who challenged the widely held perception is Bimala Law in his article "Nirvana and Buddhist Laymen," published in 1933,[6] in which he found that the non-monastic follower may access the spiritual goal that bhikkhu/bhikkhunī accesses. In 1945, Nalinaksha Dutt published an article "Place of Laity in Buddhism,"[7] which remarked the spirituality of the people as manifested in the Pāli canon. He found that the lay follower are clearly discriminated from the monk and the nun, who are the members of monastic order that the Buddha has founded for his *official* followers, as ethical teachings in the canon are clearly prescriptive to the monastic people, not the people outside the order. In this way, the non-monastic follower should not be reckoned Buddha's followers in the

6 Law, Nirvana and Buddhist Laymen, pp. 80–86.

7 Dutt, Nalinaksha: Place of Laity in Buddhism, In: Indian Historical Quarterly 21, 1945; referred in: Samuels, View of Householder and Lay Disciples in Sutta Pitaka, p. 231.

sense of those who practically obey the teaching for the spiritual goal that the Buddha has given.

In 1994, Reginald Ray in his book "Buddhist Saints in India,"[8] studied in Buddhist scriptures the important persons that he, following Catholic tradition, called *Buddhist saints*. In the book, he placed the people in the "threefold" model that comprises "monastic" monk (or village monk) and forest monk. He found that the non-monastic people are involved in "*a complex web of interdependence*," in which the three groups of the Buddha's follower depend on one another: the Buddhist householder relies on both village and forest monks; monastic monk on the householder and forest monk; and forest monk on village monk.[9] The relation within the community is hierarchical in that the importance of forest monk is located at the top, the village monk in the middle, and the householder at the base of the complex web.[10] In this relation, the non-monastic gives material donations towards the monastic and receives some teachings as well as meditational instructions in return.[11]

The thesis on the position of non-monastic follower in Buddhist community was once more raised by D.C. Ahir in his book "The Status of Laity in Buddhism," published in 1996.[12] Ahir, neglecting the negative viewpoint on the non-renunciation in the Pāli canon mentioned in Dutt's article, presented the discipleship of the lay follower in relation to the Buddha and his community. In the book, he, raising the humanist principle in the Buddha's doctrine in Pāli canon, argued that the people are Buddha's disciples who have potential to develop spirituality to reach Nibbāna as well. In 1999, another consideration about non-monastic follower according to Pāli canon was made again by Jeffrey Samuels,[13] who pointed to both of the negative and positive aspects of the people, previously mentioned by Dutt and Ahir respectively. He noticed that the

---

8 Ray studied other scriptures apart from Pāli canon that represents Indian Buddhism.

9 Ibid., p. 437.

10 Ibid., p. 438.

11 Ibid., p. 436.

12 Ahir, The Status of Laity in Buddhism, p. 171; referred in: Freiberger, Oliver: Salvation for Laity?, p. 35.

13 Samuels, View of Householder and Lay Disciples in Sutta Pitaka, pp. 231–241.

two images of non-monastic religiosities, which sharply oppose to each other in the canonical, are unambiguous in the sub-canonical by raising the monastic value. From this fact, he surmised that the reaction in the later tradition probably aimed to defend the followership of monastic people in objection against the spiritual success of the non-monastic people, which should have appertained to the interpretation of Mahāsāṇghika and partly existed in the old canonical.[14]

In 2002, two articles raised questions on the spirituality of the lay follower in the Pāli canon. First, on the attainment of *jhāna*,[15] in the article "The Jhānas and the Lay Disciple according to the Pāli Suttas" by Bhikkhu Bodhi,[16] and the second, on the spiritual path of the householder, in the article "The Path of the Householder: Buddhist Lay Disciples in the Pāli Canon" by Robert Bluck.[17] Bhikkhu Bodhi in the article demonstrated how the jhāna plays a significant role in the lay achievement of spiritual attainment.[18] According to Bhikkhu Bodhi, the noble followers, both monastic and non-monastic, should have acquired the right concentration, which is essential for the achievement of a stage of spiritual attainment in Buddhism. However, he paid more attention to the philosophical question about the role of the mystic experience playing in the achievement, so the article did not provide in particular, how and why the non-monastic people managed to develop the concentration successfully without living in the monastic order, where the practice of meditation was taught and learned.

Bluck's article gave more reflection on the spirituality of non-monastic follower. Arguing over the superiority of bhikkhu in Buddhism supported by former scholars, he defended that the non-monastic follower was not the "second-class Buddhist" by surveying the status and role of the

14 Ibid, pp. 238–239.
15 Humphreys, A Popular Dictionary of Buddhism, p. 99. Jhāna is defined as a state of serene contemplation attained by meditation. Buddhism recognizes eight states of the Jhāna.
16 Bodhi, The Jhānas and the Lay Disciple According to the Pāli Suttas in Buddhist Studies, p. 64. Available online at http://www.budsas.org/ebud/ebdha267.htm (last access 12.08.2013).
17 Bluck, The Path of the Householder, pp. 1–18.
18 Bodhi, The Jhānas and the Lay Disciple According to the Pāli Suttas, p. 3.

people in the Pāli canon.[19] In the survey, he found that the lay follower is in parallel to the monastic follower in different ways, viz. in the Buddha's propagation of the doctrine at early time,[20] in the sermons delivered to followers,[21] in the description of spiritual development in Buddhism[22] and in the reference of the followership within the scripture.[23] He concluded at the end that the division of the monastic and non-monastic followers merely lies in the *quantitative* difference, as the monastic life provides a better opportunity for the spiritual development, not the *qualitative* difference, as the monastic life is more special than the lay life.[24] The conclusion emphasizes the individualism in that the achievement of spiritual development depends on individual effort to follow the Buddha's path rather than on the enjoyment of a status as the condition.

In the same year appeared the first academic research on upāsaka/upāsikā, namely "Indian View of the Buddhist Laity: Precepts and Upāsaka Status," conducted by Giulio Agostini. The study objectively investigated the definition of upāsaka/upāsikā in existing canonical and post-canonical literature of Buddhist schools, in order to observe the status of the people and their religiosity. Similarly found in every school, the status of non-monastic follower is promoted merely by taking Three Jewels for refuges. On observance of the precepts, however, each school maintains different opinions: upāsaka/upāsikā may take merely one of the five precepts;[25] while some schools may reserve the term for the lay Buddhist who

19 Bluck, The Path of the Householder: Buddhist Lay Disciples in the Pāli Canon, p. 1. "I will look in turn at: the relative status of lay people and monastics; the teachings offered to lay people by the Buddha himself and by his senior monks; the categories of spiritual progress which could be made; and examples of both ordinary and exceptional lay people in the texts."

20 Ibid., p. 4.

21 Ibid., pp. 5–7.

22 Ibid., pp. 8–10.

23 Ibid., pp. 11–17.

24 Ibid., p. 18.

25 The five precepts "pañcasīla" are the vows of moral guidelines of Buddhist householder, abstaining from (1) harming living beings, (2) stealing, (3) sexual misconduct, (4) verbal misconduct, and (5) intoxication.

observes the total eight precepts[26] only.[27] From this perspective, the precepts taken by the people signify the stage of discipleship in approaching the spirituality: the more precepts the householder scrupulously observes, the nearer he is to the spiritual path. As reflected in his work, upāsaka/upāsikā is designated to non-monastic follower who takes the Three Jewels for refuge as well as strictly observes the total five precepts. The designation "upāsaka/upāsikā" is thus the superior status of householder. Some lay followers may not be regarded as upāsaka/upāsikā because they are not in the position to make the spiritual path perfectly. For example, moral defect because of not having the total five precepts observed, or having abnormal sexual orientation, which tradition considers 'incapable' to reach a stage of spiritual attainment in this life.[28] Upāsaka/upāsikā as viewed by Agostini signifies a degree of faithfulness and spirituality of householder rather than simply reference to the lay Buddhist.

Shortly after Agostini's research, Oliver Freiberger, who did a doctoral thesis about Buddhist order in Sutta Piṭaka "Der Orden in der Lehre,"[29] mentioned the non-monastic follower in relation to the order.[30] He also launched two articles concerning ethics and soteriology of the people according to Pāli canon.[31] Freiberger called the two distinctive images of the people, which Samuels[32] remarked as sharp opposition in his article, "tendencies," namely individualistic (or non-institutional) tendency and institutional tendency. He demonstrated that each tendency has its own

---

26 The eight precepts "aṭṭhasīla" are the vows of advance moral guildlines of Buddhist householder, abstaining from (1) harming living beings, (2) stealing, (3) having sexual activity, (4) lying, (5) intoxication, (6) eating at the wrong time (or eating in the morning, before noon), (7) singing, dancing, playing music, attending entertainment performances, wearing perfume, and using cosmetics and garlands, and (8) using luxurious places for sitting or sleeping, and overindulging in sleep.

27 Cf. Upāsaka/upāsikā in Thai Buddhism particularly denotes the lay people who observe the eight precepts.

28 Agostini, Indian Views of the Buddhist Laity, pp. 169–175: Summary no. 1, 2.

29 On scholars' opinions about the spiritual goal of lay follower, pp. 147–153.

30 Freiberger, Der Orden in der Lehre, pp. 140–212.

31 Freiberger, Salvation for Laity?, pp. 29–38.

32 Samuels, View of Householder and Lay Disciples in Sutta Pitaka, pp. 231–241. Already mentioned at p. 3.

spiritual goal and practical way to the goal.[33] The "individual tendency" points to the potential of everybody, no matter if they are inside or outside the monastic order, to develop with their own effort the spirituality to Nibbāna; whereas, the "institutional tendency" defines the Buddhist in terms of social obligation, i.e. the Buddhist fosters the spiritual aim on their chosen lifestyle. In connection with the institutional tendency, monastic follower learns and practices for Nibbāna, while the non-monastic follower supports the monastic follower for a better rebirth.[34] Considering the two sides of the non-monastic follower, he criticized the one-sided presentation of the people that Ahir had made.[35]

Freiberger assumed that the spiritual attainment in parallel to that of monastic follower was attributed to the lay follower on the purpose of institutionalizing him into the Buddhist order. This indicates an ecclesiological phenomenon, in which tradition legitimized the lay follower in the community for the steady supports.[36] Freiberger was of the opinion that, although the lay follower is a category of Buddha's follower, monastic lifestyle should be a requisite for the spiritual development and the attainment of Nibbāna. Concluding in this way, he viewed that bhikkhu/bhikkhunī is exclusively the follower of Buddha fostering the spiritual path, while upāsaka/upāsikā is mentioned as the follower in the scripture as a result of the institutionalization.

After 2000 there were some works about non-monastic follower in Pāli canon that bring a similar result. Gayatri Sen Majumdar, in 2009 conducted a study "Early Buddhism and Laity." Her finding conformed to the traditional axiom that the householder is from the outset a part of Buddha's community with patronage that built on the foundation of the order. However, the work did not offer any new idea about the spiritual side of the people, for Majumdar paid more attention to the role as supporter in the community. Furthermore, the category into two categories: gahapati/gahapatinī, which refers to married householder, and upāsaka/upāsikā, to celibate householder, is false and not supported with

33 Freiberger, Der Orden in der Lehre, p. 150.
34 Freiberger, Profiling the Sangha, p. 11.
35 Freiberger, Salvation for Laity, p. 35.
36 Freiberger, Profiling the Sangha, p. 11.

reference, so far the author has investigated the words in the canon.[37] In 2011 John Kelly in his article "The Buddha's Teaching to Lay People," based on his Master's degree thesis, investigated the Buddha's teachings delivered to householder in the five Nikāyas with orientation on the demographic characteristics of the hearers. In the study, he focused in particular on hearer who is an ordinary householder, not an ascetic, non-human deity and demon who are depicted to be Buddha's follower,[38] in order to make the study more realistic. The result conformed to his expectation that Buddha's teaching varies in accordance with age, gender, and class of the hearer. The theme of the teachings, as he found, rather emphasizes the worldly goal, orientating towards the good conduct by body, speech, and mind for the achievement of happiness in the present life and a better rebirth.[39] The finding clearly points to the goal and the path to the goal divided exactly over the status that the tradition casted to the non-monastic follower.[40]

From the early period of Buddhist Studies until nowadays, a topic on non-monastic Buddhist in Pāli canon has noticeably challenged scholars to work into different perspectives despite not very much data provided. The findings give a wide range of reflection, from the sociological to the humanistic view. Nevertheless, the religious freedom is maintained under the classification of monastic and non-monastic followers. Indeed, the "religion" as described in the Pāli discourses offers anybody the chance to learn and practice the doctrine and to receive the outcome with his own wisdom and effort.[41] Therefore, the concept of non-monastic follower cannot simply be summarized in a fixed religiosity because it can be various, as Freiberger commented: "*Die uneinheitliche Begrifflichkeit in den Texten, die unterschiedliche Nähe der erwähnten Personen zum Samgha*

37 Sen Majumdar, Early Buddhism and Laity, pp. 88–89; See 1.4.1.

38 Kelly, The Buddha Teaching to Lay People, pp. 6–7.

39 Ibid., p. 37.

40 Apart from the academic studies that I presented here, there are other handbooks, which particularly handle the sermons on Buddhist spirituality for the non-monastic Buddhist in a systematic way. A good book is Der Buddha sprach nicht nur für Mönche und Nonnen by Fritz Schäfer.

41 As we have seen in Pāli canon, some non-monastic Buddhists consulted the Buddha or a monk about a problem of a doctrine or a practice.

und die Vielfalt ihrer Praktiken macht es somit unmöglich, die Gruppe der „buddhistischen Laienanhänger" exact zu bestimmen oder abzugrenzen. Hinzu kommt, dass Individuen ihre buddhistische Identität offenbar durchaus uneindeutig empfinden können."[42] The activities mentioned in the scriptures are merely some exemplary activities that the non-monastic Buddhist might do from their intention. For this reason, the conception of the non-monastic follower is not simply to achieve from the religiosity mentioned in a sermon or in a scripture of the canon.

It seems that the consideration into two different tendencies as Freiberger suggested is the appropriate strategy to deal with the variety of the non-monastic follower prevailing in the text. The two tendencies are significant to understand the people in light of individuality, in which the Buddhist is free to do a good deed for their spiritual development on one hand, and in light of institution, in which he carries out a good deed to support the monastic order, on the other. The method is helpful in systematically categorizing the ideas that shed light to the explanation of each tendency. The individualistic tendency points to the freedom in carrying out religiosity on the spiritual path, and the institutional tendency indicates the close interrelation of the people within the community, as Ray and Freiberger have suggested. Monastic follower receives donation from the non-monastic follower and instructs him in Buddha's teaching while the non-monastic follower donates and hears the teaching in response. Nevertheless, the problem about collision of the images of non-monastic follower as argued by the former scholars is not handled. For instance, the question as to whether, in which extent, and how upāsaka/upāsikā is also an *official* follower of Buddha. Despite the fact that Vinaya does not advocate the lay follower, tradition does record many sermons delivered to lay follower about the spiritual path.[43] As individual who has an intention to reach the Nibbāna, the lay follower may learn and practice an advanced teaching with the instruction of the Buddha or a monk and can be successful with their effort. They have no commitment and no punishment in

---

42 Freiberger, Ein Vinaya für Hausbewohner ?, p. 242.

43 Kelly, The Buddha's Teaching to Lay People, p. 27. He found that 33% of the teaching devotes to the goal of happiness in this life (12%) and good rebirth (31%), while 39% to the goal of stream-entry (10%) and Nibbāna (29%).

the observance of precept, but they might control themselves under beliefs and morals that Buddha suggested. The only difference between the non-monastic and the monastic followers is the obligation to observe monastic rules and customs given in Vinaya.

Due to this fact, the discourse reveals two kinds of obligations that followers in the community have to fulfill.[44] One is the *monastic obligation*, viz. rule, customs, monkhood, etc. which is imposed on the people in the order, bhikkhu/bhikkhunī. This obligation is expressly mentioned in Vinaya-piṭaka while a little in Suttapiṭaka. The instruction, especially in the Vinaya-piṭaka, essentially connects the monastic people with the ideal that the Buddha has established for some benefits.[45] As the member of the community, the monastic follower has to accept this condition while the non-monastic follower does not have to. The other one is the *Buddhist obligation*, viz. spiritual goal, spiritual path, belief in the Buddha, observance of precepts, etc. any religiosity in relation to the Buddha and his teaching which is rather arbitrary to any people. Following the religiosity, the individuals, monastic and non-monastic follower alike, have the unity in some basic belief, goal, and path and hence appear to be associated with one another. With this kind of obligation, the people feel motivated to carry out the religiosity by themselves or in connection with the community without enforcement or punishment.[46] This is the inherent tendency among the people in Suttapiṭaka. In this obligation, a monk or a nun may keep the monkhood or leave his monkhood at will. Likewise, a non-monastic follower may go to visit the Buddha or a monk for a conversation, make a donation, or even revere other mendicants outside the order. He feels free to contact the monks or carry out the activities at will, not for duty.

44 Cf. Freiberger, Der Orden in der Lehre, pp. 236–239.

45 Book of the Discipline Vol. I, pp. 37–38. Buddha's ten reasons on setting forth a monastic rule: 1) for the excellence of the order, 2) for the comfort of the order, 3) for the restraint of evil-minded men, 4) for the ease of well-behaved monks, 5) for the restraint of the cankers belonging to the liere and now, 6) for the combating of the cankers belonging to other worlds, 7) for the benefit of non-believers, 8) for the increase in the number of believers, 9) for establishing dhamma indeed, 10) for following the rules of restraint.

46 Cf. Freiberger's individual or non-institutional tendency, which denotes the individual freedom to approach the religion.

Both monastic and non-monastic Buddhists fulfill this obligation as long as they have the belief in the Buddha and his teaching.

Both the 'monastic obligation' and the 'Buddhist obligation' affiliate with the followership under the Buddha. With the regular contact and the activity in relation to the Buddha, his monastic disciple, the order, and even the lay followers who claimed themselves Buddha's follower, the people are recognized as Buddhist, Buddha's follower, and the behaviour is considered as *ideal* that the Buddhist in later generations should follow. However, from the purely narrow viewpoint, Buddhism viewed as the monastic obligation is the path to salvation exclusively for the member of the order. In this view, only monastic followers are exclusively the Buddhist, as they join the community and adhere to the rule and custom of the community; any people outside this community are considered simply outsiders. This viewpoint is however too extreme in Suttapiṭaka because the non-monastic followers regularly contacted with the monastic order for debates, conversations, and activities throughout the texts. The *duty* according to the obligation that involves the people with the Buddha, his teaching, or the monastic order is significant at this point, as it makes the followership in a wider sense. In this view, the social mechanism as mentioned in the text manages the followership at two levels. Primarily, it reserves the proper place for the salvation in monastic order; secondarily, it relates to the society where the monastic order settles for the support and the supply of successor for the next generations in the order.

In this connection, there is another crucial question about how to perceive the followership of upāsaka/upāsikā as mentioned in the Suttapiṭaka. In fact, the word upāsaka/upāsikā appears rather limited in text, especially in Dīgha-and Majjhima-nikāya. There are merely two contexts that the word is regularly used: first, in the context in which the hearer of a sermon asked the Buddha or a monk to let him become a pupil in the order or to bear them one of his followers at the end of a discourse, and second occasionally in the sense of non-monastic follower as the composite of Buddha's community.[47] Dealing with the meaning of the term, the author pays attention to the first context that intrinsically *portrays* the picture of

47 Dialogues of the Buddha, Part II, p. 120; Part III, p. 117 ff.

how the people comply with the Buddhist obligations. Lay follower in the second context is ascribed to be another group of Buddha's follower, as a result from the first context. In this view, *the concept of the lay followership* can be framed: *why they become Buddhist, how they become Buddhist, and what they do as the Buddhist*. This is the *stereotypical* image reinforced in the discourses, which one cannot simply read from the scripts.

The stock phrases which signify the declaration of belief in response to the Buddha's sermon must convey the concerning meaning in some ways in relation to the sermon. Unfortunately, the stock phrases in this context have never been in attention of scholars, unlike stock phrases denoting the Arahatship.[48] On the contrary, the stock phrases is often criticized as not relevant to the conversion, viz. to become a follower. This is a problem in "Religionswissenschaft" to investigate systematically from the phenomena, why and how the people commit to the followership, as well as, the relation between the people and the community.[49] In this direction the study has been developed.

1.2 Purpose of the Study

The study aims at investigating the concept of non-monastic follower, represented behind the religiosity described in the discourse of Pāli tradition. The focus is primarily to find out "the Buddhist obligation," viz. the *spiritual aim and mission of becoming a lay follower under the Buddha,*

48 Stock phrases denoting Arahatship and the development of the spiritual attainment in Pāli discourse are observed by Jan Ergardt (1977) in "Faith and Knowledge in Early Buddhism" and Nathan Katz (1982) in "Buddhist Images of Human Perfection." The former investigated the stock phrases in Majjhima-nikāya, while the latter the stock phrases in the first four Nikāyas. Both aim at achieving the concept of Arahatship by studying meaning of the words, symbols, metaphors, literally and contextually. Likewise, Schmithausen (1981) in "On some aspect of descriptions or theories of 'liberating insight' and 'enlightenment' in Early Buddhism" and Bronkhorst (1986) in "The Two Traditions of Meditation in Ancient India" paid attention to the teaching and practice represented in stock phrases. The latest similar work is an analysis of spiritual way of the monk in "Sāmaññaphala- die Frucht des Entsagers: Armut und Nicht-Anhaften als Weg zum Heil beim Buddha und Franziskus von Assisi" by Bernhard-Maria Janzen (1997).

49 Cf. Stolz, Grundzüge der Religionswissenschaft, pp. 80–81.

implied in the portrayal of the confrontation and conversation between the people and Buddha ending with the declaration of followership under the Buddha. In other words, the study observes the *process of Buddhist obligation* developed in the presented stories, which has a stereotypical pattern. Next, it is to investigate the discipleship of the people from religiosity and devotion to the Buddha and his community. The concept of the people will thus be framed from the questions: what and why they do the activities relating to *the Buddhist obligation*. With the questions, the study expects to see all aspects of lay religiosity in the narratives as the manifestation of the Buddhist obligation. The study expects to conceptualize the Buddhist followership mentioned in the discourses, which should contribute in some extent to the basic understanding about the ideal of social structure and mechanism of Buddhist community in the Pāli canon, especially in Suttapiṭaka. The knowledge is essentially basic to the understanding of Buddhist community and the interpretation of Buddhist phenomena in different contexts.

The study investigates the long discourse of Suttapiṭaka, viz. Dīgha-nikāya and Majjhima-nikāya, which is one of the oldest parts of the Buddhist canon. The name of the two Nikāyas implies that the codification of the two sections might have been created from the same basis.[50] A shared similarity is that they present the Buddhist followership in the same pattern. To deal with the discourses, the study in line with the knowledge on oral literature focuses on the meaning revealed from the structure and components of discourses repeatedly communicated in oral transmission. The study hence leads to an alternative answer about the non-monastic follower.

1.3 Methodology

The study is a philological study to grasp the meaning of the Nikāya discourses in line with the nature of oral tradition, in which the text was developed and propagated and to understand the relationships constructed

50 Norman, Pāli Literature, p. 30. Dīgha- and Majjhima-nikāya is collected and codified with the length of the text, while Saṃyutta Nikāya and Aṅguttara Nikāya should have been grouped and ordered due to the theme and the number of dhamma in the sermon.

in the narratives. In detail, the author presents in three items: philological study of Pāli discourse, orality of Pāli discourse, and theory of religious experience.

1.3.1 Philological Study of Pāli Discourse

As the question of the study is the inquiry into the concept of non-monastic Buddhist from the perspective of oral tradition in the presentation of discourse, the study concerns the definition of the Buddhist and the religious organization in substantive term. The method thus relies on the specialized knowledge about language and literature of ancient Indian. Nevertheless, the aim and question of the study makes the study the subset of "Religionswissenschaft," as the study needs other helpful approaches after a lack of success achieved in the textual investigation of religious concepts, which the canonical traditions may not directly address through the scripts. The name "philology" here thus merely refers to the method dealing with language and literature.[51]

Upāsaka/upāsikā or non-monastic follower is a topic which seems to be one of the most problematic in the philological study, as the author has shown the history of the study above. The reason concerns some particularity of the people, the scripture, and the relationship between them. First, the lay follower does not 'juridically' involve with the order, but tradition mentions them as a part of the Sangha throughout many parts of Suttapiṭaka. At a place,[52] upāsaka/upāsikā is reckoned a part of Buddha's community, whereas at another place the people outside the order are distanced, secluded and, even rejected.[53] Second, the relation between the Pāli canon and the Buddhist is problematic about the position in the community and the role on the people. Generally, the religious scripture exert ideological influence in some ways on the religious people through the hearing and the reading. In this principle, the monastic follower, who follows *buddhavacana* "the word of the Buddha," in the canon should be the Buddhist, the follower of the Buddha, only; whereas, lay

51 Cf. Norman, A Philological Approach to Buddhism, p. 10.
52 Dialogues of the Buddha, Part II, p. 120; Part III, p. 117 ff.
53 Freiberger, Der Orden in der Lehre, pp. 154–164.

follower is not the Buddhist because the Buddha's doctrine on lifestyle and practice as given in Vinaya-piṭaka is not prescriptive to them. However, if the canon is the scripture exclusively for the monks to learn and instruct people in the community, the lay follower can be reckoned Buddhist because the canon collects sermons for the lay follower as well. Third, the meanings of non-monastic follower grasped from different places in the text may bring into conflict with one another. The definition of the word is exactly given in a discourse,[54] but the people portrayed in other discourses have another character. The mention about of the people is various and inconsistent, and as a result, the result of study on lay follower can be different depending on the perspective and personal notion of how the people should be like,[55] and on which part of the Pāli canon should at best reflect the concept of the people. To deal with this, the author focuses on religious meanings *implied at large* in the texts, *not directly given* in a place of the texts, for the followship is not necessarily referred in a teaching, but mentioned in the background and situation behind a sermon. The reference of the people is essentially the image from the perspective of the tradition. Therefore, the approach to the text for the answer is not merely to *read the message from the text*, but actually to *interpret the meaning communicated by the text.*

1.3.2 Orality of the Pāli Text

The problem about orality of the Pāli text that the author poses here deals with the interpretation of the *message* transmitted in the Nikāya discourses, which is a product of oral tradition. The word 'oral' in the study concerns the "basic distinction" in communicating a message of the oral narrative, which is different from that of written tradition.[56]

54 The Book of the Gradual Sayings, Vol. IV, p. 149 ff. The definition of Upāsaka given by the Buddha in the conversation with Mahānāma here is mostly cited as the definition of the Upāsaka in Buddhism.

55 Samuels, Views of Householder and Lay Disciples in the Sutta Pitaka, p. 231. At least two standpoints of the scholars can be noticed: 1) Based on religious activities and obligation such as Nalinaksha Dutt, Max Weber, Etienne Lamotte; 2) Embracing the traditional view-Akira Hirakawa.

56 Cf. Lord, The Singer of Tales, p. 5.

With this awareness, the text should be approached appropriately for the sense that the tradition has transmitted to its audience in an oral performance. Specifically, the study deals with the question, as to how to conceptualize the lay followership in the oral transmission from the text that we now read.

Scholars have been long aware that Pāli canon is orally composed and transmitted from the outset. The learning and transmission of the scriptures obviously involves vocal activities.[57] It is also found that no mention of writing in ancient India that is older than 258 BCE, when King Ashoka let the edicts build up.[58] Besides, Pāli canon apparently contains a number of stylistic features that indicate the oral literature such as usage of metrics, formulas or stock phrase and repetition, similar to other texts in the Indian tradition and in other traditions of the early age.[59] Scholars generally "perceive" the orality of Pāli canon to be an efficacious method that contributes to preserve the old sermons and stories in the tradition.[60] As a result, they, in favour of the notion in spite of the fact that the supporting reason is not very sound,[61] rejected other considerations concerning this point, such as Cousins' challenging question, as to whether the oral techniques existing in the canon may indicate the oral performance as found in other oral traditions.[62] Following the notion, later scholars raising the result of researching the formulaic language in the discourses defended

57 Collins, Notes on Some Oral Aspects of Pali literature, pp. 122–127.

58 McMahan, Orality, Writing, and Authority in South Asian Buddhism, p. 252; cf. Gombrich, Theravada Buddhism, p. 20; Allon, Style and Function, p. 1: footnote no. 6.

59 Allon, Style and Function, p. 1.

60 Hinüber, Untersuchungen zur Mündlichkeit früher mittelindischer Texte der Buddhisten, p. 15; Freiberger and Kleine, Buddhismus, pp. 174–175.

61 Wynne, The Oral Transmission of Early Buddhist Literature, p. 99.

62 Cousins, Pali Oral Literature, p. 9; referred in: Allon, Style and Function, p. 6. Cousin's work was based on Lord-Parry's finding about the oral literature in Serbo-Croatian culture, which emphasizes the creative or dynamic role of 'individual performer' in the composition (or in the performance). In this way, the theory was not accepted to view Buddhist literature, for in case of Buddhist literature the monastic 'institution' should have played the role on the composition and transmission of the teachings in corpora and therefore been not the work of individuals.

that the language should particularly have functioned as the memorizing aid for the preservation of scripture than the device for a live performance. As Bhikkhu Anālayo working on the comparative study of Majjhima-nikāya from different traditions mentioned with supports from Heinz Bechert and Mark Allon: "*In contrast (to other oral literatures), the purpose of the early Buddhist oral tradition was the preservation of sacred material, for which free improvisation is inappropriate. Moreover, recitation was often undertaken communally by the reciters, which leaves little scope for free improvisation.*"[63] By some errors which have similar sounds in corresponding texts from different traditions, he was convinced that the orality in Buddhist tradition emphasizes on verbatim transmission.[64] Obviously, the advantage of oral transmission that scholars support lends the validity to study the texts with literary criticism, as viewed that the formulaic techniques are supposed to preserve the original words precisely from the Buddha's time. In fact, it cannot be definite to us, whether the styles were intended to aim at the verbatim or the conveyed meaning, as the texts, originally oral texts, leave the clues *not enough and even impossible* for the reconstruction, and subsequently, not for a reliable answer about the history of the text. They could be, at the very beginning, composed *in* performance or *for* transmission? The scriptures left in traditions nowadays *might* be merely an outcome of the transmission(s) which spreaded in the regions and was accepted by the teachers in the schools. A history of the transmission and textual development can be reckoned merely with the exisiting evidences in the text, based on personal belief of the scholars.

In this way, scholars mainly discuss on the mnemonic techniques that help the memorization of the text and preservation of the original meaning and the establishment of relation to other scripture in other traditions.

63 Anālayo, A Comparative Study of the Majjhima-nikāya Vol. 1, p. 17. After the comparative study, Analayo concluded from the variations found in the texts from different traditions that the oral recitation and transmission in early age of Buddhism plays a crucial role in the precision of the textual memory. See volume 2, conclusion, pp. 855–891.

64 Ibid. Anālayo referred to the article of George von Simson (1965) "Zur Diktion einiger Lehrtexte des buddhistischen Sanskritkanons." The author finds the conclusion too hasty, for the mistakes merely show the role of hearing in learning the teaching in the old times.

From the history of studying classical Indian literature, the investigation of the oral styles started since 1917 as the work launched by Oldenberg in "Zur Geschichte der altindischen Prosa."[65] With the main question of philological studies focusing on the origination and transmission of the text, however, scholars examined the features to understand the form of the text[66] that may shed light to its origination and development in relation to the parallel texts in other traditions.[67] With this approach, they managed to develop methods for some philological questions, for example, to date the age, determine the relationship between scriptures and to identify the school producing scripture.[68] Furthermore, the spelling of words was observed, for the process of writing down might affect some changes to the word and the meaning.[69]

Cousins' proposal on oral literature should have reminded to concentrate rather on meaning and function than the exactness in preserving the text. The tradition self implied in the teachings rejects the decisiveness in the learning as mentioned in the Vinaya that Buddha forbade the Vedic pronunciation of teaching in learning the doctrines.[70] The doctrine

---

65 Allon, Style and Function, pp. 6–7. The history of studying oral stylistics in Pāli canon is given in the dissertation in detail. After the publication in 1997, there are some articles addressing the oral characteristics in Pāli canon: Orality, Writing, and Authority in South Asian Buddhism: Visionary Literature and the Struggle for Legitimacy in the Mahāyāna (1998) by David McMahan; The Oral Transmission of Early Buddhist Literature (2004) by Alexander Wynne; Oral Dimensions of Pāli Discourses: Pericopes, Other Mnemonic Techniques and the Oral Performance Context (2007) and The Vicissitudes of Memory and Early Buddhist Oral Transmission (2009) both by Bhikkhu Anālayo. (See bibliography).

66 Gombrich, Recovering the Buddha's Message (2005); Wynne, Oral Transmission of Early Buddhist Literature (2004); Berkwitz, Buddhist Manuscript Culture (2009).

67 Gethin, The Buddhist Path to Awakening, pp. 8–9.

68 Norman, Review of Hinüber, Untersuchung zur Mündlichkeit früher mittelindischer Texte der Buddhisten, p. 309 referred: in Allon, Style and Function, p. 3.

69 Norman, A Philological Approach to Buddhism, pp. 107–116.

70 The Book of Discipline Vol. V, pp. 193–194. Horner translated chandaso "in metrical form" which Buddha had forbidden, in opposite to "according to his own dialect." Likewise, Buddha had forbidden "with a long-drawn plain-song sound" in The Book of Discipline Vol. V, pp. 145–146.

of Mahāpadesa also alluded to the prohibition of decisive authority, as the right meaning of a teaching is more important than the origin of the teaching.[71] In this way, scholars were obviously focusing on the orality with aspects from literary criticism, with a little consideration on learning the meanings during the transmission.

In fact, studying the oral text requires another set of knowledge *"to read or interpret in its own term"* in order to get the meanings of the text communicated in a performance.[72] Few scholars realized this aspect of the orality in the Pāli text that may affect the understanding of the meanings transmitted in its oral format. T.W. Rhys Davids, one of pioneer scholars in Pāli philology, for example, noticed that the text of Pāli canon is not the book *in the modern sense* – "never intended to be read." In the introduction of Dīgha-nikāya that he edited, he complained the stylistic of orality, as it is not fit for publication that requires stylistic of written language.

> The inclusion of such *memoria technica* makes the Four Nikaya strikely different from the modern treatises on ethics or psychology. As they stand they were never intended to be read. And a version in English, repeating all the repetitions, rendering each item in the lists and groups as they stand, by a single English word, without commentary, would quite fail to convey the meaning, often intrinsically interesting, always historically valuable, of these curious old documents.[73]

He noticed that the oral text fails to give the main idea to the reader because of the mnemonic language.

---

71 Dialogues of the Buddha Vol. II, pp. 133–136. Nevertheless, the teaching of Mahāpadesa is viewed by some scholars as the evidence of authority in Buddhism. Cf. McDermott, Scripture as the Word of the Buddha, pp. 26–27. McDermott referring to George Bond (1975) claimed that the authoritatively trustworthy teaching according to the teaching of Mahāpadesa must fulfill two criteria. First, the teaching must have been heard directly or "face to face" from one of four possible sources: Buddha, a community of Sangha headed by a venerable elder, a number of well-learned senior monks, or a single elder monk of wide learning. Second, the teaching must be considered in comparison with the Sutta and the Vinaya. The teaching of Mahāpadesa, as the author views, does not determine the origin of teaching as authority; the thesis lies in the self-consideration and judgment in comparison with the Vinaya and the Sutta, which the hearer has learned, no matter where the teaching is from, even from the Buddha.

72 Foley, "Reading" Homer through Oral Tradition, p. 4.

73 Dialogues of the Buddha Vol. I, p. xxi.

> It is no doubt partly the result of the burden of such *memoria technica,* but partly also owing to the methods of exposition then current in North India, that the leading theses of each Sutta are not worked out in the way in which we should expect to find similar theses worked out now in Europe. A proposition or two or three, are put forward, restated with slight additions or variations, and placed as it were in contrast with the contrary proposition (often at first put forward by the interlocutor). There the matter is usually left. There is no elaborate logical argument. The choice is offered to the hearer; and of course, he usually accepts the proposition as maintained by the Buddha. The statement of this is often so curt, enigmatic, and even – owing not seldom simply to our ignorance, as yet, of the exact force of the technical terms used—so ambiguous, that a knowledge of the state of opinion on the particular point, in North India, at the time, or a comparison of other Nikāya passage on the subject, is necessary to remove the uncertainty.[74]

To make the text understandable in written language, it seems a lot of work to convert the mnemonic language of the Pāli canon into a *European style.* Rhys Davids imagined how the oral text should be managed.

> It would seem therefore most desirable that a scholar attempting to render these Suttantas into a European style – evolved in the process of expressing a very different, and often contradictory, set of conceptions – should give the reasons of the faith that is in him. He should state why he holds such and such an expression to be the least inappropriate rendering: and quote parallel passages from other Nikāya text in support of his reasons. He should explain the real significance of the thesis put forward by a statement of what, in his opinion, was the point of view from which it was put forward, the stage of opinion into which it fits, the current views it supports or controverts. In regard to technical terms, for which there can be no equivalent, he should give the Pāli. And in regard to the mnemonic lists and groups, each word in which is usually a crux, he should give cross-references, and wherever he ventures to differ from the Buddhist explanations, as handed down in the schools, should state the fact, and give his reason. It is only by such discussions that we can hope to make progress in the interpretation of the history of Buddhist and Indian thought. Bare versions are of no use to scholars, and even to the general reader they can only convey loose, inadequate, and inaccurate ideas.[75]

At the first glance, one may shallowly regard Rhys Davids's complaint as dissatisfaction with the oral characteristics in the English translation that are awkward in published form. By the word "European style," he did

74 Ibid., pp. xxi–xxii.
75 Ibid., p. xxii.

not mean only the translation, but also the way and logic of the text. He truly showed in the complaint this effect about the understanding of the meanings by reading because Pāli canon does not offer the reader the philosophical points, arguments, explanation, etc. in the way that the reader may expect from a scripture of religious doctrine or philosophy.[76] As he stated "*They are memorial sentences intended to be learned by heart, and the whole style and method of arrangement is entirely subordinated to this primary necessity*,"[77] the language style can affect the meaning perceived by the reading. The problem at this point is that some meanings known by the reciter and the audience in the oral transmission may never be achieved with reading the scripts. The excerpts above seem to be the only remark concerning the complexity of orality in Pāli canon in relation to the understanding of the reader. After the publication of Pāli text and translation, the text is the material to read, to analyse, to understand the doctrines and concepts. This is the problem addressed by a scholar in oral literature,

> (t)he scholarly focus on texts had ideological consequences. With their attention directed to texts, scholars often went on to assume, often without reflection, that oral verbalization was essentially the same as the written verbalization they normally deal with, and that oral art forms were all intents and purposes simply texts, except for the fact that they were not written down.[78]

This statement raises the necessity to understand the mechanism in communication and distinction between the oral and the written tradition. The unawareness of the particularity of the oral text pertains not only to the modern scholars in the study of Pāli canon, but also to the medieval scholars like Buddhaghosa. In this way, the text, which was composed in the

---

76 Cf. Ong, Orality and Literacy, pp. 36–57. Ong gave the characteristics of orality based on thought and expression: (i) additive rather than subordinative; (ii) aggregative rather than analytic; (iii) redundant or 'copious'; (iv) conservative or traditionalist; (v) close to the human lifeworld; (vi) agonistic toned; (vii) empathetic and participatory rather than objectively distanced; (viii) Homeostatic; (ix) situational rather than abstract.

77 Dialogues of the Buddha. Part 1, p. xx.

78 Ong, Orality and Literacy, p. 10. Cf. Vansina, Oral Tradition as History, p. 56; Lord, The Singer of Tales, p. 126. "The idea of obtaining an accurate text of a given performance is comparatively recent because heretofore the concept of a fixed text somewhere in the background tended to minimize the importance of any single given performance."

oral tradition with some typical characteristics in conveying the message generally served in the oral performance, is read and treated like written texts with expectations generally satisfied in the written tradition.

The important mechanism of the oral text lies in the style and structure: stock phrases, metrical rhythm, repetition, etc., which have some functions in the oral transmission. In relation to these points, it is necessary to mention some concerning theories: first, the "Oral Formulaic Theory" developed by Milman Parry and Albert Lord;[79] second, the influence of the oral literature to the written tradition by Eric Havelock in investigating the oral characteristics that significantly influences to Plato's thought in his book *Republic*. The two findings greatly contribute to the knowledge that oral literature conveys messages to the people in the tradition with the stylistics and the way of transmitting the text.

Albert Lord, following his teacher, Milman Parry,[80] about the oral literature in Greek culture, has known from his study of living storytelling in Serbo-Croatian culture that the usage of stock phrase in repetition generates the *theme*[81] of the text. "*Anyone who reads through a collection of oral epic from any country is soon aware that the same basic incidents and descriptions are met with time and again. ... The reader's impression of repetitions would be closer to the experience of the singer himself and to that of the singer's audience were he to read first the song in the repertory of a single singer and then those from singers in the same small district.*"[82] The composition of the themes in certain order and in repetition causes the

---

79 Parry and Lord's theory, despite critics about the view about oral tradition, is regarded as pioneer pointing to the distinction of oral tradition from written tradition. The author, referring to their theory, focuses only on understanding the meaning of the text, not the dynamic aspect in the production (or performance) of the text.

80 Lord, The Singer of Tales, p. 3. Milman Parry in 1928 for the first time analysed the language of oral text in Illiad and Odyssey in his work *L'Epithète traditionnelle da Homère* and tried to develop theory about the 'form' of the oral text distinguished from the written text in a study of Serbo-Croatian epics. Parry had begun the latter work a little before his death in 1935 and Albert Lord continued it until it is finished, which was his dissertation "*The Singer of Tales.*"

81 Lord, The Singer of Tales, p. 4. "By theme I refer to the repeated incidents and descriptive passages in the songs."

82 Ibid., p. 68.

logic of the narrative and the consequent force of habitual association that internally holds the complexes together.[83] Not only to the understanding of the hearers in the oral tradition, this also affects their thought process[84] or thought pattern[85] that heritages to people as evidenced in the literature of written tradition. When people have heard the literature, which consists of the stock phrase and repetition in a specific way, they "*determine the kind of thinking that can be done, the way experience is intellectually organized.*"[86] The meaning is the true message of oral text that influences to the thought of the reciter or the hearer. As Eric Havelock found out, oral literatures in Hellenic culture significantly influence Plato's ideas in his work *Republic*, by which the formulaic language and style transmitted and stored in the tradition as cultural book provides some standardized conceptual thoughts.[87] This indicates that, in the process of transmission, the hearer absorbed the meaning through the regular usage of oral stylistics. "*The formulaic style characteristic of oral composition represented not only certain verbal and metrical habits but also a cast of thought, or a mental condition.*"[88] It is not to neglect, the use of the oral styles results in the worldview of the people from the repetition of stock phrases and sentences.

Pāli discourse or Sutta that consists of certain structure and stock phrases should be taken into consideration in the similar way. It does not only convey the detail of philosophical teaching with the dramatic scenes, but also represents a single story of Buddha's mission describing how a person encountered the Buddha and finally became his follower. With the use of oral stylistics in a precise pattern, more discourses can be created constantly. In this way, the discourses leave no trace of facts behind the language style. What appeared to the audience was a story redirected to support a new main idea. In Buddhist literature, some stories in Jātaka were created by adapting tales, known widely from the great epics, such as

83 Ibid., pp. 96–97.
84 Ong, Orality and Literacy, p. 33.
85 Ibid., p. 35.
86 Ibid., p. 36.
87 Ibid., p. v. Cf. Henaut, Oral Tradition and the Gospel: The Problem of Mark 4, p. 86.
88 Havelock, Preface to Plato, p. viii.

Kaṭṭhahārika-jātaka vs. the story of Śakuntalā in Mahābhārata, Dasaratha-jātaka vs. Rāmāyaṇa. There are several stories in Jātaka, which plots can be found parallel to collection of legend, fable, and parable of Indian. As the background of the discourses is unlikely to investigate the origin or the history behind the language of the oral text, the question on the redirection, rearrangement, or the new meaning established in the composition for the Buddhist tradition should be more important and worthy of focus.

Discourse in this perspective points to the characteristic of *epic* in the Suttapiṭaka.[89] Namely, each consists of the theme of Buddha's mission and the gaining of followers.[90] Collectively, they present the motif that Buddha attempts to propagate his doctrine "for the benefit and happiness of the people." The effort in the mission is regarded by tradition as the great mission to the humankind. This idea conforms to another designation of the Buddha *sammāsambuddha*, "the wise man who discovered the dhamma and propagated it to the world," whose role is much greater and more important than *paccekabuddha* and *anubuddha* "individual Buddha" and "following Buddha" respectively.[91] This claim makes the clear distinction that *sammāsambuddha* has the mission after his enlightenment while the others do not. Commentary clarifies this point in terms of Buddha's *mercy* in the revelation of the discovered dhamma to the world, in which he had made a great effort in telling the truth to a person. Thus, Buddha's effort in the propagation, from the view of the tradition, is not the desire to win acceptance and reverence of the people.[92] The image corresponds to the

89 The usage of the word 'epic' here needs a little more explanation. According to Lord in The Singer of Tales (p. 4), the word 'oral'and 'oral epic' is defined as "*the narrative poetry composed in a manner evolved over many generations by singers of tales who did not know how to write; it consists of the building of metrical lines and half lines by means of formula and formulaic expression and of the building of songs by use of themes.*" The term epic is applied to the stylistics of Nikāya discourses comprising regular structure and formulaic language.

90 Lord, The Singer of Tales, p. 94.: "The theme in oral poetry exists at one and the same time in and for itself and for the whole song. This can be said both for the theme in general and also for any individual singer's forms of it."

91 Tradition has it that the effort in the propagation of the doctrine is the great work. Sammāsambuddha is thus most revered by the Buddhist in this way.

92 Traditional attitude to Buddha's mission, see introductory verses of commentary texts, such as Samantapāsādikā, Papañcasūdanī, Sāratthappakāsinī, etc.

metaphor in which he compared himself to be a doctor who cures the sickness.[93] In this connection, the worldly suffering in the human life is a kind of sickness that needs the cure from him. Dhamma that he discovered in the enlightenment is compared with the medicine. Giving the technique to the followers, Buddha taught the people to reach benefit and happiness.

In sum, the orality of Pāli discourse handled in the study concerns thc problem to achieve the concept from the oral text, as the text is by nature composed with a distinctive attitude. First, the concept about religious people or thing in the originally orally performed literature is not directly given in a statement, but portrayed in the story. Second, the information presented in the recitation rather emphasizes on meanings intended to communicate to the audience serving on the purpose of instruction and transmission of the doctrine in the tradition than giving historical facts. Third, the orally performed literature is orientated towards some concept in relation to the presented motif. From these facts, the author concludes that the discourse should have represented the imagery of Buddha's mission, in which he has instructed people, as it conveyed a sermon text in tandem. Presented in the discourses, the non-monastic follower can be viewed as the 'outcome' of this mission. The story should be understandable from itself and not essentially connected with the reality or the historical fact because the structure and formulaic language of the oral text cannot extensively bear the historical trace of evidence or leave the reliable clues for a reconstruction. In order to clarify this point from this aspect, the study following the suggestions above pays attention to the concept of non-monastic follower revealed behind the stylistics in the discourse: the arranged outline, the repetition of sentence and phrases, the usage of the stock phrase, and repetition. To understand the meaning, it is necessary to know how the elements are arrayed in the discourse. The understanding of the discourses in this fashion should better reflect the meaning in the canon.

1.3.3 Theory of Religious Experience

In the study, theory on religious experience will be applied to analyse the meaning constructed in the discourses with the usage of predictable

93 The Middle-Length Saying, Vol. II, p. 99 ff.

pattern and formulaic language, i.e., the sermon delivered by the Buddha and the hearer's expression in reaction to the delivered sermon, in the conclusion of discourse. The theory applied in the study was developed by Ann Taves in her book "Religious Experience Reconsidered." Therein, she proposed a framework on the study of religious experience for the benefit of comparative religion. The religious experience is the process of seeing, hearing, or experiencing of a thing or event deemed holy, ideal, anomalous, and thus special for the person who perceives the thing or the event.

Theory of religious experience was first adopted and adapted in the study of religion during the first half of the twentieth century. William James, the psychologist, defined the meaning in English as "*the feelings, acts, and experiences of individual men in their solitude, so far as they apprehend themselves to stand in relation to whatever they may consider divine.*"[94] Connected with the systematic theology, religious experience mentioned in religious traditions is regarded as the religious meaning.[95] Therefore, religious experience from various traditions is unique and inherent in the context.[96] It does not allow a comparison between the traditions. To solve this problem, Taves suggested the idea that "*religious or mystical or spiritual or sacred "things" are created when religious significance is assigned to them.*"[97] On this principle, the religious experience is not regarded as inherent and substantive in a particular religion, but it is a meaning to a thing or an event given by an individual or a particular group, who has experienced it. Stating this intention clearly, she avoided the sense *religious experience* as used in theological study and defined it instead in terms of *experience deemed special.* As followed, religious experience according to Taves is another thing from the classical 'religious experience,' which she called *religious experience in sui generis model.*[98] As the experience in the classical model is the mystic experience relating to the *holy* claimed by the pious in the religious community, the experience is

94 James, The Varieties of Religious Experience, p. 32.
95 Cf. Stolz, Grundzüge der Religionswissenschaft, pp. 20–21.
96 Cf. Wulff, Psychologists Define Religion, p. 208.
97 Taves, Religious Experience Reconsidered, p. 8, 17.
98 Ibid., p. 18: see Table 1.1 in the book.

inherent and constant to people in the tradition. The new developed model considers the religious experience as individual or group's religious consciousness developed in the ascription of things that a person or a group of people deem special. The figure below is Taves's summary of the phenomena categorized due to the person who has experience (individual or group) and the type of ascribing the experience (simple or composite ascription).[99]

Figure 1: Taves's Categorization of Religious Experience

Variations in the Nature of Experience by Ascriptive Unit and Type of Ascription

		Ascriptive Unit	
		Individuals	*Group*
Type of Ascription	Simple	• Individuals deem a particular thing or event as special. • The experience of individuals in contact with the thing or present at the event counts as evidence for ascriptions, though others may not consider it plausible.	• Groups constitute themselves as such by reaching interpretive consensus regarding a particular thing or event. • The experience of those in contact with the thing or present at the event (witnesses, disciples) counts as evidence for ascriptions
Type of Ascription	Composite	• Individuals perpetuate an initial thing or event deemed special by re-creating it through practices they deem efficacious. • Individual experience counts as evidence for the efficacy of practices relative to the goal, though others may not consider it plausible.	• Groups perpetuate an initial thing or event deemed special by agreeing on how it can be re-created. • The re-creation of thing/event rests on group consensus regarding the efficacy of practices relative to the special goal, which outsiders typically do not find convincing.

The ascription as simple and composite is the attitude and activity to the special experience after encountering it. A special experience once encountered by a person or a group of persons may simply be remembered as special. The ascription in this case is called 'simple,' as it does not further to other activities concerning the special thing or event. However, when the special experience is followed by an attempt, for example, to investigate the experience, to re-create or to imitate the experience with the purpose to relate, connect, or call for the experience or the

99 Ibid, p. 53.

achievement of the experience once more. The activities are the cause of organizing ideas or process on the method, process, or path systematically to achieve the goal determined in relation to the experience. This is 'composite' ascription, which paves the way to religious organization. In short, in her words: "*A focus on things deemed religious in turn allows us to make a distinction between simple ascriptions, in which an individual thing is set apart as special, and composite ascriptions, in which simple ascriptions are incorporated into more complex formations, such as those that scholars and others designate as 'spiritualities,' or 'religions.'*"[100]

Figure 2: Taves's Model of Religious Experience "Simple Ascription"

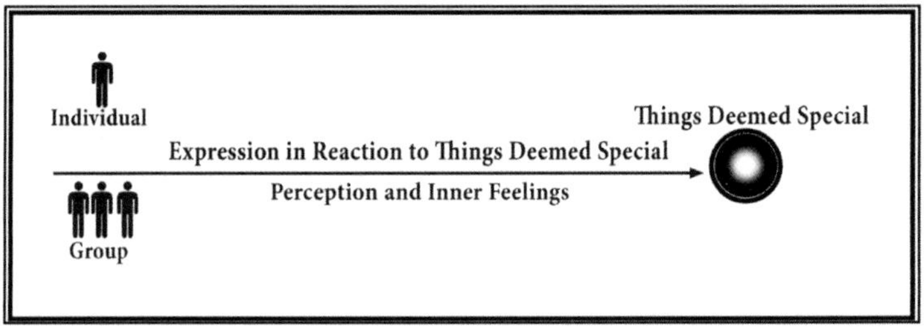

Taves called the process *simple ascription*, by which the people may have the religious experience with the things deemed special variously, and express in response with different behaviours and actions. The consciousness from the single ascription can become more complicated when those who have had the experience perpetuate the thing or event deemed special. Taves called the action *composite ascription*. See the figure 3.

Figure 3: Taves's Model of Religious Experience "Composite Ascription"

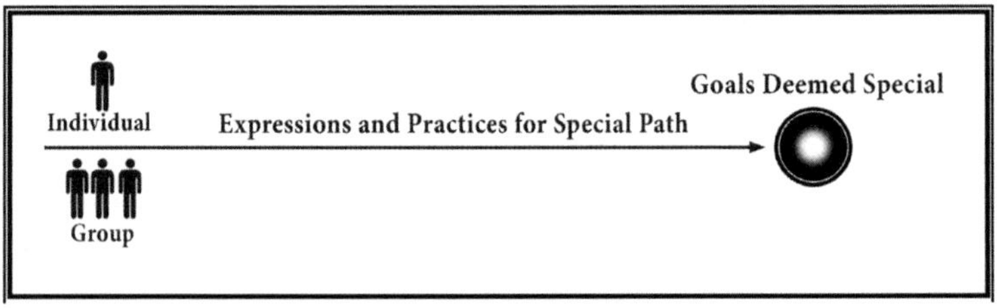

100 Ibid., p. 9.

In figure 3, the encountered experience inspires the people to search for the significance in ways relating to the specialness and some higher power.[101] To achieve the goal, those who have had the experience arrive at a consensus about the goal and the mean, which is developed into religious path. A religious experience may inspire several paths, when the people disagree with the goal or the means of the other paths and redirects the goal and the means for themselves. In this way, one may reconstruct the development of sect or religion that consists of several paths, in which an individual or a group of people shares the same goal, set as the center of the paths. It can be seen that the people are behaving in the similar direction.

Figure 4: Formation of Ascriptions in Making of Religion

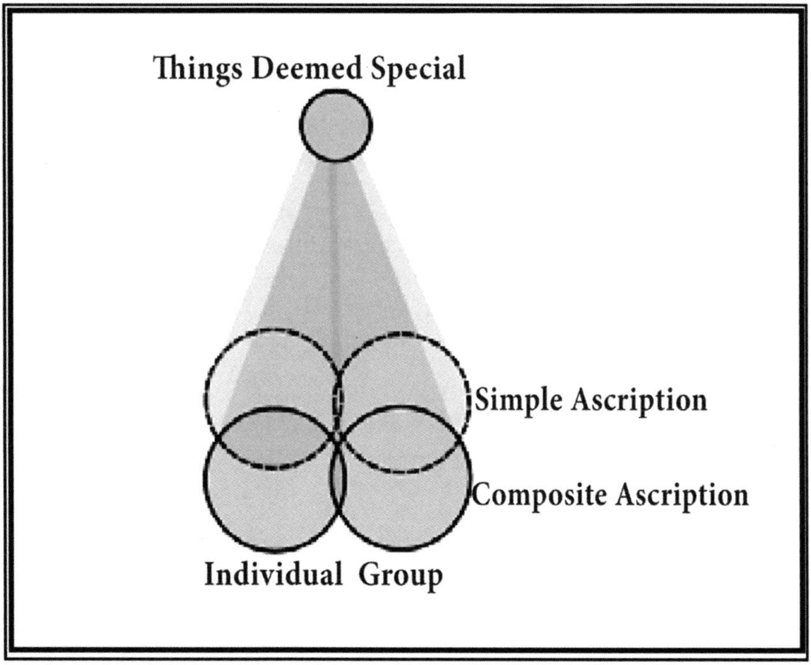

From the figure above, different paths followed by individuals and groups of the people, who have encountered the experience, may be

101 Ibid., p. 51.

developed in relation to the goal set as the center. To achieve the goal, they follow the paths developed on the purpose. In summary, the simple ascription is the building block constructing composite ascriptions that create a larger religious denomination in relation to the thing that the people deem special, which consists of the variations of paths together.

Taves's model on the religious experience excellently sheds light to the way to interpret the followership depicted in the Nikāya discourse, which offers the picture of instructing an individual follower in contribution to the making of religious community. First, Buddha's sermon in each discourse is regarded as *specialness*, to which Pāli tradition exclusively assigns the religious significance inspiring a hearer's decision to become a follower. Second, tradition has with it the structure and the use of stock phrases that Buddha's followers, monastic and non-monastic alike, had theoretically passed on this *experience*. In this light, it is thus possible to understand the process behind the declaration of belief and even the religiosity carried out by the lay follower with the theory of religious experience.

In doing this, the Nikāya discourses are approached in the following ways:

1. The discourse constructs the plot that unfolds an idea about development of belief and "conversion" presented in the discourse.
2. The theory is applied to analyse the pattern, by which people were motivated to declare the followership under the Buddha.
3. The theory is applied to understand thought and feeling of the people, expressed stereotypically in stock phrase, in reaction to *religious specialness*

The first point can be problematic in that the discourse is not a true account of description by those who claimed to have had the experience.[102] The term experience is applied to the feeling to believe in Buddha, which is depicted as the reaction to the encounter with the Buddha. The language, constructed plot, and method to convey a teaching the doctrine reveal some idea about "Buddhist" and the making of the Buddhist, which is a unified and systematized form of religious expression.[103] This is the way

102 Taves, Religious Experience Reconsidered, p. 69: Types of Data.
103 Wach, Types of Religious Experience Christian and Non-Christian, p. 39.

that the oral literature presents some abstract ideas with situations.[104] The discourses, which are developed in a certain theme and repeatedly told in the same pattern, reveal the ideas on the Buddhist belief: as to what should have happened to people, how they should have felt and expressed in response, etc. when they have encountered the Buddha and heard his sermon. The regularity of the incidents is the fact about the Buddhist that tradition tells the audience.

The second problem concerns the theory of religious experience applied to interpret the meaning of discourse, which is about a motivation, not the religious experience generally understood as the encounter with the Holy. In theistic religions, the experience is the encounter with God or any conscious contact, by which a person perceives the existence of the God in some way. Whereas, in Buddhism, atheistic religion, the sacred experience is meant to the attainment of spiritual experience, such as the mind disciplined with *jhāna* 'contemplation,' the experience of *nirodhasamāpatti* 'attainment of cessation of consciousness,' the mental status of the spiritual people in Theragāthā and Therīgāthā, etc. In this way, religious experience in Buddhism merely points to any experience connected with a spiritual practice. Richard Gombrich, relying on this principle in the investigation of the religious experience in Pāli canon, found that the forms of religious experience mentioned in the canon are uncertain and even unreliable, as they depend on the context, where an experience is claimed to have occurred. Some of them should not be an extraordinary experience, but a kind of hallucination.[105] In this manner, he even seemed to question about the concept as such with a question mark after the name of his article.

In the study, religious experience is defined in terms of the consciousness developed by something ascribed as special that inspires religious motivation. It is applied to understand the behaviours of the people in the development of belief and the process of conversion. This is the way that tradition *symbolically* presents Buddha and his sermon as the specialness, to which a hearer at the end is determined with stock phrases to behave in reaction in a particular way. With regard to the application, some may argue, the general understanding of the conception 'religious experience'

---

104 Ong, Orality and Literacy, p. 49.
105 Gombrich, Religious Experience in Early Buddhism?, p. 146: conclusion.

may be distorted and thus misleading from the classical concept, which particularly denotes to the summit of consciousness from a religion. The adaptation of the concept into the religious motivation can be explained in the following way.

Religious experience in the general sense cannot be compared with the religious experience in Buddhism because of the atheistic nature of the religiosity. Without God as subject to experience, Buddhism, as manifested in the scripture, indoctrinates people with dhamma, the truth, the contemplation, and meditation for the development of *vijjā* 'knowledge' and the sight of the world reality. In this way, the religious experience in Buddhism is not subject to compare with that in any other tradition. However, as Pāli discourse is structured to present Buddha's sermon as the ascribed specialness, the cult, in which people were described with satisfaction and declared their belief, can be defined as "religious experience" in the fashion that it inspires motivation and conversion into the religion. The question here is, as the pattern tells, how the people experience the Buddha and believe in him. The analysis should bring a new model of the understanding about the relation between Buddhist and the religion.

Last, the study of religious experience in Pāli discourses must deal with some typical styles of language in oral text, which is limited to describe incidents or explain concepts. Once more, the religious experience, which is the consciousness in reaction to the delivered sermon, is **not account of real experience of the people,** but the stereotypical image that the tradition ascribed to the Buddhist followership in the structure and language pattern, presenting the followership in the oral performance.[106] The details about behaviours, feelings, activities, etc. are the image that the tradition projected, of how one became the lay follower and what they as the lay follower should have done. This is the definition of followership offered by the oral text, not a clear definition given in a sermon as in written tradition. The study must analyse from the narratives the relation between the hearing of sermon and the outcomes achieved after the activity reflected from the structure and formulaic language of Pāli discourse.

---

106 Cf. Ong, Orality and Literacy, p. 49.

1.4 Definition of Key Terms

The words *upāsaka/upāsikā*, *bhikkhu/bhikkhunī*, and *Sangha* need more explanation in the corresponding English term; for they are often easily coloured by the acquainted concepts from the language and Christian culture that the original sense of terms can be misleading.

1.4.1 Laity; Non-Monastic Follower – *upāsaka/upāsikā*

The English word *laity*, *layperson*, *laypeople* or with genre *layman/laywoman* generally represents the Pāli word *upāsaka* (m.) and *upāsikā* (f.) denoting the Buddhist or Buddha's follower who is not bhikkhu/bhikkhunī, living the ascetic life under the monastic discipline. There are two kinds of upāsaka and upāsikā: the celibate and the married.[107] The married status of householder may relate to the precepts that the people ordinarily observe: the celibate observes the eight precepts while the married observes the five precepts.[108]

The word upāsaka/upāsikā in Pāli and Sanskrit literally means "sitting down near," which Theravada tradition interprets into "sitting down near the Three Jewels."[109] Noticeably, the word is coined in a similar fashion to the word *upaniṣad,* the name of philosophical scripture in Vedic tradition,[110] in which debate and discussion on heterogenic doctrines were compiled.[111] The word upaniṣad is explained to mean "sitting down near," clarified further as "sitting down near the teacher *to hear a sacred knowledge*." The meaning represents the pedagogical tradition of the forest dweller and renunciants, in which the sacred knowledge was told privately to some able pupils that had been passed down through

107 Cf. Lamotte, History of Indian Buddhism, p. 65; Dialogues of the Buddha Part II, p. 112; Dialogues of the Buddha Part III., p. 117ff.,; The Collection of the Middle Length Sayings Vol. II, p. 47, p. 169, p. 209: "layman who is white-clothed and celibate householder," "layman who is white-clothed and married householder," "laywoman who is white-clothed and celibate householder," and "laywoman who is white-clothed and married householder".

108 Walters, Moral Discipline, p. 536.

109 Sumaṅgalavilāsinī Part I, p. 234.

110 Mahony, Upaniṣads, p. 9480.

111 Slaje, Upaniṣaden, p. 814.

the generations.[112] In this way, the word contains the esoteric tone to the extent that the doctrine was not general to other people.[113] Interestingly enough, the people attending the debate or discussion portrayed in the upaniṣad scriptures were not always a Brahmin or an ascetic. They might be a man, a woman, a child, ordinary people who were simply interested to debate or discuss on a metaphysical doctrine. This image reminds the character of upāsaka/upāsikā: 'anybody' who had a philosophical talk with the Buddha and accepted the point that the Buddha had given.

The word upāsaka/upāsikā appears rather in limited context.[114] Generally, Buddha or a monk called a householder, the person who lived the wordly life, gahapati/gahapatinī, no matter the householder was his follower or not.[115]. The designation gahapati/gahapatinī means "the owner of house or family," particularly denoting seṭṭhī "treasurer" or "a man of higher rank in the third caste," which is opposite to the *anāgārika* or "ascetics who had sacrificed the property and severed the connection with the society in order to live the religious life."[116] Sometimes, the word gahapati may be applied to call a Brahmin to emphasize his lifestyle in that he still possessed property and social life in some degree.[117] In this way, the word gahapati/gahapatinī is a common noun, which is not specific to the status or role in the Sangha or a religious institution.

In Dīgha- and Majjhima-nikāya, the status of upāsaka/upāsikā can be promoted to *every people* after hearing a sermon or accepting Buddha's answer given to their question, by declaring to a witness the Three Jewels – Buddha, dhamma, and Sangha- for refuge, and asking to be a follower under the Buddha, like a person to be *bhikkhu.* As surveyed from the

---

112 Monier-Williams, A Dictionary of Sanskrit-English, p. 201.: "the sitting down at the feet of another to listen to his words (and hence secret knowledge given in this manner; but according to native authorities Upanishad means 'sitting at rest ignorance by revealing the knowledge of the supreme spirit)."

113 Mahony, Upaniṣads, p. 9480.

114 See p. 9.

115 Barua, An Analytical Study of Four Nikāyas, p. 70.

116 Cf. Barua, An Analytical Study of Four Nikāyas, pp. 68–69; Humphreys, A Popular Dictionary of Buddhism, p. 31.

117 The Collection of the Middle Length Sayings vol. II, pp. 25–26; cf. Gombrich, Introduction: The Buddhist Way, p. 12.

discourses, the characteristics of the person under the name upāsaka/ upāsikā can be concluded in the following points, which the study will investigate and discuss.

1. He is the person who passed on the process of hearing a sermon. He encountered and debated with Buddha or a monk about a philosophical point. Buddha or the monk then delivered a teaching from their standpoint. At the end, the person was convinced to leave his former belief and follow the offered standpoint.[118] As implied from the text, he was a follower of the Buddha by accepting and revering the teaching of the Buddha *in some degree.*
2. The process of hearing the Buddha's sermon above (1.) was not always successful. Some people did not declare the followership after a sermon while some people who had asked for the followership might change the decision at the last minute.
3. The concept of non-monastic follower should relate to the meaning of the stock phrases at the end of the discourse. From perspective of oral literature, the stock phrases should be the body of the doctrine of Buddha's followership upheld in the Pāli tradition.
4. After the declaration, some non-monastic follower still kept their former social status or remained the former religious life. In this way, *upāsaka/ upāsikā* might be a householder with a profession such as merchant, carpenter, or even religious people from other religious community like Brahmin, mendicant, wanderer. The lay follower who was Brahmin still kept the profession of Vedic teacher and his Vedic school after the declaration of the followership.[119] Likewise, some of wandering *paribbājaka,* who announced the followership under the Buddha, remained ascetic in their school.

---

118 This is clear in DN5, in which Brahmin Kūṭadanta agreed to make worship (Yañña) in Buddha's version; and DN31, in which Sigāla agreed to follow the worship of six directions as Buddha suggested.

119 Pokkharasādi, after declaration of belief, was a lay follower who strongly believed in the Buddha that his name was mentioned in the hearsay concerning Buddha's qualities. It can be seen that a householder can claim themselves Buddha's follower while remaining in their own social and religious status. See DN4, DN5.

In the sub-canonical literature, however, the word upāsaka/upāsikā is used to denote lay follower with restriction to an individual householder "*gahaṭṭha*," (particularly not a wanderer ascetic from other religious group) who has declared going to the Three Jewels for refuge and become a follower.[120] He observes the five moral precepts and has a suitable profession, which path does not conflict to the moral precepts. In Dhammapadaṭṭhakathā, the word usually appears, for example, as vocative in the context, where the Buddha or a monk summons a householder. The meaning of the word points to the institutional tendency, where the monastic is distinguished from the non-monastic in that monastic follower represents themselves as the learner, practitioner, and successor of the Buddha's teaching while ascribes the householder to be the supporter of the monastic community. Therefore, the meaning given in commentary is different from the meaning given in Pāli discourse in that it *implies*, not *states*, the duty in connection with the religious life that the scriptural tradition ascribed to the Buddha's followers.[121]

The understanding may partly arise from the usage of the English term *laity*, for the origin of the word *laity* or *lay* in European language is connected with the meaning "folk" or "people" in Greek *laïkós*, and Latin *laicus*. Particularly in Old Germanic, the meaning of the word *lay/Laie* is synonym to "inexpert" or "illiterate,"[122] which is connected with the tradition of religious education in the Middle Age. In this way, the word *laity* is used to denote the mass of people whose religious knowledge was low in opposite to that of the Christian priest, who were educated in the Church

120 Sumaṅgalavilāsinī Part I, p. 234.

121 The view about the duty should come from the sociological perspective that the monastic and non-monastic followers dependently correlate. As the result, some scholars regarded the activity of one in response to the other one as 'duty.' Cf. Prebish, Laity, p. 468: "It is also a responsibility of the laity to provide for the welfare of the monastic community through offerings of clothing, food, and the like." In fact, in the Pāli canon mentions no duty of the householder to provide the gift to the monastic, but the monastic promotes their profile to propagandize the good outcomes achieved from the donation to the well-learned and well-behaving practitioner like the Buddha's order.

122 Ritter and others, Laie, pp. 378–399.

and associated with God.[123] In this fashion, *laity* has to depend on the knowledge of the priest in a sacrament or a religious ritual. This is not the character of lay followership in Buddhist tradition, viz. in Pāli discourse. As Sir Charles Eliot addressed this problem:

> The word (upāsaka) may be conveniently rendered by layman although the distinction between clergy and laity, as understood in most parts of Europe, does not quite respond to the distinction between Bhikkhus and Upāsakas. European clergy are often thought of as interpreters of the Deity, and whenever they have had the power they have usually claimed the right to supervise and control the moral and even the political administration of their country. Something similar may be found in Lamaism, but it forms no part of Gotama's original institution nor of the Buddhist Church as seen today in Burma, Siam and Ceylon.[124]

In this way, the word "laity" ascribed to the mass people is coloured by the connotation concerning the religious knowledge, the chance of education, the social status in the religious institution, and even the spiritual connection with the Supreme Being. In Buddhism, the word is suitably applicable to the Buddhists in the institutional tendency, in which monastic Buddhist is religiously educated, able to be the well learned and achieve Nibbāna while the non-monastic Buddhist is dependent to the monastic on religious activity and instruction and has a limited chance for the spiritual attainment. As a composite of Buddha's community, the non-monastic Buddhist are perceived as the supporter of the monastic follower for *puñña* "merit" that is believed to cause the good rebirth and happiness in the next life as well as create the chance for the monkhood and the spiritual attainment in the future. However, the author considers the concept impractical to the lay follower in Pāli discourse and thus tries to find the meaning behind the relation between the people and the religion.

1.4.2 Monk; Monastic Follower – *bhikkhu/bhikkhunī*

Another term that needs special attention because of cultural differences between Christian and Buddhist culture is the term *monk* and *bhikkhu.*

123 Cf. Hauschild, Laien, p. 17.

124 Eliot, Hinduism and Buddhism: An Historical Sketch Vol. I, p. 249; referred in: Barua, An Analytical Study of Four Nikāya, p. 71.

In Pāli, bhikkhu (m.) and bhikkhunī (f.) literally means *beggar* because they were ascetic who had neither possession nor profession in the society to crop or earn money and thus begged for food. The ascetic was called collectively *samaṇa*, the religious people who were outside the society in opposite to *brāhmaṇa*, the religious people who were specialist in the Vedic hymns and ritual of the society. Like other ascetics in other contemporaneous schools, bhikkhu had no house and wandered in different places, alone or in-group. They devoted lifetime for the religious doctrine, spending time on the practice or philosophical discussion with other ascetics. Buddhist tradition distinguishes ascetics from the schools with different names. Bhikkhu/bhikkhunī is the name reserved for the male and female ascetics particularly under the Buddha's doctrine[125] while outside the community other terms are used such as *acela or acelaka, paribbājaka*. Ascetics might be called in connection with the leader of the school, such as *Nigantha* the ascetic pupil of Nigantha Nāṭāputta. The Buddhist monks self were called by others *sakkaputta samaṇa* "the ascetic who is the son of the Sakka or the Buddha."

From the literal meaning, the word *bhikkhu* applied to Buddha's follower obviously emphasizes the *dependent* aspect of the ascetic life in that they ordinarily live on donation. This means that they never lived on their own or separated themselves to live in a distance forever. According to Nissaya, the doctrine of the most basic life told to a new-ordained monk, the members of the monastic order live poorly on the food that they begged on their walking and luck.[126] Even in Dhutaṅga, which is regarded as the doctrine of austerity allowed by the Buddha, the begging of food is made more difficult by limitation on the begging and the place where the food is received.[127] It appears neither that the monastic people grow the crop nor prepare the food by themselves. Nor are they allowed to be a vegetarian or to choose favourite food. In this way, the life of the monk and the nuns is always dependent on other people's generosity. Living on the donation, they are thus expected by the society, the donator, to live and behave

125 In the first sermon, Buddha called the five ascetics with the word 'bhikkhu,' despite the fact that the ascetics have not asked to become a monk.

126 The Book of the Discipline, vol. IV, p 75.

127 The Path of Purification, pp. 66–69.

modestly and poorly, as far as they are the beggar in the society. On this principle, the monastic rules were developed to control the monk to prevent luxurious life and live modestly after some of them had expressed some inappropriate lifestyle and received critics from the society.

The fact that the 'bhikkhu' has severed the connection with the worldly society to live on the monastic rules, which enforce on the poor lifestyle, leads to the adoption of the word *monk* in Christian culture, which is derived from the Greek *monachos* "solitary, single," for the English translation. In fact, the monastic traditions from the two cultures are found similar in several aspects, in which some scholars observed from the perspective of cultural contact.[128] In Christianity, the word signifies to the Christian in Catholic tradition who left the society to live an ascetic life for the grace of God. In the early period, the Christian monks lived alone in desert far from the society. Later, monastic disciplines were developed to regulate the austere life within the monastic community after more people later had joined the living. In this connection, the word bhikkhu in Buddhist tradition, who likewise lives under the monastic discipline, is translated into *monk* in English or other derivations in European languages; whereas, the words representing other Indian ascetics are translated into English *mendicant, recluse, wanderer* that emphasizes the aspect of wandering ascetic whose lifestyle is unclear about the institutionalization and regulation.[129] In so doing, the Christian concept of monk colours the image of Buddhist monk in our perception into a kind of *disciplined ascetic, poor, austere* life, which is problematic in Buddhism,[130] because life of bhikkhu is never always considered as austerity. The life in the monastic order may be hard in comparison with the life of householder, but from the perspective of ascetics together, the life is considered light, as some

---

128 The similarity of monasticism in Buddhist and Christian tradition is addressed in Neu, Die Analogie von buddhistischem und christlichem Mönchtum. Eine sozialgeschichtliche und religionswissenschaftliche Untersuchung, pp. 97–121, and discussed in Freiberger, Zum Vergleich zwischen buddhistischem und christlichem Ordenswesen, pp. 83–104.

129 Freiberger, Zur Verwendungsweise der Bezeichnung *paribbājaka*, p. 121.

130 Cf. Freiberger, Anmerkungen zur Begriffsbildung in der Buddhismusforschung, p. 140.

contemporaneous ascetics had criticized.[131] Buddha self criticized the austerity and self-mortification as the extreme life that should be avoided and in this way regulated the community life on the middle way, which is neither too extreme in worldly happiness nor austerity.[132] In fact, life of Bhikkhu is sufficient, but as observed from outsider, it is a poor life because it still depends on the donation and thus lives on the uncertainty of the donation.

The study emphasizes the difference between the two kinds of followerships in Buddhism and thus stresses the distinction of the two significations in spite of the fact that the Pāli term is at best represented by the Pāli tradition.[133] To represent the word bhikkhu, the author applies the word *monastic follower* to denote both bhikkhu and bhikkhunī because the word *monk*, which is frequently used in the scientific works, rather has a connotation of the male members of the Sangha in the tradition.[134] The translation reduces the sexism and makes a distinction between the two kinds of followers, who live on the monastic rules (Vinaya) and not on the rule. The antonym non-monastic follower or non-monastic Buddhist is also suitable for the study, as it is neutral and not connected with the special practice of celibacy and observance of the eight precepts.

1.4.3 Monastic Order - *Saṅgha*

The word *saṅgha* literally means group or assembly. In Buddhist literature, the word denotes the assembly of monk and nun or *monastic community* under the Buddha in particular.[135] To represent the concept clearly in a

131 Dialogues of the Buddha Part I, p. 223–224; The Collection of the Middle Length Sayings. Vol. II, p. 55. The discourses evidence the Buddhist acceptance that ascetic life in other schools was much harder than in Sangha that lived in the middle way.

132 The Book of Discipline Vol. IV, p. 15.

133 Cf. Freiberger, Anmerkungen zur Begriffsbildung in der Buddhismusfoschung, pp. 143–146. The word 'monk' is problematic in history of Buddhism because the monastic followers in the Buddhist traditions have a wide range from ascetic practitioner to non-celibate practitioner.

134 Freiberger, Anmerkungen zur Begriffsbildung in der Buddhismusfoschung, p. 143.

135 Humphreys, A Popular Dictionary of Buddhism, p. 167; cf. Wijayaratna, Buddhist Monastic Life, p. 1.

European language, it is better to represent with the term *order,*[136] although the word "community" is also acceptable. The order may settle in an area such as *ārāma* 'forest,' *vihāra* 'pavilion,' *pāsāda* 'mansion,' which may simply be called monastery as seen nowadays. According to Pāli canon, the community in the early age, like other ascetic communities under other teachers, wandered from place to place except in the rainy season. Despite receiving a place to live, the ascetics groups kept wandering after the rainy retreat.[137] All of them lived under monastic rules and some communal customs determined by the Buddha. Nevertheless, the community consisted of sub-groups headed by a monk who was the great instructor of the group of monks with similar interest and skill.[138] Wandering in the countries, the community lived on donation from local people and occasionally had a contact with other communities. With the monastic rules and instructions, they separated themselves definitively from other ascetic communities and householders, including Buddhist householders, in order to control behaviour and lifestyle effectively.

Sangha in the wider sense may be perceived in term of abstract concept of Buddhist, in which the spirituality is counted for the membership.[139] Lay follower who reached a stage of spiritual attainment is thus a member of the Sangha as well, like a monk. Sangha in this tendency symbolizes the followership of the Buddhist in that they followed the spiritual path and reached the goal that the Buddha had pointed. The membership of non-monastic Buddhist in the abstract Sangha indicates that people outside the monastic order is considered Buddha's follower and has the potential to develop themselves on the spiritual path.

In the study, the word Sangha will be generally applied in the meaning of monastic order. However, the author tends to avoid the word and uses instead the English translation "order" to represent the monastic community, so that the word Sangha exclusively represents the ideal community, which is not specific to the monastic follower.

---

136 Cf. Gombrich, Introduction: The Buddhist way, p. 9, 13; Freiberger, Der Orden in der Lehre, p. 29.

137 Wijayaratna, Buddhist Monastic Life, p. 29.

138 The Book of the Kindred Sayings Vol. II, pp. 108–109.

139 Freiberger, Der Orden in der Lehre, pp. 237–238.

1.5 Other Regulations in the Study

1.5.1 Orthography

The study is based on Pāli scripture, so any name and Buddhist terminology is thus in Pāli orthography. For example, the study uses the form *dhamma* instead of *dharma*, *Nigantha* instead of *Nirgrantha*. The name of people, towns, and other proper noun is spelt in Pāli form such as *Rājagaha* instead of *Rājagṛha* in Sanskrit, *Sakka* instead of *Śākya*, *Sāriputta* instead of *Śāriputta*. Some Sanskrit words that are known in English in Sanskrit form are spelt with the popular form such as *karma* instead of *kamma, which* is the Pāli counterpart.

1.5.2 Reference to Pāli Canon

The study is based on the Pāli text and translation of Dīgha-nikāya and Majjhima-nikāya offered by Pāli Text Society. As the study mainly deals with Pāli discourse, the discourse is identified with number. In referring a paragraph from the canon, the author mentions the volume, the page, and the row of the text respectively while in referring translation, the author cites the source like a book: the English name of the scripture, volume, and page, as given in the example below.

Example on the references:

DN2 refers to the second discourse of Dīgha-nikāya or Sāmaññaphalasutta.
MN56 refers to the seventy-sixth discourse of Majjhima-nikāya or Upālisutta.
Pāli text: MN I 318, 6–7 refers to Majjhima-nikāya Vol. I, p. 318, line 6–7.
Translation: The Collection of the Middle Length Sayings Vol. II, pp. 379 ff. refers to the English translation of Majjhima-nikāya published by Pali Text Society.

All references of Pāli text are collected in the indices at the end of the study.

1.5.3 Reference to Stock Phrase

The study approaches the Pāli discourses as oral literature and thus mentions some terms about oral literature. One of the terms, which the study directly addresses, is the word *formula* denoting one or two sentences up to one paragraph that regularly appear throughout an oral text. As defined by Milman Parry and supported by Albert Lord, formula is *"a group of words which is regularly employed under the same metrical conditions to express a given essential idea.*"[140] The formula is the useful device for rapid composition of the text. With the idea about the text production, Lord called the production of oral literature in terms of "performance." Many scholars later have adopted the idea in their work and invented new terms representing the word, so the word has many synonyms such as mnemonic formula, cliché, stock expression, stereotyped phrase,[141] pericope, formulaic expression, standard phrase.[142] Mark Allon has questioned the difference identified by the names and the used contexts and found that the definition of the word used by scholars in contexts is not consistent.[143]

Among the choices, the author uses the word *stock phrase,* which *literal meaning of the word refers to its function as supplied passage* that represents a fixed meaning in a making of oral texts, i.e. in a recitation.[144] However, for the orality in Pāli canon, scholars tended to concentrate on the question or discussion concerning the *production* of the text, such as the aid of transmitting the text,[145] or on the learning of teaching.[146] The author has shown above[147] that the oral text needs another set of knowledge and approach to understand the concepts that the text actually conveys, and on this focus, it should be possible not to discuss on the used term implying the idea about the development of the stock phrase and the text. Any question on the function of the stock phrase in the history or the development of the Buddhist literature will not be mentioned in the study. As the text to read nowadays, the stock phrases in the parts of discourse, which play an important role on the meaning of the Nikāya discourse, are neglected. The author thus pays attention on the essential idea that phrase

140 Parry, Studies in the Epic Technique of Oral Verse-Making, p. 80; referred in, Lord, The Singer of Tales, p. 30.
141 Allon, Style and Function, p. 9.
142 Anālayo, A Comparative Study of the Majjhima-nikāya Vol. 1, p. 16.
143 Allon, Style and Function, pp. 9–12.
144 A recitation can be reckoned a making or a production in view of the audience because it makes the meaning new in a context.
145 Allon, Style and Function, p. 7.
146 Gethin, The Mātikā: Memorization, Mindfulness, and the List, p. 155; referred in: Allon, Style and Function, p. 7.
147 See detail in 1.3.2.

or word group represents which is significant to the understanding of the discourse as oral literature.

The stock phrases are studied on its appearance in the first chapter. They will be referred in the following chapters with the number in parentheses. The numbers and the represented texts are shown in the appendix III.

1.6 Outline of the Study

Each chapter of the study is developed in the following way.

In the second chapter, the author poses the question about the the *meaning* of oral form in Nikāya discourse conveyed to the audience while they were transmitted: read aloud, rehearsed, or told to another person, like oral epics in other oral traditions. In this connection, the scripture should be approached in line with the knowledge about oral literature in order to understand the religious concepts reflected in the tradition. The chapter devotes on structural study and analysis of the discourses with a particular focus on the conclusion that provides the resolution of the given story in formulaic language. To support the author's argument that the Nikāyas discourses do not merely convey a text of sermon, it demonstrates that the discourses form an epic of Buddha's mission containing sub-stories of Buddha's delivery of sermon to different people. In each sub-story, his sermon is presented to satisfy or surprise the hearers as well as to change many of them into a follower, both monastic and non-monastic.

In the third chapter, the study of lay follower begins with the micro level of the analysis of the individual, which is the foundation of religious community. The development of Buddhist belief will be traced in the narrative of the discourses along Taves's *model of simple ascription*. As the oral text communicates a concept with story, the chapter observes the development of the belief in the Buddha that occurs at two stages: first by hearing or seeing visible qualities of the Buddha and second by hearing Buddha's sermon. The outcome of hearing the sermon in the conclusion will be categorized and defined. Following Ann Taves's theory of religious experience, the author considers the process parallel to the structure of religious experience, on which the belief and religiosity is founded. The chapter aims at analyzing the *experience deemed special* expressed in the development of belief aroused by the two kinds of *things deemed special:* first, the visible characteristics of the Buddha, and second, the sermon of the Buddha respectively.

Finally, the chapter discusses on the relation between the things deemed special and the reverence towards the Three Jewels, expressed in the stock phrase denoting the declaration of belief and followership.

In the fourth chapter, the study focuses on the construction of individual belief into a larger structure of religious community. Religious activities of non-monastic follower in Pāli discourse are investigated in Taves's *model of composite ascription* with the aim to find the direction of spiritual intention and goal after the declaration of lay followership. With the *experience deemed special* in the simple ascription, the non-monastic follower perpetuated the experience by carrying out activities in relation to the Buddha and his community, which the author calls *religiosity*. The religiosity comprises three activities: the act of declaring the belief and followership, or *Buddhist conversion*; the praising of Buddha's qualities; and the religious devotion. The activities mentioned in the discourse will be observed in connection with the analysis in the third chapter to understand the *behaviours and feelings* to the community. This is the *religious meaning*, the ideal of lay religiosity in the Pāli discourse, which points to the *followership of the non-monastic Buddhist* in relation to the Buddha and his monastic order.

The last chapter concludes the followership of the non-monastic follower as investigated in the Pāli discourse and suggests ideas about researching Buddhism from the finding and the experience in the study.

With the different perspective on studying Pāli discourse, the author ventures critics from scholars who are used to the classical methods. However, it is hoped that the study would present some different ideas. Primarily, we should be more aware of the meaning of orality in the Buddhist traditions. Particularly, the pattern of text and the use of stock phrases, which are not achieved merely by reading or following the scripts. The succession of the literary tradition from oral to written tradition results in the adoption of some styles in the literature of later tradition. Likewise, the Buddhist followership and their religiosity, which are mentioned in the text, should be a focus for a wider discussion for an understanding of the tradition, both the scripture and the people. A study of Buddhism in this direction should contribute to a new way of analyzing concepts of this religion in particular and offer perspectives of the religion in comparison with others.

Chapter II: Discourse as Imagery of Buddha's Mission

Discourse or *sutta* is an episode of Buddha's sermon, collected in the Nikāyas of Suttapiṭaka in Pāli canon. It depicts situations attributed to the Buddha's lifetime, telling how the Buddha or one of his chief disciples delivered a sermon and, in respond to the sermon, how the hearer became a follower of the Buddha. Containing the teachings, Pāli discourse is a crucial source of doctrine and religious concepts in Buddhism. However, according to the perspective of oral tradition, some of the doctrines or concepts are not to achieve simply by reading because they are not directly given within the text composed particularly for oral performance or transmission, as the text is structured to convey meanings to the audience in a particular way that dovetails with the vocal. To understand its meaning is thus simply not to read and follow the written scripts, but also to understand with the knowledge about mechanism of oral literature in conveying the meaning to the audience. On the other word, it is necessary to know the system of oral text that functions on communicating meanings in a performance. In the beginning, the author surveys the structure and language, which basically relates to the presentation of followers in relation to the Buddha's delivery of sermon.

2.1 Remarks on Pāli Discourse as Oral Literature

Pāli discourse is viewed as a collection of Buddha's sermon delivered in different situations.[148] From the perspective of the reader, the idea and the teaching given in the sermon is considered as the significant *message* of the discourse, while the situations are the minor component in the presentation. As the discourse is rather complete and informative about the incidents and the teachings, scholars *read* the oral text as written text focusing on stories and teachings, often without attention on the meaning of oral-formulaic language, which actually has a function while the

148 For example: Norman, Pāli Literature, p. 30.

text was uttered. The oral-formulaic languages[149] are considered merely as the mnemonic *device* for the memory of the text and transmission of some significant concepts. Without consideration of other possibility in the transmission, this opinion is clearly given from perspective of written tradition. The scholars hardly suspect the elements in the text that convey some meaning in particular.

As a genre of scripture in Navaṅgasatthusāsana, Sutta is traditionally reckoned a certain form of scripture containing a teaching of Buddha or his disciples in dialogue, prose, or verse in a situation.[150] Sutta may merely refer to a collection of Buddha's teaching, as mentioned in Mahāpadesa, DN16.[151] Apart from the term, there is another similar word *suttanta*, such as in *suttantapiṭaka* 'basket of *suttanta*.' The word is the compound of *sutta* and *anta*: *sutta* or *sūtra* 'tread' in the old tradition that denotes the short sentence on a gist of doctrine for memorization, as in the study of Pāṇini's grammar. Compounded with *anta* 'end,' the word signifies to a text at the end of the collection.[152] The word *suttanta* can be understood in term of *commentary of sutta*, i.e. the teaching elaborated with story of people and background.[153] From the characteristics comparable to Bhaṣya,

---

149 In Foley's article "Word-Power, Performance, and Tradition," the word is sometimes called "grammars of phraseology and narrative pattern (p. 279)," "textual libretto" (p. 280), "grammars of 'words'" (p. 282).

150 Rhys Davids, The History and Literature of Buddhism, p. 36. In this way, a single episode of sermon in Khuddhaka Nikāya may be regarded as Sutta as well, such as Sutta Nipāta. Traditionally, Sutta as one of nine aṅgas in canonical texts classifies all the sermon in verse as gāthā, while sutta may denote scriptures composed in verse such as sutta in Dīgha- and Majjhima-nikāya, Niddesa, Khandhaka, Parivāra, etc. See Norman, Pāli Literature, pp. 15–16.

151 Klaus, Zu den buddhistischen literarischen Fachbegriffen *sutta* und *suttanta*, p. 524.

152 Ibid., pp. 524–525. Surveying other compounds ending with –anta in Sanskrit in comparison with the single word without the suffix, Klaus considered that the suffix does not make a different meaning. With supports from differentiated names of Buddha's teaching, which does not represent specific characters, he concluded there should be no significant difference in meaning between sutta and suttanta. Both simply represent Buddha's teaching.

153 Cf. Tub and Boose, Scholastic Sanskrit, p. 173. The author does not agree with the Tub and Boose's statement that "This format is based both

it can be supposed that the discourses might be a commentary work composed with some influence from the structure of the commentary in the Vedic tradition.[154] The presupposition about the origin of the discourses may be true to form, but there is no evidence which supports it, i.e., the *sutta*, the short tread believed to be the original text, does not exist in any tradition. From this perspective, Buddhist discourse is theoretically regarded as a commentary but practically still canonical. This is probably the new meaning that tradition gave in the old text to represent some meanings in the community.

The study of Laurie Patton in "Myth as Argument" pointed to the fact that a composition of commentary may generate another meaning. In his study, he examined the nature of Bṛhaddevatā together with the original text Ṛgveda. He found that, despite theoretically the commentary of the Ṛgveda, Bṛhaddevatā forms the coherent and well-categorized knowledge that supports the stories of people in Ṛgveda.[155] The finding led him to raise two significant points about commentary in Indian tradition: First, the canonical commentary can occur in more various fashions and functions than the commentary in the European culture that emphasizes on philosophical explanation. Second, a question on Indian commentary should be related to its function to observe "*the nature of commentarial totalization*," in which the commentary may function as encyclopedia in life.[156] Obviously, Bṛhaddevatā is not only the elaboration of the hymns in Ṛgveda, but also contains other knowledge significant to the learning and ritual purpose within the tradition.

---

historically and stylistically on oral debate..." The incident is not necessary from a real debate, rather a stylistic presenting philosophical arguments in oral tradition. Also, there is no evidence to prove that the debate really occurred as the text describes. A debate can be at best understood in terms of supposition based on the objection of the other side because debate can occur in any situation, in which the conflict of ideas is handled.

154 Ibid.: "Traditionally, discussion of meaning takes the form of a dialog in which the commentator allows opponents to raise various objections against the texts or against his interpretation of it and then proceeds to refute these objections."

155 Patton, Myth as Argument, p. 442.

156 Ibid., p. 443.

As a result, he interestingly called the Bṛhaddevatā from this perspective that the text represents "*destiny of the Veda,*" how a commentary can redirect the meaning of the Vedic tradition. At this point, Patton gave the questions about the process of representing a canon of any tradition in narrative or visual media. "*How is the collectivity of verses, or images, or canonical objects, depicted? What power is claimed for that collectivity? When can the symbolic whole of the canon stand for it representations inadequate? What are the interpretative and contextual reasons for a visual, as distinct from a verbal, representation of canon?*"[157] In this way, Pāli discourse, which depicts incidents of encounter and conversation as the scene for an explanation or debate of a teaching according to the commentary tradition, may offer a new meaning and function in the Buddhist tradition. Despite no archetypal texts pointing the beginning of the tradition, the use of the unique stylistics generates or reinforces some ideas in the literary tradition unconsciously. Structure and formulaic languages of Pāli discourse which strongly shapes a sermon text or Buddha's teaching[158] may shape a new "destiny of Buddha's teaching" that the discourses play another role in the tradition. In this light, the meaning of the Nikāya discourse in Theravada Buddhism should be observed.

From the function on transmission, a discourse is however viewed as a part of Pāli canon preserving the teachings and major incidents. Since the writing down of the Pāli canon in the palm leafs in the reign of King Vaṭṭagāminī Abhaya in 29–17 BC,[159] the scripture in the tradition should have been approached from the view of written tradition. When Buddhaghosa went to Ceylon for the translation of Sinhalese canon and commentary into the language *Māgadhī,* he did not seem to be aware of the orality of the text and its particular way of communicating meaning. As tradition

157 Ibid., p. 446.

158 Hinüber, A Handbook of Pali Literature, p. 26.

159 Lang, "Pāli Canon" in Encyclopedia of Buddhism, p. 584. The year is calculated according to tradition: Buddhist teachings were brought to Sri Lanka by Mahinda at a year of his lifetime 282–222 BCE, and were written down in the reign of King Vaṭṭagāmaṇi circa 29–17 BCE. This means, the teachings were learned and transmitted orally for around 200 years in Sri Lanka, and it is therefore impossible to know what the canon looked like. It could be different from the present version.

has it, he came there to learn commentary, wrote Visuddhimagga, which is the summary of Buddha's teaching in the canon, in order to convince the community of Sinhalese monks that he was qualified to work on their scriptures, viz. their commentary in Sinhalese language.[160] Certainly, he worked on the canonical texts verbalized in the written form as he normally dealt with other scriptures.[161] After that, his works contributed to the religious education and production of literature. Until today, Pāli canon with its commentary is religious scripture published and distributed to read for the learning of the contents, teachings, stories, etc. transmitted in the tradition. People, viz. the Buddhist, hence view the canon as the collection of books and the contents as the historical incidents. In study of religion, Pāli canon has the status like other religious scriptures which are to be read for the understanding of the doctrines and concepts given in each sentence. Some scholars construed the text as the records of words and situations, as to how the Buddha propagated his doctrine.[162] In sum, a discourse is *raised* as the religious constitution for the teaching contained and *read* for the presented contents. Sermon is perceived to be philosophical and historical information or the 'message' of text that the transmitter preserved and transmitted in the tradition.

Several scholars attempt to understand the text from the nature of oral literature, which has nothing with the scripts. They are of the opinion that the text should be approached with an impression of hearing in that the concentration should focus on the meaning received by hearing, not the signs received by seeing. For example, Ray mentioned the flexibility in understanding the oral literature, "*Oral tradition in Buddhism, when it is not fixed in authoritative texts and a set canon, retains a certain fluidity. But when teachings are fixed in authoritative form, particularly in writing, orthodoxy and standardization can more easily become dominant concern.*"[163] Likewise, Griffiths suggested, in reading the religious text as such, grasping the *gist* of the message presented in the text,

160 Norman, Pāli Literature, p. 120, pp. 128–130.
161 Cf. Ong, Orality and Literacy, p. 10. The author quoted his statement p. 18.
162 Langer, Sermon Studies and Buddhism: A Case Study of Sri Lankan Preaching, p. 1.
163 Ray, Buddhist Saints in India, p. 34.

not the *verbatim*.[164] In somewhere else,[165] he recommended considering the significance of literacy and the relation to the orality. In practical, however, the meaning perceived in context of performance is ungraspable because the tradition has forgotten the senses since the adoption of writing in the transmission.[166]

To deal with the original meaning of the text, scholars in oral literature and ethnography suggested that the meaning of the oral literature can be investigated from words which are the basic elements forming the literature.[167] Reading can approach to the text with the awareness of its oral form and performance. "*'Reading' is what the signs are and how texts and performances inhabit mutually exclusive worlds.*"[168] Foley accepted the power of the word in studying the meaning of oral literature in that "*words engage contexts and mediate communication in traditional oral narrative.*"[169] This means, the meaning of the words and stock phrases in the text concerns to the meaning conveyed in the performance and in the tradition. In the transmission, the reciters who transmitted the texts must have known or understood the words in the literature well, as they were in the context of oral performance or recitation.[170] The words are the source of the old meaning concealed in the oral tradition, as he stated

> ... Multiformity, as expressed in formulas, themes, and story patterns, provided the synchronic solution to the ongoing challenge of performance. This approach led to the discovery of elaborate "grammar" of phraseology and narrative pattern that subtended the languages of traditional oral poetry. It became a tour de force

164 Griffiths, Religious Reading, p. 51.
165 Ibid., pp. 28–29.
166 Cf. Foley, Word-Power, Performance, and Tradition, p. 290. "Because the texts are already removed from the performance, and preserve only a limited and decontextualized record of that performance, they in effect make even the scholar closest to them an "outsider" who can never recover the multifaceted reality that lies behind them."
167 As John Foley claimed, Milman Parry, Albert Lord, Richard Bauman, Dell Hymes.
168 Foley, Signs, Texts, and Oral Tradition, p. 21.
169 Foley, Word-Power, Performance, and Tradition, p. 278.
170 No matter the text had been created 'for' or 'in' a live performance; every time of recitation should be regarded as a 'creation,' because the text is given in another context.

to "count the formulas" or to map the themes in given versions of given songs, and thus to begin to glimpse the traditional multiformity that was available as a communicative medium...[171]

In its appearance, the words do not exist alone. Particularly, they form into formula or stock phrases, systematically in certain order and context, referring to some meaning in the way that is understandable to the audience.[172] Thus, for Foley, the formulaic languages "*cannot be dismissed simply as "dead letter." The integers of expression and perception, the cognitive categories that function optimally only within the enabling event of performance, retain in their textual forms a rhetorical vestige of that performance that cannot be ignored.*"[173] In sum, stock phrases found in the text should not be considered merely as the mnemonic aid. In the theory of oral literature, it may function as referent of some meanings known in the tradition.

From this perspective, to understand the concept of non-monastic follower given in stock phrase at the end of the discourse, it is significant to approach the "grammar" or the system, in which the literature lies in the communication of the meaning in the performance. However, this theory has been criticized by Mark Allon, who considered the use of stock phrases as the mnemonic aid exclusively. Supporting arguments from other studies in different traditions, he proposed that a systematic theme represented by the use of stock phrases is not consistent. "*The epic narrative consists of an enormously protacted concatenation of individual facts, each of which carries the same apparent 'weight' as all the others, regardless of the importance to the story.*"[174] This should true or false, depending on the role of the stock phrase playing in the text. However, a fact, of which he might have not been aware, is that Pāli discourse consistently depicts the scene of the propagation of teaching, i.e. the delivery of sermon and the outcome.

The discourses, when recited regularly, reveals the 'messages' that the tradition aimed to present to the people. First, it tells the story that the Buddha

171 Ibid., p. 279.
172 Ibid., p. 287.
173 Ibid., p. 293.
174 Smith, The Singer or the Song?, pp. 149–150; referred in: Allon, Style and Function, p. 13–14.

or a chief disciple delivered a sermon to people. Second, it always ends with the hearer's reactions given in certain stock phrases. In this connection, the declaration of the lay followership under the Buddha is given in stock phrases. However, it is still doubtful in many aspects as the exact meaning of stock phrases is unknown. Particularly, the declaration of belief in the Buddha that follows a sermon text as the outcome is illogical and thus implausible. Many scholars do not think that the motif at the end of the discourse should be reckoned the act of conversion or the act of assent to the religious belief, as the tradition has it.[175] This will be the main question of the study, with the open-mindedness about the particularity of lay follower in the discourse, to find the relationship concealed behind the usage of the words in the stock phrases.

In this way, the *oral forms* in the Nikāya discourses concerning the declaration of the followership must be studied in detail. If the discourses are approached as understood by the audience in oral tradition, how stable the use of pattern, formulaic language, and stock phrases are, so that the language elements are the keyword to understand the traditional concept of Buddhist in this way? Despite the fact that it is unknown about how the meaning was actually understood by the audience, it is necessary at the primary stage to understand the basic meaning presented in the groups of word. This also has a risk because we never know exactly what the Buddhists have learned from the vocally performed literature in the old tradition. With the imperfect, the study cannot tell the facts from the history of tradition. The study should merely result in some contribution to some understanding based on the formulaic language as presented in nowadays.

2.2 Overview of Discourse Structure

For the knowledge about structure and components of the discourses and the meaning, the study investigates 186 discourses: 34 in Dīgha-nikāya and 152 in Majjhima-nikāya. The language and structure of the two Nikāyas are found similar to some extent that the Majjhima-nikāya should be developed in connection with the Dīgha-nikāya.[176] Structurally, a discourse has four

175 Griffiths, Problems of Religious Diversity, pp. 26–30.
176 Franke, Majjhima-nikāya und Suttanipāta, p. 261.

components:[177] the reference to the way the sermon was received, stated in stock phrase "*evaṃ me sutaṃ;*" introductory story giving the background of the sermon, message or the sermon text; and conclusion mentioning the hearer's reaction to the sermon, given in different stock phrases.

Figure 5: Outline of Pāli Discourse in Dīgha-nikāya and Majjhima-nikāya

1) evaṃ me sutaṃ "Thus I Have Heard."

2) Introductory Story

- Where is the Buddha?
- Who is the Sermon Giver?
- Who is the Hearer?
- What is the Incident Leading to the Sermon?

3) Text of Sermon

- The Message Delivered to the Hearer

4) Conclusion of the Sermon

- What is the Hearer's Expression in Response to the Buddha's Sermon?

2.2.1 Reference to the Way the Sermon Received

Every discourse of the first two Nikāyas begins with the stock phrase *evaṃ me sutaṃ* "thus I have heard." Scholars paid attention on the phrase

177 Compared with the study of Manné in Debates and Case Histories in the Pali canon, the analysis of the discourse structure is basically the same. However, she did not regard the stock phrase as a part of the discourse.

and tried to find out its meaning in relation to the discourse. Based on Tibetan tradition, Brough interpreted that the discourse was once heard.[178] Bhikkhu Anālayo considered the stock phrase emphasizes on the verbatim transmission in Buddhist tradition.[179] Jonathan Silk thought that the stock phrase is rather a *ritual formula* signifying a teaching of the Buddha than the indication that the text was really produced by the Buddha.[180] Nevertheless, it is difficult to judge which interpretations are correct because the exact meaning perceived in the old times is unknown. The interpretation on the literal meaning of the stock phrases seems to be the best way at this point. As the syntax rule and the deduction, which does not allow other interpretation,[181] the sentence is rather perceived at best as the marker of direct Buddha's saying, which means *a logo of originality* in some degree.[182]

As the tradition has it, the sentence was spoken by Ānanda,[183] as he began reciting the text retold by Buddha, Ānanda is a close attendant of him who heard every sermon, which Buddha had preached to people in his lifetime, and transmitted them to the assembly of monks in the First Council.[184] In the Pāli canon, Ānanda was several times acknowledged as excellent in his personality and knowledge that he was beloved in the community of monk, nun and householder. In the sub-canonical, the detail about him is elaborated even more to make him more distinguished with the experience of Buddha's sermons. Ānanda's profile emphasizes on his opportunity that he when serving the Buddha must have learned the sermons from the Buddha every day. Ānanda, as told in the tradition, had

---

178 Brough, "Thus I have Heard," pp. 416–426; referred in: Silk, A Note on the Formula of the Buddhist Sūtra, p. 158. Brough's interpretation is systematically demonstrated in Klaus, Zu der formelhaften Einleitung der buddhistischen Sūtras, pp. 310–313.

179 Anālayo, A Comparative Study of Majjhima-nikāya Vol. 1, p. 22.

180 Silk, A Note on the Formula of the Buddhist Sūtra, pp. 161–162.

181 Klaus, Zu der formelhaften Einleitung der buddhistischen Sūtras, p. 317.

182 Ibid., p. 321. The word is translated from "eine Art Echtheitssiegel der Texte."

183 Each word in the sentence is elaborately glossed in Sumaṅgalavilāsinī Part 1, p. 31.

184 In Sumaṅgalavilāsinī Part I, pp. 13–14 Ānanda uttered merely Dīgha-nikāya, Majjhima-nikāya, and other parts of the canon were uttered by others.

asked the Buddha for the opportunity to learn sermons delivered on a day to prevent blame from others that he did not know anything about the Buddha while being his attendant.[185] In this regard, the statement indicates an attempt to legitimize the teachings in the Nikāya discourse in that they are perfectly transmitted and reliable with the expert who was near the Buddha.[186]

Referring to the excellence of the reciter, the statement affirms that the tales and the teachings are true story that once happened in the Buddha's lifetime and the monk had remembered and told in the First Council. With the view of written tradition, the stories in the oral tradition are perceived in term of *history* which once occurred in the course of time. The background story is interpreted with the doctrine of karma and cosmology in Buddhism. In this way, some Buddhist nowadays still consider the story as history and even use it in the promotion of morality and merit doing in some Buddhist community.[187]

The author views the statement 'evaṃ me sutaṃ' as equal as the English idiom, "as the tradition has it" or "according to the tradition." In the context of performance or recitation of the text in an assembly, the statement is given from the perspective of the reciter who merely presented the discourse to the audience, and not others. With this regard, the statement might not necessarily concern Ānanda as the first hearer of the story from the Buddha. Instead, it should denote anyone in the tradition who told those who were reciting the text or an unidentifiable source from which the monks had learned the text. As previously said, Buddhaghosa tended to approach the oral text from the perspective of people in written tradition. As the reader, one directly receives the text from the composer, which is believed to be the person near the Buddha. It is thus convinced that there were those who retold the teachings. On the contrary, in the context of

185 Story about Ānanda is given in several places of commentary literature. About his eight wishes, in which Ānanda asked Buddha for hearing sermons every evening, is for example in commentary of Juṇhajātaka.

186 Cf. Klaus, Zu der formelhaften Einleitung der buddhistischen Sūtras, pp. 321–322.

187 For example, in media of Dhammakāya community in Thailand, the teaching of Karma is illustrated by stories in Pāli canon and commentary, especially Dhammapadaṭṭhakathā.

oral transmission the reciter is simply the third person to the retold story. Nikāya discourses should be presented from the perspective of the reciter in the oral tradition. Not only is the story shown in the discourses but also religious concept about the Buddha's followers is actually told from the perspective of the reciter.

2.2.2 Introductory Story

Pāli discourse after the statement of the reference begins with the description of the scene that leads to the delivery of sermon text. It also gives the detail about the place where the Buddha stayed while the following sermon was delivered,[188] the participants, and their situations. The people who involve the situation may be monk(s), a householder, or an ascetic of another community. Likewise, the causes leading to the sermon are various, ranging from a curiosity leading to a conversation to an ideological conflict leading to a discussion or a debate. Offering the logic of the incidents and people's action, the introductory story is connected with the following sermon as narrative clarifying the reason why the sermon was delivered, the theme of the sermon, the level of difficulty, the use of metaphor, etc. The introductory story is thus in principle significant and indispensable to the extent that it exposes the background of a discourse. However, it is sometimes found that the introductory story may not be very significant. With the degree of the significance, the discourses can be categorized with emphasis on the incidents leading to the sermon and on the message of discourses.

1) Discourse presenting the introductory story, the sermon text repeated

The discourse in this group particularly gives colourful details of the introductory story while the sermon text may be the same as in other discourses. It can be noticed that the description of the location, the presentation of the opponents and their credentials, the development of debate from challenge,

188 Cf. discourse delivered by a monk in the Buddha's lifetime MN76 and after the lifetime DN23. But some discourses do not have this reference such as MN52, MN94.

refutation and defeat is described deliberately in the introductory story.[189] For example, how the hearer was attracted to the Buddha, what he thought about the Buddha, how he challenged the Buddha, etc. Manné called the discourses '*dramatic debate*,' because it is a *drama*, describing the occasion, in which the Buddha and religious leaders encountered to each other and "*put knowledge and prestige to the test in public.*"[190] In the discourses, she made a notice, "*In the text, individual speeches are recorded so that the development and the course of the argument can be followed verbatim.*" The details obviously indicate the emphasis that the discourses actually present. In this case, the story of the encounter between the Buddha and the people and the process in which Buddha defeated them is more significant than the sermon that the Buddha delivered to them.

Discourses within the first book of Dīgha-nikāya,[191] for example, presents a text of sermon on the spiritual development in the disciplined lifestyle, meditation, and wisdom[192] respectively, delivered by the Buddha to different people and in different situations. Therein, the people, Ambaṭṭha (DN3), Soṇadaṇḍa (DN4), Maṇḍiya and Jāliya the ascetics from other schools (DN7) are depicted to hear the same sermon. Interestingly, the three discourses handle the people and the situations, how the people encountered the Buddha and heard the sermon, in a different fashion. Ambaṭṭha is the pupil whom his teacher Pokkharasādī sent to observe the Buddha's signs of Great Man.[193] In the journey, he, having challenged the Buddha, was argued back and finally sermonized at length by the Buddha. Soṇadaṇḍa had visited the Buddha and became his lay follower. At the end, he however arranged with the

189 Manné, Debates and Case Histories in the Pali Canon, pp. 19–26.
190 Ibid., p. 19.
191 DN3, DN4, DN5, DN7, DN9, DN12.
192 The text of sermon concerns the teaching of Sīla: Cūla-, Majjhima-, and Mahāsīla, Jhāna, and Ñāṇa.
193 In Rhys David's translation in Dialogues of the Buddha, Part III, p. 1, the word purisalakkhaṇa is translated into "the marks of the superman." However, the author prefers the English word "the signs of Great Man" with capital letter to denote the particularity of the man according to the mentioned tradition.

Buddha about the gesture of reverence in his way.[194] Likewise, the two ascetics in DN7 are convinced to hear the text of sermon despite asking another question. In MN41 and MN42, the Buddha delivered the same sermons to the people in towns with different names,[195] in which the situation and the content of the sermon are the same. The examples indicate that the tradition intentionally presents in the discourses the various incidents of propagation, in which Buddha had encountered different people debating with them in several contexts, not only delivering a sermon.

Likewise, MN131, MN132, MN133 mention the same text of sermon, the verses on *bhaddekaratta* "those who have a great night," told by different people. In MN131, Buddha delivered the sermon to the community of monk, and in MN132 Ānanda delivered to the community of monk. In MN133, a deity, who had learned the sermon, told the sermon to a monk, who did not know the meaning of the sermon, so he visited Kaccāna, a chief disciple, for an explanation of the sermon. The discourse then provides the account of explanation given by Kaccāna. Among the three discourses, the way the text is sermonized and explained is made distinguished to demonstrate some characteristics of the preacher and situations: the sermon givers, the way the hearer was called, the way the sermon was delivered and explained to the hearer. In comparison between MN132 and MN133, the two monks differently handled the sermon: Ānanda delivered the sermon in the same way the Buddha had delivered, but Kaccāna developed the explanation of the sermon in his fashion. This feature emphasizes some image of the two monks in the tradition: Ānanda was the expert in the memorization of the sermon that he had heard from the Buddha[196] while Kaccāna was the expert in the explanation of doctrine in full of brief teaching.[197] With the variation of the teachers, the subject matter of the sermon was created more interestingly.

194 This arrangement is mentioned on p. 164.

195 Translation of Pāli Text Society offers the translation of the two discourses one time.

196 The Book of the Gradual Sayings Vol. I, pp. 19–20: Ānanda is chief among Buddha's disciples who are of wide knowledge (bahusutta), of retentive memory, of good behaviour, resolute, and personal attendants.

197 Ibid., p. 17.

The appearance in the discourses as such is not a mistake in the codification if we trust the traditional compilation.[198] The creation of variously colorful stories must concern a purpose in oral tradition that is unknown in our written tradition. The commentary of the discourses merely remarked the repetition by referring to the explanation of the previous text, in which the messages of the sermon have been already commented. It does not discuss on the cause of the repetition. In the commentary of the first book of Dīgha-nikāya, the explanation of the words in the discourse is given in commentary of Sāmaññaphalasutta, the first discourse that mentions the sermon text. Likewise, the commentary of MN42 refers to the explanation of every point to the commentary of MN41. This is clearly a character of oral literature which cannot manifest itself in the world of written tradition. The differently enumerated accounts of people, scene, and situation are the '*content*' that the discourses represent, not the text of sermon.

2) Discourse presenting sermon text, the introductory story is insignificant

The discourses in this group are generally recognized by the present readers, as they convey the sermon text with a little detail about the scene, where and to whom the text was delivered. With emphasis on the sermon text, the introductory story is succinct and, occasionally, merely stereotypical in order that the discourse is attributed to the format of the section. Noticeably, the discourses often claim the Buddha as the sermon deliverer, the Sangha as the hearer, the monastery Jetavanārāma and the town Sāvatthī as the place where the Buddha delivered the sermon to the community. The incident and motivation that leads to the delivery of the sermon is not described in detail. Without the colorful story, the sermon is nevertheless complete and understandable per se because the significant message is the sermon text, the teaching.

Some discourses in this group offer a unique sermon that gives the detail about the cause in the introductory story. Without the introductory story, it is difficult to understand the intention, characteristic, and

198 Norman, Pāli Literature, p. 30. As Norman pointed, this may also come from a problem of codification, in which the reciters of the discourse could not agree on the allocation of the text.

metaphor of the sermon. A good example is Sigālovādasutta (DN31), in which the Buddha delivered a sermon to Sigāla, a householder, about appropriate conducts to six different groups of people, which is represented in the metaphor of six directions.[199] The metaphor in the discourse cannot be understood without the introductory story that provides the context why Buddha preached the sermon in this way. First, Buddha talked about the moral life for householder, although he normally did not raise the topic in the Sangha. Second, Buddha used the metaphor of directions in reference to the position of people from perspective of householder. The introductory story gives the depiction that Buddha met by accident a young man who had been paying worship after the instruction of his parents to the several quarters of earth and sky: to the east, south, west, and north, to the nadir and the zenith.[200] The Buddha then instructed him to "worship the six quarters" in this fashion, so he mentioned with the metaphor of the six directions how to deal with the people from different positions correctly.

The two types of introductory story in Pāli discourses indicate the content that a discourse aims to present. Apart from the sermon text, the discourse may present the stories of mission, debates, conversation, and instruction within the community of Sangha, as raised in the example above. This points to the fact that a discourse is not only the sermon text but often a kind of entertainment that offers stories about the Buddha including his disciples, his personality, his quality, his mission, etc. This is a typical characteristic of the long discourses in Dīgha- and Majjhima-nikāya. In a discourse of Saṃyutta Nikāya and Aṅguttara Nikāya, a sermon text is simply presented with a few details of introductory story. This indicates that the development of Dīgha- and Majjhima-nikāyas and the other two Nikāyas should be based on a different principle. The introductory story of the Dīgha- and Majjhima-nikāyas is supplement to the delivered sermon, while in Saṃyutta- and Aṅguttara-Nikāyas the delivered sermon is the core message.

199 The six directions, which consist of the east, the south, the west, and the north, the nadir and the zenith, denote to the six groups of people around the person, who are teachers, husband or wife, friends and acquaintances, parents, Brahmins or spiritual teachers, and servants respectively.

200 Dialogues of the Buddha Part III, p. 173.

2.2.3 Message of the Discourse

As religious scripture, the sermon text is recognized as the message of the discourse, the most important part, for it represents a teaching, debate, or discussion raised from the Buddhist standpoint. As the canon was transmitted, the teaching extended to other areas of the religion, pertaining to the people in the Sangha which preserved the teaching that is called Buddhism.[201] Hence, despite the claim that every sermon is for the spiritual path to reach Nibbāna,[202] the themes of the sermon in Pāli discourses are not always specific to the spiritual path. They range from the doctrine on the spiritual path to the moral lifestyle that leads to worldly happiness. Although the story of religious life can be compared with the Catholic saints, as done by Reginald Ray, the messages in the Pāli discourses focus on knowledge and techniques in the learning and practice or the understanding of the doctrine. Their virtue and sanctity from the experience in religious life are subject to revere and mention as the role model for the Buddhist in the tradition.[203] In connection with the function, the discourses might have supported the learners in the foster of spiritual development. Biography of several chief disciples in the discourses, which describes the journey to the Buddhist community from the first encounter with the Buddha until the success in the spiritual practice, offers a good inspiration in the religious life. Together with the learning, the story could be an entertainment in the community as well.

In relation to the introductory story, the message of discourse is presented as the Buddha's answer following the question posed by the hearer, although it may also appear that the Buddha declared himself in order to give a sermon.[204] Manné considered the interrelation between Buddha and the hearer in term of *challenge*.[205] *It* is noticeable that Manné used the word 'challenge' in context of intense debate made by the two people from different ideological standpoints. Whereas, in another discourse, in which a monk or a lay follower engaged, she used the word *'question'* to

201 Bronkhorst, Der indische Buddhismus und seine Verzweigungen, p. 26.
202 The Book of the Kindred Sayings. Part V., p. 370.
203 Ray, Buddhist Saints in India, p. 1.
204 Manné, Debate and Case Histories in the Pali canon p. 24.
205 Ibid., pp. 23–24.

refer the points raised in the conversation.[206] The selection of the word reflects her attitude about the encounter of the Buddha with a stranger and acquaintance despite the fact that the two words do not offer any difference in the literary function. The world *challenge* signifies the aim to win the opposition, while the word *question* has the more neutral sense in the relationship between the expert and the learner. It appears that whether the talk is a sermon, a conversation, or a debate, the *challenge* or the *question* is necessary for the direction and determination of the sermon delivered or argument deployed. An explanation or a sermon needs a leading question that raises the argued point, before expanding the detail. In this way, the challenge or the question brings about the Buddha's answer. In the other word, the hearer was active to the Buddha with a question while Buddha was passive with the answer to the question. This is an attitude of Buddhist monk that the monk does not deliver a sermon to a person who has not asked him for the sermon or paid no respect to him verbally or behaviourally.[207]

Presenting question and answer about a teaching was an effective way to educate people during the oral transmission. It is a method to convince the audience, how the Buddha was wise and superior to other teachers in his doctrine and the way of answering the question. Following the recited text, the audience got several points at first, considered each point, and agreed with the Buddha's last answer. Moreover, it offered the chance for the audience to 'experience' the Buddha, especially his wisdom in answering a question. Hearing and considering the text in oral transmission, the learner could achieve more meanings behind the answer and scene from the text recited. Namely, sermons were '*naturally*' composed as retold stories of meeting and conversation carried out by the characters, who defended for their standpoint. The story for learners in the tradition is the subject to consider and analyse for 'theses' behind. Whereas, we, in the written tradition, see merely the 'appearance' of the text: the content of the doctrine, the level of difficulty, the genre of hearer, etc., from which the Buddha, his personality, his doctrine, etc. that a reader can assess. To achieve other meanings implied in the oral

206 Ibid., p. 29.

207 Cf. Sekhiyavatta in Vinaya-piṭaka on the delivery of sermon.

text, we should focus on the format under the presented scripts rather than on the scripts.

2.2.4 Conclusion of Discourse

Pāli discourse ends with a result of the encounter describing the feeling and act of the people expressed in response to the delivered sermon in form of certain stock phrase. The stock phrase at the end of the discourse has two types: The first type denotes a satisfaction with the delivered sermon and the second type denotes the declaration of followership. The presence of the two stock phrases suggests *success* of the Buddha or a preacher in his missionary activity that he could develop the hearer to have more understanding or turn them to become his follower with the sermon,[208] for there is also in some discourses no usage of the stock phrases. Apart from stock phrase, some discourses may end with verses, which summarize the content of Buddha's sermon. This reminds that the presence of the stock phrases is meaningful in some way. The details of each stock phrase and its existence is significant to the study of lay followership in the discourse. The author focuses on the study of each stock phrase in 2.3.

Nevertheless, the stock phrase in the conclusion is questioned about the meaning and its relation to the Vedic tradition of composing commentary.[209] Set up in the scene of conversation or debate, especially in case of the debate between the Buddha and a challenging stranger, a discourse ends with the stock phrase that denotes the declaration of the followership under the Buddha. This seems to be a 'ritual' in debate according to Vedic tradition, in which the loser has to acknowledge being the follower of the winner. Specifically, there is a rule in the debate that "*(i)f one does not know the answer, the only honorable way out of the predicament is to become the pupil of the winner in the discussion.*"[210] Witzel clarified this motif in some Pāli discourses, in which the opponents had to accept the Buddha's argument, after they could not defend themselves. Some of them

208 Cf. Manné, Debates and Case Histories in the Pali canon, p. 18, pp. 29–30.
209 Witzel, The Case of the Shattered Head, p. 381.
210 Ibid., p. 370.

confessed to the Buddha that they must acknowledge the point argued by the Buddha; otherwise, his head would be shattered.[211] Manné, connecting this tradition with the meaning of the stock phrases, concluded that the expression as such is a kind of *acknowledging the defeat* in the debate.[212]

In this view, Buddha's mission presented in Pāli discourses was often understood in relation to the establishment of his religion in the social context, in which Brahmin's ideology was influential.[213] His debate with the Brahmin was perceived as an attempt to gain respect from other ideological schools and the society. The idea particularly concerns the discourses with a *long* introductory story, especially in the first book of Dīgha-nikāya, where Buddha debated Brahmins and won their followership. In the discourses, the social status and religious knowledge of Brahmins was mentioned at length, as if it was to emphasize symbolically the superiority of the Buddha in parallel to that of Brahmins who were the leaders of religious community at that time.[214] The presentation of the debate as such shows that the Buddha was successful in the propagation over the Brahmins. He managed to spread his spiritual doctrine and received acceptance even from the old Brahmin teachers, who ideologically influenced over the Brahmin society at that time.[215] In other words, his religion, the doctrine of the Buddha, was established firmly with the

211 Ibid., pp. 381–382. Witzel referred to several parts of Pāli canon that refers to allusion. In DN3, Ambaṭṭha was forced to acknowledge the defeat because of seeing a demon raising an axe to beat his head. In DN5, Kūṭadanta unwillingly accepted the Buddha's answer; he knew, his head would be shattered when rejecting it.

212 Manné, Debates and Case Histories in the Pali canon, p. 25.

213 Gombrich, Theravada Buddhism, pp. 36–37; Chakravarti, Social Dimension of Early Buddhism, pp. 41–46.

214 Manné, Debates and Case Histories in the Pali canon, pp. 20–21.

215 Johannes Bronkhorst in Greater Magadha (2007) and Buddhism in the Shadow of Brahmanism (2011) proposed the new theory of about the settlement and the demographic extension of Buddhism in India. According to the theory, Buddha's order should have been originally a religious group among others in Magadha, located in east of Prayāga, which had a typical characteristic on religion and culture such as the ascetic cult, funerary practice, etc., before it extended to the northern area, where Brahmanism was strongly-stamped and hence influential to the Buddhism.

support of his lay followers who were the religious leaders in the country. The story is viewed as history left in the tradition and thus interpreted in relation to the foundation of the community.

However, the main point of the study is the question, how the Brahmins became Buddha's follower and why tradition determined the process to them so. Considering the use of the Vedic tradition from the perspective of oral tradition, the use of stock phrases in the discourse proposes a new meaning in the Buddhist tradition.[216] In this way, other meanings from the tradition adopted in the composition of discourse were forgotten; the only meaning left in the tradition is how the Brahmin became Buddhist, and as the outcome, what is the meaning of Buddhist represented in the process. Despite the origin from the Vedic tradition or other unknown tradition, Pāli discourse as established in the oral tradition adopted the traditions in the story of Buddha's mission and initiation of his follower. The sense of history is not important at this point, but the new meaning in the declaration of the followership.

As the answer in response to the Buddha's sermon, the conclusion of discourse demonstrates an idea in Pāli discourse that the sermon is meaningful and influential to individual belief. Sometimes, the hearer may achieve '*Dhammacakkhu*' from the hearing. Some discourses mention that the hearer attained Arahatship after a sermon.[217] This can imply from the text that the teaching and the ability in a conversation is the 'strength' of Buddha that truly attracts people to become a new follower.[218] The idea is influential to the sub-canonical literature. At the end of Buddha's sermon, explained in Dhammapadaṭṭhakathā, several thousands of lay followers attained Sotāpanna and thousands of monks attained Arahatship. Despite composed in written tradition the book clearly imitates the structure of the Nikāya discourses that repeatedly represents the scene of Buddha's delivery of Dhamma with the similar ending. These obviously show the

216 Cf. 2.1, Patron's ideas about the new meaning of commentary.

217 The Collection of Middle Length Sayings Vol. III, p. 70.

218 It is never known to us the true purpose of the constructed plot with the scene of debate, conversation or instruction. Presented in a recitation, the plot is significant to the cognition of the hearer: the religious concepts are transferred to the hearer through repetition of the stories.

image of Buddha reinforced in the tradition exclusively as the sermon giver for the world. In this regard, the role of dhamma and sermon handed down in Theravada tradition indicates its status, not only as authority but also as an important religiosity, among the followers. Sermon is the instrument that may influence the people, from the disbeliever into the convert, and from the convert into another stage of the spiritual path.

2.2.5 Conclusion

Viewed from perspective of oral characteristic and function within the Sangha, Pāli discourse is 'religious scripture' conveying Buddha's doctrine and religious concepts in format of oral text. Consisting of the four parts, discourse suggests the theme of Buddha's *missionary activity*, in which Buddha turned adversary into follower and promoted some follower to achieve more understanding or to reach a spiritual attainment.

Every part plays an important role on introducing the ideas to the audience. First, a discourse contains a reference to an undesignated origin of the following story and sermon, which indicate the perspective of third person. Tradition has claimed that the third person is Ānanda, the Buddha's close attendant, who was a well-learned monk. Considering the perspective of the reciter, the author is of the opinion that the reference should mention 'tradition' in general, where he had learned the discourse. Second, the introductory story mentions people, situation, and incident that lead to a sermon. In this part, a question or a challenge was posed to the Buddha to determine the direction of the discourse. The emphasis on the part of discourse may indicate the *content* presented by the discourse. The introductory story may sometimes be more emphasized to demonstrate Buddha's wisdom in controlling the situation and defeating his opponent. Third, the text of sermon is the Buddha's answer in response to the question or the challenge posed by the people. So, it is recognized as the core of the discourse. Viewed as debate, the sermon is the last *stratagem* to defeat the hearer to accept the Buddha's superiority in wisdom and decide to become a follower after a long discussion. Lastly, the people after hearing the sermons or answers acknowledged the righteousness of the answer and request for the followership under the Buddha. At this stage, those who are new to Buddha officially declared the followership in front of him and in the public. With the regular use of pattern and language, some religious ideas such as the idea of Buddha's mission and followership, connection between the *Buddha's followers*, those who asked to become a monastic or non-monastic follower, and the appreciation of teaching given in the sermon delivered by Buddha, etc. can be grasped from the story.

The theme in the oral literature is thus not the element to overlook. It is the core or the foundation, from which the oral text is developed by adding other elements. In the analysis of Serbo-Croatian literature, Lord surmised that a singer of oral poetry should receive the theme from his father who is the prime teacher and thus most influential to the singer's performance. However, the idea of the theme could be developed when the singer was more skillful in the performance and in the active listening of other singers. At this point, he concluded for the Serbo-Croatian culture: "*Transmission at this early stage must be differentiated from transmission of a song at a later period in the singer's development.*"[219] In the Nikāya discourse, the theme, which particularly illustrates the Buddha's mission and the gaining of followers, should remain the same throughout from its beginning. No matter if the discourses were original from the Buddha's time or newly composed at a time after his death, the stories of people and the sermons are allocated in this formulaic language that makes the discourses look the same. The reactions of the hearer are closely similar up to the same point that the sermon is the last stratagem to win the followership.

Apart from the ideas, the discourses significantly revitalize two qualities of the Buddha in this missionary activity. First is his wisdom in the encounter and debate with a person who had challenged him. The presentation in the introductory story obviously shows that Buddha is more interesting than other teachers are. This enhances the feeling of reverence for the Buddha and the motivation to visit him. Second, Buddha's effort in the missionary activity shows his mercy in the world beings in the propagation of his doctrine to help the beings liberate from the fetters of rebirth and death in the circle of birth. Along these lines, the act of explaining a teaching or defeating the challenging person in the mission is, rather than the *gain* of

219 Lord, The Singer of Tales, p. 78.

reverence, the *help* in that Buddha pointed the people to go on the right direction in gradual progress.[220] Buddha's activity is thus regarded by later tradition as the practice for the good and welfare of others.[221]

2.3 Expressions at the Conclusion of Discourse

The use of stock phrase is considered noticeably common in Nikāya discourse,[222] or even typical in Buddhist literature.[223] For example, the stock phrase mentioning the process of Arahat attainment, or the stock phrases denoting the declaration of Buddhist followership in response to Buddha's sermon, as the author here is dealing with. Nevertheless, the research that devotes on this method is scarce,[224] probably because it is understood that the result does not contribute to the history of Buddhist canon or the understanding of the religion. In 2.2.4, the study partly mentioned *conclusion of discourse* as a part of Pāli discourse. As it provides the results of the delivered sermon in the missionary episode, in which Buddha finally won the hearer with a sermon, the conclusion is a significant part, especially in Dīgha-nikāya and Majjhima-nikāya.[225] Unfortunately, the stock phrase is merely a short sentence that cannot give the expressions exaggeratedly like in written tradition, in which description of feelings and emotions is in script. This part devotes a study on the stock phrases to understand the meaning and implication about the conclusion of the discourse better.

---

220 The Collection of the Middle Length Sayings vol. III, p. 52.

221 In sub-canonical literature, the virtues of the Buddha are mentioned twofold: *attahitasampatti* 'accomplishment of one's own welfare' and *parahitapaṭipatti* 'practice for the good or welfare of others' and the threefold: *paññāguṇa* 'wisdom' *visuddhiguṇa* 'purity' and *karuṇāguṇa* 'compassion.' The source is the commentary of Visuddhimagga, which is unfortunately neither in Roman version nor in English translation. The author got this information from Buddhist Dictionary by P.A. Payutto. Available at http://www.84000.org/tipitaka/dic/d_seek.php?text=%BE%D8%B7%B8%A4%D8%B3&original=1 (in Thai) (last access 08.09.2013).

222 Hinüber, Untersuchung zur Mündlichkeit, p. 17.

223 Cousins, Pali Oral Literature, p. 96.

224 Hinüber, Untersuchung zur Mündlichkeit, p. 17; cf. Footnote 48.

225 In other Nikāyas: Saṃyuttanikāya, Aṅguttaranikāya, and in some sections of Khuddakanikāya, the conclusion is occasionally given, often even dropped.

There are mainly two types of the conclusion: first, in context of acknowledging the sermon or explanation, the hearer is represented with stock phrase *satisfaction*, and second, in context of *spiritual promotion*, in which stock phrase denoting the declaration of belief in the Three Jewels and his followership under the Buddha.[226] Occasionally, some hearer is mentioned with another stock phrases that denote the experience of *Dhammacakkhu*. Therefore, the author categorizes the stock phrases in three types: type I denoting the hearer's satisfaction, type II denoting formal declaration of belief in Buddha, and type III denoting *Dhammacakkhu* or a spiritual attainment.

Figure 6: Table Showing Conclusion of Discourses in DN and MN

Results	DNI	DNII	DNIII	MNI	MNII	MNIII	Total
Leading to Satisfaction	4	4	7	40	22	45	122
Leading to a Reaction	9 (2)*	1	3 (1)	8 (1)	24 (1)	3 (1)	48 (4)
I. *Dhammacakkhu*	2	1	-	-	3	-	6
II. Request for Monkhood	2	-	-	1	4	-	7
III. For Lay Followership	9	-	1	5	20	3	28
Unsatisfying Sermon Unsuccessful Conversion	- 	1 -	 2	 5	 3	 -	1 10
Legend	-	5	1	2	4	4	16
Sum total of discourses	13	10	11	50	50	52	186

*The number in parentheses means the number includes more persons, as some discourses mention more than one hearer. In some discourses more than one hearer are mentioned. For example, in DNI Sīlakkhandhavagga, 9(2) means the among the 11 hearers from 9 discourses who reacted in some way to the Buddha's sermon, 3 of which became a monastic follower and 9 of which became a lay follower; the other 2 persons are counted from some discourses which mention more than one hearer.

In 186 discourses of Dīgha-nikāya and Majjhima-nikāya there are 170 discourses which depict a single story of mission undertaken by Buddha and his chief followers.[227] The discourses end with a type of stock phrase

226 See 2.3.4.

227 Apart from the discourses, there are 16 discourses, which characterize like legend or retold story ending without reaction of hearer or conversation participant. The legend discourses are thus not included in this study.

representing a reaction after a sermon. 122 Discourses end with the first type stock phrase, while 48 with different reactions. The first type discourse ends with a satisfaction with the delivered sermon while the second type ends with the declaration of followership. In the latter, it sometimes appears the mention of the experience *Dhammacakkhu* (I.), the request for the monkhood under the Buddha (II.), and the declaration of the lay followership under the Buddha (III.). The use of stock phrase also occurred in opposite meaning: no use of stock phrase denoting the understanding, acknowledgment and declaration of belief or negation of the stock phrase.

2.3.1 Stock Phrase Denoting Hearer's Satisfaction

Among 122 discourses depicting the mission, there are 117 discourses that end with the stock phrase denoting the hearer's satisfaction. The 103 of which the hearer are the member of the monastic community, while the 14 of which the hearer is the outsider of the community, viz. householder or other ascetics. Only 5 discourses end with others. The stock phrase is the *standard concluding formula*, as Manné referred in her monograph.[228] It denotes that the hearer or participants were *satisfied* with the sermon, the explanation, or the advice, which the Buddha or a senior monk had given. The stock phrase consists of the word *(su)bhāsita* "(well) said" and the conjugated verb *abhi √nand* "to rejoice" or other synonyms denoting to great happiness.

> (1) Idam avoca [Bhagavā], attamanā [te bhikkhū] [Bhagavato] bhāsitaṃ abhinandun-ti[229] (DN1)
> Thus spoke [the Exalted One]. Delighted [these monks] rejoiced in what [the Exalted One] had said.

The formula can be applied in other contexts, in which other sermon giver and hearer are mentioned.

> (1a) Idam avoca [bhagavā]. Attamano [āyasmā Ānando] [Bhagavato] bhāsitaṃ abhinandîti[230] (DN 14)
> Thus spoke [the Exalted One]. Delighted [Venerable Ānanda] rejoiced in what [the Exalted One] had said.

228 Manné, Debates and Case Studies in the Pali Canon, p. 18.
229 DN I 46, 27–28.
230 DN II 71, 28–29.

(1b) Idam avoca [āyasma Sāriputto]. Attamanā [te bhikhū] [āyasmato Sāriputtassa] bhāsitaṃ abhinandun-ti.[231] (DN34)
Thus spoke [Venerable Sāriputta]. Delighted [these monks] rejoiced in what [Venerable Sāriputta] had said.

The stock phrase is regular and unvarying except the name of the hearer it contains. The hearers, viz. the monks who listened to the Buddha(1), Venerable Ānanda(1a), and the monks who listened to Venerable Sāriputta(1b) respectively were satisfied with the delivered sermon. Occasionally, it has variant form with identical meaning, containing derivative of the keywords in the standard concluding formula.

(2) Itiha te ubho [mahānāgā] aññamaññassa subhāsitaṃ samanumodiṃsûti.[232] (MN5)
In this wise did each of these [great beings] rejoice together in what was well spoken by the other.

In (2) Sāriputta and Moggallāna, the Buddha's chief disciple, exchanged the ideas on a dhamma topic to each other, and felt satisfied with the exchanged answers. The ending sentence does not follow the formulas presented in the pattern (1), but remain the same meaning with the synonyms: *itiha* for *idamavoca*, and *samanumodiṃ* for *abhinanduṃ*.

Figure 7: Sermon as the Thing Deemed Special

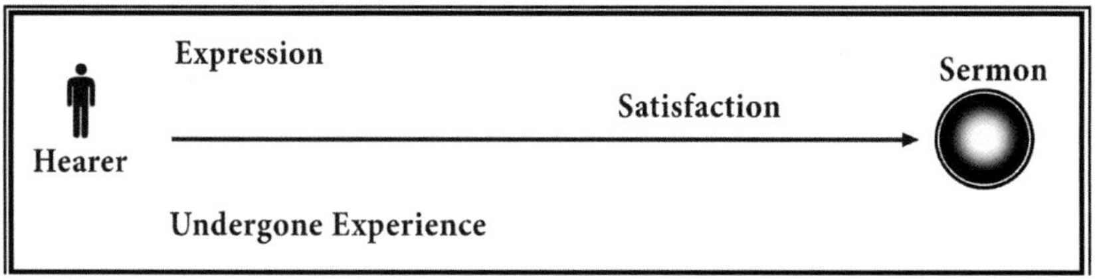

The stock phrases can be understood in terms of experience: the hearer considered the sermon responsive to their curiosity in some way and thus felt satisfied with the answer. In this relation, the experience may not directly concern the special deeming. It merely represents the relation between the hearer and the sermon that an extraordinary feeling occurs

231 DN III 292, 6–7.
232 MN I 32, 33–34.

from the subject, which the hearer has perceived. In the other word, the hearer is motivated to be satisfied with the sermon as the agent.

In this perspective, the stock phrase is the marker denoting that the hearer acknowledged what the Buddha or the disciple had said.[233] Considering contexts, the satisfaction can be interpreted as a positive feeling in response to explanation or advice that Buddha had given to their challenge or question in the introductory story.

> "When this had been said, the venerable Abhiya Kaccāna spoke thus to Pañcakaṅga the carpenter: 'It is a gain for you, householder, it is well gotten by you, householder, that you got rid of the doubt you had and also obtained a chance to hear this disquisition on *dhamma*.'"[234] (MN127)

In the discourse, Anuruddha instructed and explained a lay follower, Pañcakaṅga, to develop a spiritual mind. During the instruction, another monastic follower, Abhiya Kaccāna, joined the conversation and asked Anuruddha the similar question. Anuruddha then gave the explanation to them. At the end, the monastic said to the lay that *he, the lay follower, was lucky with the explanation*. From the text, it is deducible that the audiences were satisfied with the explanation because they had removed the doubt. They understood more about the teaching. The monastic should have found that the explanation is sensible and advantageous for the disciples to know, so he thus regarded the chance of hearing the explanation as the *gain*, with which one, like the lay follower, should be satisfied. In this way, he considered the sermon 'special' to him at the moment. The satisfaction with the answer can be compared with the compliment of King Pasenadi to the Buddha's answer after the king had asked him many questions.

> "We, revered sir, questioned the Lord about the omniscience; the Lord explained omniscience, and because it was pleasing to us and approved we are delighted. Revered sir, we questioned the Lord about the purity of the four castes, and because it was pleasing to us and approved we are delighted. Revered sir, we questioned the Lord about the *devas*; the Lord explained the *devas*. And because it is pleasing to us...we are delighted. Revered sir, we questioned the Lord about Brahmā; the Lord explained about the Brahmā, and because it was pleasing to us and approved we are delighted. And revered sir,

---

233 Ibid., p. 18.

234 MN III 152, 19–22; The Collection of the Middle Length Sayings vol. III, p. 197.

whatever it was we questioned the Lord about, that very thing the Lord explained, and because it was pleasing to us and approved we are delighted..."[235] (MN90)

The extraordinary feeling in response to the sermon can be understood in relation to the previous incidents constructed in the certain outline: the sermon, explanation, or advice presented in the discourses. The relation of the message deliverer/advisor and the pupil/asker, shows the process of giving, viz. teaching, explanation, answer, suggestion, etc., in response to the other side, who had asked or requested for it. The giving of the information as such fulfils the wish to know the answer from the people they trust on the one hand. On the other hand, the answer in the moment resolves the doubt over a fact, the curiosity about some story, the obstacle that blocks one to proceed with an activity, etc. These are the understanding that relieves the 'annoyance,' which the pupil/asker had struggled to overcome. In this way, the satisfaction ascribed to the hearers at the end of the discourses can be interpreted not only as the expression of acknowledgment, but also as representation of any positive feeling in response to the given answer or sermon, which is abbreviated into mnemonic formula, as the stock phrases (1).

It is also possible that the stock phrase is negated or omitted with the aim to represent that the given answer or the sermon does not satisfy the hearers. Mūlapariyāyasutta (MN1) is the single discourse, which ends with stock phrase denoting non-satisfaction of the monks after having heard Buddha's sermon.[236] Commentary explained that the Buddha delivered a difficult sermon to suppress the monks' false view that they were intelligent in the learning.[237] The sermon delivered with this attention was not understood by the hearer and thus not satisfying for them because the hearer could not learn or gain anything from it. Likewise, in Gopakamoggallānasutta (MN108), in which Brahmin Gopakamoggallāna had asked Ānanda a question, there is no use of the stock phrase to represent the asker's satisfaction at the end of the discourse.[238] Not long

235 The Collections of the Middle Length Sayings Vol. II, pp. 313–314.

236 See discussion on this point: Anālayo, A Comparative Study of the Majjhimanikāya Vol. I., pp. 26–27.

237 The negation is mentioned in the commentary, Papañcasūdanī part 1, p. 59.

238 The Collection of Middle Length Sayings Vol. III, p. 65.

after Ānanda had answered the Brahmin, Vassakāra came and joined the conversation. The monk and Vassakāra debated with each other that satisfied Vassakāra at the end. Gopakamoggallāna seemingly did not understand the answer, which the monk had given before Vassakāra's arrival, so the Brahmin asked the monk again for the answer. Then, the monk gave the same answer, which he had given at first. The discourse ends with this answer without the stock phrase or a sentence denoting on Gopakamoggallāna's reaction. The lack of the reaction implies that Ananda's answer did not improve the Brahmin's understanding. He was simply left with the doubt; he should therefore not be satisfied with the given answer.

Therefore, the stock phrase *satisfaction* in relation to the context of the story may really signify "satisfaction" or a positive feeling in reaction to the answer or the sermon although the detail of how the hearer was satisfied and responsive to the answer is omitted. It means the attention to present that the sermon is well said, understood and accepted by the hearers in the story, in opposite to some discourses that mention none of the stock phrase. It has finally become symbolic that the delivered sermon or the given explanation in the discourse is complete and will thus be satisfying for the hearer.

2.3.2 Stock Phrase Denoting Formal Declaration of Belief in Buddha

The discourse may end with another stock phrase after a conversation or debate with the Buddha or a senior monk. The stock phrase consists of three main sentences, comprising: the hearer admires the answer or the sermon (3), announces to take the Three Jewels for refuges through their life (4) and asks to be a lay follower (5) or a monk (6) respectively.[239] It is to notice that the stock phrases particularly appear in this position in the conclusion of discourse, and in this order. Whenever the stock phrase (3) about the value of the teaching is mentioned, it is always followed by the admiration, appreciation and reverence of the Three Jewels.[240]

---

239 Cf. Manné, Debates and Case Studies in the Pali Canon, pp. 25–26.

240 Commentary of the text (3) (4) (6) is given in Sumaṅgalavilāsinī Part 1, pp. 228–236; Commentary of the text (5) is given in Sumaṅgalavilāsinī Part 2, p. 362.

1. Admiration of the instruction

(3) Seyyathā pi bhante nikkujjitaṃ vā ukkujjeyya paṭicchannaṃ vā vivareyya mūḷhassa vā maggaṃ ācikkheyya andhakāre vā tela-pajjotaṃ dhāreyya: "cakkhumanto rūpāni dakkhintî" ti evam eva Bhagavatā aneka-pariyāyena dhammo pakāsito.[241]
Most excellent, Lord, most excellent! Just as if a man were to set up that which has been thrown down, or were to reveal that which is hidden away, or were to point out the right road to him who has goes astray, or were to bring a lamp into the darkness so that those who have eyes could see external forms – just even so, Lord, has the truth been made known to me, in many a figure, by the Exalted One.[242]

2. Taking Three Jewels for refuges

(4) Esâhaṃ[243] bhante Bhagavantaṃ saraṇaṃ gacchāmi dhammañ ca bhikkhu-saṅghañ ca.[244]
And I, even I, betake myself as my guide to the Exalted One, and to the Doctrine; and to the Brotherhood.[245]

3. Ordination or lay discipleship requested in front of Buddha or the chief disciple, with whom the hearer had debated.

(5) Upāsakaṃ maṃ bhagavā dhāretu ajjatagge pāṇupetaṃ saraṇaṃ gataṃ.[246]
May the Exalted One accept me as a disciple, as one who, from this day forth, as long as life endures, has taken his refuge in them.[247]
(6) Labheyyāhaṃ bhante bhagavato santike pabbajjaṃ, labheyyaṃ upasampadan-ti.[248]
I would fain, Lord, renounce the world under the Exalted One; I would fain be admitted to his Order.[249]

---

241 DN I 85, 8–12; cf. DNI 176, 7–12.

242 Dialogues of the Buddha Part I, p. 94 cf. p. 135. The former is the translation from DN2, uttered by King Ajātasattu, while the latter from DN 3 by Pokkharasādī. The Pāli text of latter applied a little different word, "*bho gotamo*" instead of "*bhante*".

243 In DN2, the word *esāhaṃ* is *sohaṃ*. DN I 85, 12.

244 DN I 176, 12–13.

245 Dialogues of the Buddha Part I, p. 239.

246 DN I 85, 14–15.

247 Dialogues of the Buddha Part I, p. 94.

248 DN I 176, 13–15.

249 Dialogues of the Buddha Part I, p. 239.

The group of stock phrases is common in the Nikāya discourses. In the 48 debate discourses, the usage of the stock phrases (3) (4) (5) denoting the declaration of belief to become a lay follower appears 37 times[250] while the usage of (3) (4) (6) denoting the declaration of belief to become a monk appears seven times.[251] The stock phrases always appear together in this form, except MN92, which is a legendary discourse ended in verse and is thus not included in the study.[252] However, it is also found that not every debate discourse ends with the stock phrases.[253] This reflects that the missions were not always successful.

The group of the stock phrases has a certain order throughout the Nikāyas. The beginning stock phrase (3) denoting the admiration of teaching is noticeably followed by certain passages: announcement of refuges (4) and a request to be either a lay follower (5) or a monk (6). This clearly points to the usage of the stock phrase (3) that it only denotes the impression of people who believed in the Buddha, his teaching, and his Sangha particularly after hearing a sermon. Similarly, the other stock phrases (4) (5) (6) mentioned above appear especially in this context and with their concurrence. They never appear out of this rule. This implies that the stock phrases exclusively function to denote a precise meaning about the belief and declaration of followership. Unfortunately, the stock phrases do not give longer detail for a clear meaning.

---

250 The declaration of belief of young Brahmins Veseṭṭha and Bhāradvāja, the Buddha's components who finally asked to become laity in a discourse, is regarded as one time. The story appears in DN13 and MN98, in which topics of the debate are different. Their story once appears in DN27, in which the two Brahmin had become monks.

251 DN8, DN9, MN7, MN57, MN73, MN75, MN79. In DN9 and MN57, two hearers after hearing the Buddha's sermon, made a different decision on the declaration of belief. One hearer asked to be a laity, another one to be a monk. In Mahāparinibbānasutta (DN16), which is secluded in the study because of its legendary characteristic, there is a mention of the stock phrase (3) (4) (6) to represent the declaration of belief of Subhadda Paribbājaka.

252 In MN 92, the ordination of Sela is depicted in form of dialogue with the Buddha, in which the stock phrases (3) (4) (6) are not mentioned.

253 DN24, DN25, DN35, MN50, MN76, MN79. See the table in appendix II.

The order of the sentence within the stock phrase points to a kind of logic from the cause in (3) to the effect in (4) and (5) or (6), i.e. the declaration of belief is made under an impression that Buddha's sermon is considered worthy in several aspects, such as the value of the teaching, the wisdom of the Buddha, and the generosity of the Buddha (that he delivered the teaching to the people). The logic of the progress in the activity may be compared with that of worship in other contexts, for example, as exemplified in King Pasenadi's remark on the Buddha's teaching that his queen mentioned.

> "It is wonderful, Mallikā, it is marvelous, Mallikā, how much the Lord, penetrating through wisdom, sees by means of wisdom. Come Mallikā, let me wash." Then King Pasenadi, rising from his seat, having arranged his upper garment over one shoulder, having saluted the Lord with joined palms, three times uttered this solemn utterance: "Praise to the Lord, the perfected one, the fully Self-Awakened One."[254] (MN87)

Queen Mallikā had explained her husband, King Pasenadi, how the sufferings could arise from the loss of son, wife, properties, etc. according to the Buddha's teaching. Her explanation fascinated the King. In tandem, it surprised the king about the wisdom of the Buddha. Before the king uttered the worship to the Buddha as in the last sentence, he admired the teaching: *wonderful, marvelous*. From the expression, it seemed that the teaching about sufferings and their causation was at first unknown to him. He became gladdened and excited with the new knowledge. No wonder, the king's expression clearly shows not only his acknowledgment of what the Buddha had said, but also his actual satisfaction in the words, which we can perceive from the context. After that, he subsequently paid homage to the Buddha. The meanings in this order indicate that worship, as it appears in the discourses, is based on *the consideration of worth and virtue of what to be worshipped*. Likewise, the decision to utter the worship and declare the followership under the Buddha could be made under the impression that dhamma and Buddha, the teacher of dhamma, is worthy of it.

---

254 MN II 111, 35 – MN II 112, 1–7; The Collection of the Middle Length Sayings Vol. II, p. 296.

Figure 8: Model of Experience Deemed Religious in Declaration of the Belief

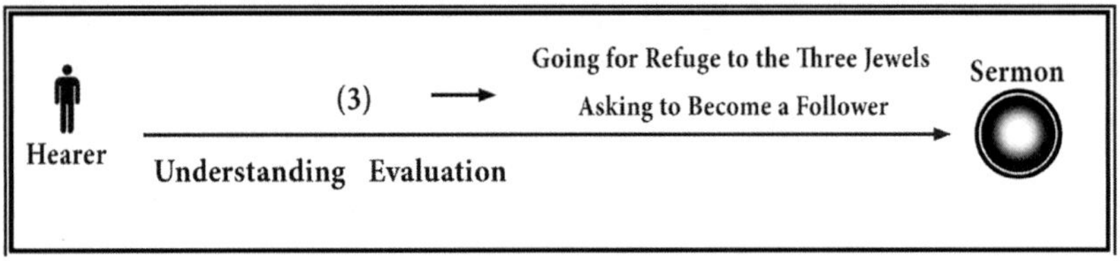

According to Taves, the feelings can be explained as the experience motivated by the perception of some things considered special. In this relation, the teaching was deemed as special because of the meaning considered extraordinary. It thus fascinated and surprised the hearer as if it was an unordinary thing. The hearer in a discourse finding the meaningful teaching thus admired the sermon in many ways, took the Three Jewels as refuge, and asked to become a follower. This is clearly opposite to his adversary feeling in the encounter at first. Therefore, the sermon can be compared with other things deemed special in other traditions – god, who had some certain *power* in the opinion of the religious people, and thus needed to be treated with reverence, to satisfy him in order to give them the wishes. The sermon, as presented in the discourse, gave an inspiration that also made the change in the hearer. The reaction to surrender the Buddha implies the perception of some worthy qualities in the sermon and in the Buddha who preached the sermon. On the other words, the hearer, having seen the qualities, deems the sermon and the Buddha as special and thus worthy of the worship.

In sum, the process of the declaration of belief can be understood in the following way.

First, in (3) the hearer understood the sermon and considered that the sermon was meaningful in some way. In this action, the hearer had evaluated the value of the dhamma and found that it is the truth of life.

Second, at the end of (3) the hearer appreciated the Buddha's gratitude in that the Buddha presented the precious dhamma to him, and in this way, he knew the truth of life.

Third, in (4) the hearer declared a respect to the Three Jewels, which consist of Buddha, dhamma, and Sangha. In relation to the context, the worship to the Three Jewels is clearly the format of respecting to Buddhist institution.

Fourth, in (5) or (6) the hearer asked the Buddha to become a follower. The hearer might ask the Buddha to join his order or to remember him as a lay follower.

The process is made stereotypical with the use of stock phrases in a discourse, where a new hearer had heard sermon and understood it. The certain usage reveals a principle in the tradition that the lay follower is the person who has experienced in some way with the Buddha's teaching and realised the significance of the teaching before asking to become a Buddhist.

2.3.3 Stock Phrase Denoting a Spiritual Attainment

It is also found that some hearer is mentioned with stock phrases referring to an extraordinary experience. In the Dīgha-nikāya and Majjhima-nikāya, there are only 5 lay followers mentioned with this stock phrase.[255] The stock phrase consists of two sections. The first section tells the incident, in which the hearer heard a sermon delivered by Buddha, followed by description of how the hearer perceived and felt in reaction to the heard sermon. The second section mentions the hearer's special perception and intensive feelings after hearing the sermon.

1. Narration of what the Buddha preached.

> (7) Ekamantaṃ nisinnassa kho [brāhmaṇassa Pokkharasādissa] Bhagavā ānupubbikathaṃ kathesi seyyathīdaṃ dānakathaṃ sīlakathaṃ saggakathaṃ kāmānaṃ ādinavaṃ okāraṃ saṃkilesaṃ nekkhamme ānisaṃsaṃ pakāsesi. Yadā bhagavā aññāsi [brāhmaṇaṃ Pokkharasādiṃ] kallacittaṃ mudu-cittaṃ vinīvaraṇa-cittaṃ udagga-cittaṃ pasanna-cittaṃ atha yā buddhānaṃ sāmukkaṃsikā dhammadesanā taṃ pakāsesi: dukkhaṃ samudayaṃ nirodhaṃ maggaṃ. Seyyathā pi nāma suddhaṃ vatthaṃ apagata-kāḷakaṃ sammad eva rajanaṃ patigaṇheyya.[256]
> Then to him thus seated the Exalted One discoursed in due order; that is to say: he spake to him of generosity, of right conduct, of heaven, of the danger, the vanity, and the defilement of lusts, of the advantages of renunciation. And when the Exalted One saw that [Pokkharasādi, the Brahman,] had become prepared, softened, unprejudiced, upraised, and believing in heart, then he proclaimed the

255 DN3, DN5, MN56, MN74, MN91.
256 DN I 109, 38 – DN I 110, 9.

doctrine that Buddhas alone have won; that is to say: the doctrine of sorrow, of its origin, of its cessation, and of the Path. And just as a clean cloth from which all stain has been washed away will readily take the dye.[257]

2. Description of what the hearer perceived and how he felt as the outcome of hearing the sermon.

(8) Evameva kho [brāhmaṇassa Pokkharasādissa] tasmiṃ yeva āsane virajaṃ vītamalaṃ Dhamma-cakkhuṃ udapādi: "yaṃ kiñci samudaya-dhammaṃ sabban taṃ nirodha-dhamman" ti. Atha kho [brāhmaṇo Pokkharasādi] diṭṭha-dhammo patta-dhammo vidita-dhammo pariyogaḷha-dhammo tiṇṇa-vikiccho vigata-kathaṃkatho vesārajjappatto aparapaccayo satthu sāsane.[258]
Just even so did [Pokkharasādi, the Brahman,] obtain, even while sitting there, the pure and spotless Eye for the Truth, and he knew: 'Whosoever has a beginning in that is inherent also the necessity of dissolution.' And then [Pokkharasādi, the Brahman,] as one who had seen the Truth, had mastered it, understood it, dived deep into it, who had passed beyond doubt and put away perplexity and gained full confidence, who had become dependent on no other man for his knowledge of the teaching of the Master, addressed the Exalted One, and said:[259]

The usage of stock phrase (7) (8) is always attached with the set of the stock phrases denoting declaration of belief (3) (4) (5) or (6). The stock phrases (3) (4) (5), together with (7) (8), clearly shows a more special degree of understanding and impression after hearing the sermon, represented with the stock phrase (8), The stock phrase (7) followed by (8) means that the person encountered the experience of *Dhammacakkhu* denoted with the stock (8) after hearing the Buddha's sermon *Ānupubbikathā* "progressive discourse" in (7), which consists of various topics ranged from the simplest issue, viz. the teaching for a better rebirth, unto the complex issue, viz. the teaching to renounce the mundane happiness. In this way, the sermon Ānupubbikathā and the experience of Dhammacakkhu must be related to each other in some way.

Unfortunately, the two texts are not especially commented in commentary, as the meaning seems clear in the context in the opinion of the commentator. In Sumaṅgalavilāsinī, the commentary of the Dīgha-nikāya, the word Ānupubbikathā is explained similarly to the text of the stock

257 Dialogues of the Buddha Part I, pp. 134–135.
258 DN I 110, 10–17.
259 Dialogues of the Buddha Part I, p. 135.

phrase.[260] Whereas in Dhammapadaṭṭhakathā, where the word is often used, the word is found in two meanings. First, the word mentioned at the beginning of the commentary denotes the progressive story that leads to the Buddha's utterance of the verse at the end.[261] Second, it means a certain progressive sermon, with which the hearer is inspired to become a monk.[262] It also appears that the sermon in this name may cause the hearer to attain Arahatship.[263]

Commentary explains that this stock phrase represents the arising of Sotāpanna experience.[264] Stated in the passage (8), the people had the *dhammacakkhu* 'having eyes seeing the truth' or 'realization of the truth.'[265] As remarked above, before achieving this experience the people had heard from the Buddha a particular sermon, so-called *ānupubbikathā* 'talk which themes developed respectively.' It comprises the subject matters of teaching ranged from a simple doctrine to a complex doctrine, i.e. the doctrine on giving, moral habit, and rebirth in heaven for a better rebirth, and the doctrine on the peril, the vanity and the depravity of the pleasures of the senses, the advantage in renouncing for the liberation respectively. According to the meaning of stock phrase (7), the sermon is delivered when the hearer is ready, i.e. he had become "prepared, softened, unprejudiced, upraised, and believing in heart." After having heard the sermon, the people, as described in the stock phrase (8), are mentioned to have seen the truth that 'whosoever has a beginning in that is inherent also the necessity of dissolution.' With the perception, they seemed to have understood all the truth about the Buddha, his enlightenment, his doctrine, and his community of Sangha so broadly and profoundly that they were not doubtful about the Buddha's doctrine and thus had a stable, unshakable belief in the Buddha and his teaching. Hence, the hearer's attainment

260 Sumaṅgalavilāsinī Part 1, p. 278.
261 Dhammapadaṭṭhakathā Vol. 1, p. 68.
262 Ibid., p. 4 l. 16, p. 56 l. 3, p. 161 l. 5.
263 Ibid., p. 207, l. 11.
264 Sumaṇgalavilāsinī, Part I, p. 278.
265 Some scholars translate *dhammacakkhu* "dhamma-insight," Malalasekera "the Eye of Truth" in Dictionary of Pāli Proper Name Vol. I, p. 33. While Masefield (p. 71) defined it, "a glimpse of sanctuary lying beyond the phenomenal world of dukkha – and the path thereto – were gained."

of the Dhammacakkhu is regarded as great success in a delivery of sermon, with which the Buddha was satisfied.[266]

The context of *Ānupubbikathā* in the stock phrases (7) should offer some clues about the meaning of the stock phrases. From the subject matters mentioned in the passages (7) that the sermon starts with the doctrine for lay follower and ends with the doctrine for monk, the sermon *Ānupubbikathā* remarkably includes all the fundamental teachings in Buddhism. It begins with the doctrine of karma on morality and charity in everyday life that an action has a following outcome, and in vice versa, the presence has a cause. As Buddha often instructed, any intended action has an effect, and along this line, in order to achieve a satisfying outcome, one has to conduct a satisfying thing to others. However, the achievement of the satisfying thing as such is still an inconsistent situation that brings a suffering. Specifically, the achievement is still the worldly pleasure that the rule of uncertainty can always affect. Buddha, having pointed to the disadvantage of the pleasure, then suggested renunciation to be a monk, the way to leave the conditioned situation for the true peace that is free from the uncertainty. In this way, as tradition points in the Pāli canon, the *Ānupubbikathā* sermon, which includes all basic themes, may be symbolic of the basic teachings of the Buddha. This also includes the meaning of ascetic life.

Considering the bold scripts of the stock phrase (7), the Buddha simply proceeds to develop his sermon that helps the hearer to understand thoroughly with a common technique of teaching.

> **Then to him thus seated the Exalted One discoursed in due order; that is to say:** he spake to him of generosity, of right conduct, of heaven, of the danger, the vanity, and the defilement of lusts, of the advantages of renunciation. **And when the Exalted One saw that [Pokkharasādi, the Brahman] had become prepared, softened, unprejudiced, upraised, and believing in heart,** then he proclaimed the doctrine that Buddhas alone have won; that is to say: the doctrine of sorrow, of its origin, of its cessation, and of the Path. And as a clean cloth from which all stain has been washed away will readily take the dye.

From the quotation above, the Buddha had a small talk with the hearer about some basic doctrines in order to prepare him to the more profound

266 Cf. The Book of the Discipline Vol. IV, p. 18.

doctrine delivered next. The process might help him learn some principles of the doctrine. At the outset, the hearer was not yet ready to listen and understand anything because they just settled himself on his seat. After some minutes passed, the hearer could concentrate on the sermon better. As the text implies, the Buddha waited for the right time in which the hearer is ready. The text compares the current condition of mind, which is free from other doubts and focusing upon the spoken topics, with a clean cloth which is the suitable material for the dye in producing the dyed cloth with best quality. Then, after the Buddha had noticed the hearer's readiness, he delivered the sermon on the main doctrine, which concerns the Four Noble Truth. The order of incidents clearly shows that the systematically ordered teaching of the teacher played an important role in the hearer's success. The characteristic appearance and voice of the teacher may attract the hearer's concentration that supports the understanding, but they are not the significant factors that the passage mentions. Instead, it is a technique for teaching which prepares for the pupil the background of knowledge and mental readiness to a more difficult lesson. This is an important character of the Buddha that his disciples did not have, *anusāsanīyapāṭihāriya* 'wonder of education,' with which a delivered sermon is successful.[267]

The meaning of the stock phrases reveals two universal claims of Buddhism as world religion. First, the Buddha's teaching proposes the problem and solution of uncertainty in everyday life that the human ordinarily encounters. None of them could reject, birth and death is the most basic condition, which human, as a being in the world, must encounter. The life condition can cause both happiness and unhappiness. Buddha considered the unstable condition the endless suffering and thus tried to find the liberation from it. For the Buddhist, the problem and the solution proposed by the Buddha are thus subject to understand and accept for every human who realises the suffering in their everyday life. Second, it points to the role of the *understanding* as the basis of the belief in the Buddha and his doctrine. Any human can learn and understand the Buddha's doctrine because it is a viewpoint about the problem of human life and solution. By learning *all* the viewpoint, the hearer will

267 Dialogues of the Buddha Part I, p. 279.

understand the Buddha thoroughly. With the explicit knowledge, they will have a stable belief (to some extent) in the doctrine and trust what the Buddha instructs about the liberation as the solution of the life suffering. The knowledge will also lead them to the status *Buddhist* standing on the path directed by the Buddha. In this connection, Buddhism is the doctrine that every human, who realises the life problem of suffering, may learn and understand and even reach the spiritual attainment successfully. The situations indicate the significance of homiletics in the development of Buddhist spirituality

2.3.4 Conclusion

Investigating the stock phrases in the conclusion of discourse, the chapter discussed on the meaning about the behaviours and emotions of the hearer in reaction to the Buddha's sermon. Although the stock phrase is short, uninformative, and stereotypical, the meaning of each is observable and distinguishable from one another with the co-appearance of the phrases and context. The stock phrases are the following:

First type: expressing *satisfaction* (1) or its synonym (2): It can be understood in terms of a positive feeling in reaction to the given answer that fulfilled the hearer's interest or removed his doubt.

Second type: *formal declaration of belief in Buddhism* consists of (3) admiring Buddha's dhamma, (4) worshipping the Three Jewels, asking for permission to become a monk (5) or a lay follower (6). The stock phrases denote the declaration of belief in Buddhism under the impression that dhamma is worthy of worship.

Third type: *achievement of a spiritual attainment* (7) hearing *Ānupubbikathā* sermon and (8) attaining an experience of *Dhammacakkhu*, which tradition means the experience of achieving Sotāpanna. The stock phrases denote an extraordinary experience in the hearing of sermon, which occasionally appears with the second group of stock phrases side by side.

It is also observable from the finding that the meaning of the stock phrases should relate to familiarity of the hearer with the Buddha, his teaching, and his Sangha. Despite not directly mentioned in the introductory story, it is predictable from the description about the people and situation. The stock phrase that denotes satisfaction signifies that the hearer had heard dhamma and been familiar with the Buddha in some extent before the visit. Visiting the Buddha for a talk, they had known Buddha's wisdom in answering a question. Hearing of Buddha's sermon thus results in the *hearer's satisfaction* with the answer of what they had doubted. However, in the others types, the hearer should not have been acquainted with the Buddha and his teaching, so he was surprised about the teaching. The discourse with this type of conclusion is presented with elaborate introduction and reactions, especially in the dramatic debate. About the Buddha, the hearer had different attitudes such as curiosity, non-confidence, non-acquaintanceship, and even sometimes, opposition. The declaration of followership at the end is symbolic of victory or acceptance of ability in the face-to-face encounter.

2.4 Summary

With the purpose to find out the concept of non-monastic follower in Pāli discourse, as the oral tradition presents to the audience, the chapter concentrated on the presentation of the text. The task began with the remarks on the discourse as oral tradition, followed by the survey of parts of discourses.

The discourse, despite containing a philosophical sermon delivered by Buddha and his followers in different situations, presents the outcome of confrontation and dialogues between the Buddha and the people, who are monastic followers, lay followers, householders, or others. At the end of the discourses the talk or the sermon, often, satisfies the hearer(s). In case of dialogues with people outside the order, viz. householders and ascetics from other communities, it logically points to the *development of belief in the Buddha*, which is concluded with an acknowledgment of the hearer. Despite the fact that the structure of the discourses *might* have a root in the Vedic tradition of commentary composition, the discourses structured in the form of delivery of sermon and debate reflects the significance of the homiletics in the missionary activity. It helped the people to understand the teaching and the qualities of the Buddha, which was the important basis of Buddhist spirituality. This knowledge played an important role on the decision to become a follower. Furthermore, it was a factor to attain a higher spirituality, viz. achievement of Dhammacakkhu, the followership with unshakable belief in the Buddha. The plot constructed in this fashion is thus effective to illustrate the role of the Buddha in propagating his teaching to his pupils and converting people. In tandem, the sermon symbolizes the dhamma, the knowledge which is claimed as the enlightened wisdom of the Buddha. The 'changed' behaviours and attitudes of the outsiders into friendliness, acknowledgment, and reverence in the conclusion support the claim of Buddha's specialness in his teaching. This is the grammar of the followership presented to the audience.

At the first stage, it can be concluded that the stock phrases at the end of discourse signify a degree of *knowledge* as well as *acknowledgment* of the Buddha and his teaching. This is the relationship that connects with outsiders: an ordinary householder, Brahmin, or even an ascetic from other schools. This fact obviously points that the concept of upāsaka/upāsikā, especially in this two Nikāyas, is distinctive from upāsaka/upāsikā in other scriptures of the canonical and sub-canonical and from *lay follower* in other religions like Christianity, in which the word denotes the inexpert or subordinate people in the church. In the next chapter, the development of the belief, which is declared at the end after the sermon, will be investigated in detail to find out the pattern of the development of the belief and the making of the non-monastic Buddhist, presented in the discourse.

Chapter III: Development of Belief and Religious Experience in Pāli Discourse

In the last chapter, Pāli discourse in Dīgha- and Majjhima-nikāya, not only represents the text of Buddha's sermon, can be reckoned the epic of Buddha's mission containing the stories of how the Buddha confronted people and converted them into his follower. This chapter aims at investigating the pattern of the conversion, starting with the first encounter between Buddha and a hearer who is the main character of the story. As depicted in discourse, the belief in the Buddha gradually increased and and reached the end that the hearer became a follower. Dealing with the depiction, the author observes the development at three stages: first, at first hearing the Buddha's reputation and seeing him in person; second, at hearing the sermon, in which the hearer might express an impression; and last, at the end, in which the hearer said and behaved in reaction to the sermon. The result, which is the concept of the spiritual development, will be discussed with the theory of religious experience in order to understand the relation between Buddha, his sermon, and the hearer, expressed with verbal and non-verbal expression presented in the discourse.

3.1 At First Hearing the Buddha's Reputation and Seeing Him in Person

The story in the introductory begins with Buddha's arrival at a community, where the hearer, the main character of the discourse, lived. Through the medium of hearsay, the reputation of the Buddha on his qualities had grown in the community that attracted the attention of the hearer. From this point forward, the hearer was depicted to obsess about the Buddha, which motivated him to pay a visit. The study observes the behaviour, thought, words, described in the discourses showing the development of belief after hearing the name and his reputation at first with the aim at understanding the development of followership, expressed in his behaviour, speech, and action in the discourse.

3.1.1 Buddha

Buddha's reputation spread in the social communication can be categorized into two types. First, the Buddha as the great spiritual teacher described in hearsay,[268] and second, the Buddha's possession of the 32 signs of Great Man that existed on the Buddha's body.[269] The types of reputation resulted in the category of people who got the message. The hearer who was attracted by the hearsay were Brahmins[270] and those in the community where Buddha and community arrived of Sangha came,[271] while only the Brahmin teachers were attracted by the rumor that Buddha possessed the signs of Great Man.[272]

3.1.1.1 Buddha's Spiritual Qualities

In the introductory story of discourse, the spiritual qualities of the Buddha were spread in a hearsay growing in the society, where the Buddha and his disciples were arriving. The hearsay is particularly posited in the introductory part of a discourse for the opening of Buddha in order to present the social status, knowledge and attainments in comparison with that of the hearer, the main character of discourse.[273] The text has it:

> That Blessed One is an Arahat, a fully awakened one, abounding in wisdom and goodness, happy, with knowledge of the worlds, unsurpassed as a guide to mortals willing to be led, a teacher for gods and men, a Blessed One, a Buddha. He, by himself, thoroughly knows and sees, as it were, face to face this universe, –including the worlds above of the gods, the Brahmas, and the Māras, and the worlds below with its recluses and Brahmans, its princes and people, –and having known it, he makes his knowledge known to others. The truth, lovely in its origin, lovely in its progress, lovely in its consummation, doth he proclaim, both in the spirit and in the letter, the higher life doth he make known, in all its fullness and in all its purity. 'And good is it to pay visits to Arahat like that.'[274]

268 DN3, DN4, DN5, DN6, DN12, DN13, DN23, MN41, MN42, MN60, MN82, MN84, MN91, MN92, MN95, MN150.

269 DN3, MN91, MN92.

270 DN3, DN4, DN5, DN6, DN12, DN13, DN91, DN92, DN95.

271 DN41, DN42, DN60, DN150.

272 DN3, MN91, MN92.

273 Manné, Debates and Case Histories in the Pali Canon, pp. 20–21.

274 Example from DN. 3, p. 109. DN I 87, 15 – DN I 88, 2; Dialogues of the Buddha Part I, p. 109.

From the hearsays and rumour, it shows that Buddha had a very good image of spiritual teacher in ancient communities of the central land and been welcome in the communities. The hearer's attitude in reaction to the Buddha described in the hearsay was obviously handled with respect. First, it significantly points to the beginning of Buddhist belief in that it could start an attention of people who had heard the hearsay by challenging them to check up the cited qualities of Buddha by himself or herself by seeing the Buddha in person and hearing his teaching. Second, Buddha was a spiritual teacher with respectable knowledge and controlled manner. The society, even the community of Brahmin, acknowledged the characteristics of spiritual teachers in this fashion. Paying a visit to the spiritual teachers with the qualities as such was worthwhile for them. The text states a community belief that the Arahat as such was worthy of a visit. "*And good is it to pay visits to Arahats like that.*" The reputations attracted the people to see and talk with him to observe the qualities by themselves.

According to Pāli canon, the term *Arahat* as construed by people was relativistic and dependent to the user to understand what the 'admirable' ascetic should be like. Both Buddhism and Jainism applied the word to denote the spiritual status of those who had been liberated from fetters. Arahat was the designation of *holy* person who had reached the highest spiritual attainment and would achieve Nibbāna after the death.[275] Different from each other was the question as to how to reach this Arahatship. As Pāli canon implies, people in the ancient society perceived the concept of Arahat in term of admirable and extraordinarily spiritual. Several ascetics outside the Sangha, especially those who practiced a hard self-mortification or strange austerity, claimed themselves as well as were ascribed by people in the society with the term.[276] With the understanding, the term included the ascetic who could perform and were expected to perform an extraordinary miracle.[277] One may surmise that the exact meaning of

275 Bronkhorst, Der indische Buddhismus und seine Verzweigungen, p. 127.

276 DN14, p. 12 The word Arahat in this context is ascribed by a misunderstanding monk Sunakkhatta to Kora, the ascetic who behaved like a dog.

277 It can be implied from the context in Pāli canon that the concept of Arahat is often believed in relation to a miracle, i.e. the ability to perform a miracle indicates the Arahatship. For example, Buddha's miracles in the hermitage of the matted hair ascetic Kassapa of Uruvelā in Book of Discipline Vol. IV, pp. 33 ff.;

Arahat particularly for householders was uncertain and even connected with the magical power.

In this way, it can be imagined that the understanding about ascetic life and Arahat for the householders should be very different from one another, and even far from a true understanding in the ascetic schools because the householder did not know their doctrine, or the dhamma that makes him so-called Arahat in each ascetic school. They did not have any knowledge for a judgment, which ascetic was the true Arahat who practiced the right doctrine. Magic, supernatural, extraordinariness could always be attributed by the householder to the ascetic who lived the spiritual life. With the reference to spirituality, the people were excited about the coming of the famous spiritual teacher. Seeing him in person, they perhaps hoped to see some miracles from him, not only to hear his teaching, as some reader may expect. In this way, the belief in the Buddha as presented in the text was connected with private belief and interpretation of people on the Buddha that arouse more motivation to see him. Buddha as perceived by the local people was probably not a philosophical teacher, but a magic performer. Sunakkhatta Licchavi, for example, joined the Sangha for the chance to observe the magic of the Buddha.[278]

3.1.1.2 Signs of Great Man in Buddha

As another alternative, a discourse, in which the main character is a Brahmin, may mention the treatise on signs of Great Man, with which attracted Brahmin's attention to Buddha. The treatise was known to several Brahmin teachers mentioned in Sīlakkhandhavagga. Because the treatise was claimed to pertain to the Brahmin self,[279] it is reasonable that the Brahmins, after having known that Buddha really possessed the signs of Great Man, became excited and curious to see him in person, in order to observe every sign on his body. Having seen the Buddha in person, they even became more submissive to the Buddha with the confidence that he

Piṇḍola Bharadvāja's miracle to take the bowl that a merchant let it hang on a tree in Book of Discipline Vol. V, pp. 149–150.

278 Dialogues of the Buddha Part III, p. 8 ff.; cf. p. 127.

279 Dialogues of the Buddha Part I, pp. 110–111. Pokkharasādi claimed that the physiognomy is learned only by Brahmins.

was the true Enlightened. The process points to the fact that the development of Buddhist belief especially at the very basic stage is first connected with the basic belief of the hearer.

As the discourses depict, some Brahmins hearing from the hearsay the coming of the Buddha in their community became attracted to the Buddha with their physiognomic knowledge of 32 signs of Great Man,[280] which they had learned in their tradition. The treatise was claimed in several parts of the Pāli Suttapiṭaka as an elite science of the Brahmin,[281] stated that the man with the 32 signs became one of the two great persons in the world: the emperor, the king of the kings or the Buddha, the teacher of the teachers, as Pokkharasādi explained to his pupil Ambaṭṭha:

> "... If he dwells at home he will become a sovran [sic!] of the world, a righteous king, bearing rule even to the shores of the four great oceans, a conqueror, the protector of his people, possessor of the seven royal treasures. And these are the seven treasures that he has – the wheel, the Elephant, the Horse, the Gem, the Woman, the Treasurer, and the Advisor as a seventh. And he has more than a thousand sons, heroes, mighty in frame, beating down the armies of the foe. And he dwells in complete ascendancy over the wide earth from sea to sea, ruling it in righteousness without the need of baton or of sword. But if he go forth from the household life into the houseless state, then he will become a Buddha who removes the veil from the eyes of the world. ..."[282]

The physiognomic knowledge was influential on Brahmin's fast judgment to the Buddhahood and decision to join the community, right after he had checked all the 32 auspicious signs on the Buddha's body, including the special tongue and penis. The discourse describes that Buddha had some organs under the cloth particularly shown to the curious Brahmin, in order to remove the doubt about the peculiarity of the organs. In Selasutta (MN92), at first hearing the word *buddha 'the enlightened'* in reference to the Buddha Gotama, the leader of the Sangha, Brahmin Sela was surprised by the designation because it denoted the person who possessed the signs of Great Man and had chosen the spiritual life for the Enlightenment and the great doctrine of the world.[283] The Brahmin was curious about

280 For detail of 32 signs of Great Man, see DN30.
281 DN3, DN30, MN91, MN92.
282 DN I 88, 32–34; DN I 89, 1–9; Dialogues of the Buddha Part I, pp. 110–111.
283 The Collection of the Middle Length Sayings Vol. II, pp. 334–335.

the signs on the Buddha's body and wanted to visit the Buddha at once. With the knowledge about the physiognomy, after having observed all the 32 signs of him, the Brahmin was certain about the Buddhahood of him and asked to become a monastic follower, although Buddha had not delivered him a sermon.

Brahmāyu (MN91)[284] is another example of Brahmin who was absolutely attracted to the Buddha and had the Buddhist belief developed with this physiognomic knowledge alone. He completely believed in the Buddha at first encounter after he had been confirmed about this fact from his pupil who had observed the thirty-two signs on his body and every manner of the Buddha through seven months. The pupil's report fascinated him greatly that he three times bowed to the Buddha and wished himself a visit. At first seeing, the Brahmin paid a great respect to the Buddha in front of public. This means, the Brahmin was not doubtful about Buddha's "Buddhahood" and his great qualities as spiritual teacher. After he had seen by himself every auspicious feature of the Buddha and talked with him, he had the belief in the Buddha developed in a short time. The Brahmin's manner after the dialogue is described in the following way:

> When this (Buddha's answer) had been said, Brahmāyu the brahman, rising from his seat, arranging his upper robe over one shoulder, having inclined his head to the Lord's feet, kissed the Lord's feet on all sides with his mouth and stroked them on all sides with his hands, and he made known his (own) name: "I, good Gotama, am Brahmāyu, the brahman." Then that company was filled with wonder and marvel, and said: "Indeed it is wonderful, indeed it is marvelous how great is the psychic power and the majesty of the recluse in virtue of which this Brahmāyu the brahman, well known and renowned, pays such deep respect."[285]

Likewise, Pokkharasādi, after having heard the report about the Buddha's signs from his pupil, he wanted to pay Buddha a visit at once. He paid no attention to the pupils' objection that he should have seen the Buddha on the next day. He went to see the Buddha in the night, in order to see the Buddha and the signs of Great Man with his eyes. On the next day, on which the Brahmin invited the Buddha for food at his place, the Brahmin asked to become a follower with *Dhammacakkhu* a spiritual attainment

284 The Collection of the Middle Length Sayings Vol. II, pp. 317 ff.
285 MN II 144, 23–31; The Collection of the Middle Length Sayings Vol. II, p. 330.

mentioned in discourse. The influence of the treatise in the development of belief in the Buddha was obviously seen in opposite to Soṇadaṇḍa, who was not attracted with the knowledge.[286] The Brahmin went to the Buddha at his place as the result of social manner that he as the great Brahmin of community should visit a spiritual teacher who arrived in his community. The visit was thus obligatory for this social status. Besides, during the conversation, he was worried about himself in responding a debate and did not recognize the signs of the Great Man according to the treatise. In this way, he was a normal convert with a request for a limitation on showing respect to the Buddha in public. As the discourse implies, his belief in the Buddha did not reach at height like the belief of other Brahmins who were attracted with the knowledge about the signs.

From the literary perspective, the description about the Buddha in this part significantly relates to the style of debate discourse. As Manné has mentioned, this part intentionally provides the information of each side before the encounter, especially that of the Buddha which created a challenge to the hearer.[287] It thus logically links to the following reactions of the hearer, depicted in the discourses. Specifically, they became curious about the Buddha and wanted to see him in person. Some of them sent their pupil to observe the Buddha to prove, whether the qualities mentioned in the rumour or the hearsay are true. In every case, after the fact about Buddha's thirty-two signs of Great Man was confirmed, the belief in the Buddha was quickly developed that they asked to become a follower at once. Sela became a monastic follower and later reached Nibbāna. Brahmāyu became a non-monastic follower and supported Buddha and his community with food through seven days while living in his community. He passed away not long after the Buddha's visit and had the rebirth that affirms his spiritual attainment. Pokkharasādī became a Buddhist lay Brahmin, whose status as Buddha's follower is well known in the Brahmin society.

No matter this fact about the Buddha was true, the constructed plot offers the sensibility in that the hearers were attracted to see the Buddha by their beliefs about lifestyle, manner, wisdom, etc. considered 'holy.' The narrative of discourses shows that the concept of *Buddha* 'the enlightened,'

---

286 Cf. 4.2.2.

287 Manné, Debates and Case Histories in the Pali Canon, pp. 20–21.

Arahat 'the admirable,' and the Great Man is well known to the people in the society, especially of Brahmin, that indicates the holiness of the person. Buddha was mentioned in the fashion that he possessed a sacred quality and thus managed to attract various people, particularly the Brahmin teacher, to see the quality in him, before making a conversation with him. Tradition clearly makes a point that a local belief or a private belief encourages to the development of belief in the Buddha. The hearer tended to trust and become more faithful in the Buddha at once after hearing that the Buddha really possessed the respectable qualities as in the hearsay. At the first encounter, the people wholeheartedly expressed the reverence in the Buddha. To understand the reaction, they may not have really known how the Buddha is sacred, as they were new to his doctrine. Instead, they, following the belief they have about what the sacred man is like, were convinced that the Buddha was truly sacred. In the process, with the physical reaction to the Buddha described in the text, it is plausible that their mind became submissive in some extent and willing to hear what the Buddha would say.

3.1.2 Monastic Follower as Representative of Buddha

Monastic follower, especially Bhikkhu, is Buddha's pupil who by duty learns and practices the doctrine for his own liberation. As a result, in the discourse, the monastic follower, especially those who were *successful* in the spiritual duty, may ably answer any question about the doctrine and practice. In Dīgha-nikāya and Majjhima-nikāya, there are 19 discourses, in which the monastic followers, bhikkhu and bhikkhuṇī, delivered a sermon or gave an advice to the Sangha, lay follower, householder, or even ascetics from other schools.[288] Noticeably, the followers were mentioned in the discourse that they helped another person understand what they had doubted. Some of them such as Kaccāna explained the teaching impressively that the hearer declared the Three Jewels for refuge and asked to become a follower.

288 See tables in appendices I, II: DN33, DN34, MN3, MN5, MN15, MN24, MN28, MN31, MN32, MN44, MN123, MN127, MN141; DN10, MN50, MN76, MN84, MN94.

A chief disciple may thus replace the position of Buddha as debater against those who challenge the doctrine. In DN23, the introductory story mentions the reputation on positive qualities of Kumārakassapa, who is one of Buddha's disciples "*wise and expert is he, abounding in knowledge and learning, eloquent and excellent in discourse, venerable too and an Arhant.*"[289] Although the qualities did not attract the chieftain Pāyāsi with great respect at first encounter, the quality, especially the skillfulness in the doctrine, attracted him to visit the monk for a conversation about some beliefs that he had doubted. The description is thus sensible to the story which particularly conveys the heatedly debate on the belief as the following incident. However, there is unfortunately only DN23 that represents the debate between a monk and a person outside the order who challenged the doctrine. Normally, the discourses depict Buddha as the religious debater whose qualities were spread in hearsay and attractive to the hearer. The case of Kumārakassapa was quite special, as it was the incident after the Buddha's lifetime and concerned the challenge of belief that was ordinary belief in Buddha's lifetime.

3.1.3 Conclusion

If the pattern of Pāli discourse reflects the abstract idea of the oral text as Ong claimed,[290] the description in this part reveals a *mechanism* in the development of Buddhist belief that starts with an attraction. The pattern, as the tradition points out, indicates that the former belief of the hearer was the basis to the development of Buddhist belief of an individual and to the making of Buddhism. The power that attracted the hearer to the Buddha rooted in the social value accepted in the society of the hearer about what the spiritual people should look like. With the attraction, the hearer after hearing the Buddha's story and the news about his arrival at his community went to see him in person. The value of the people was dependent to their family and society. Ordinary people, householders, were attracted to Buddha with qualities in the hearsay that could make first impression at first meeting. Whereas the Brahmins, who had learned the physiognomic treatise,

289 DN II 317, 8–11; Dialogues of the Buddha Vol. II, p. 350.
290 See detail in 1.3.2.

were attracted to the Buddha with the characteristic signs of Great Man. The visible, observable qualities spread in the hearsay or rumor created a very good image about the Buddha that makes a visit in the discourses reasonable.

The impression at first sight played a very important role in Buddhist spirituality. The discourse obviously shows how it contributed to the belief in the community. Buddha was remarked that he was well supported because of his good-looking characteristics.[291] However, this quality was particular to a person. It was temporary and even problematic to the Buddhist spirituality that supports the effort to self-development in every way. As a result, Buddha encouraged his pupils to possess the respectable qualities and images concerning the knowledge and manner that everyone can improve with intention and effort. The definition of *thera* from Buddha's perspective focuses on the achievement of the spiritual life, viz. the more maturity in knowledge and manner, *instead of* on the number of the years of spiritual life.[292] In this way, tradition gives prominence to knowledge and manner that monastic follower had learned and practiced in the Buddha's community,[293] and as the result, it regards them more worthy of visit and donation than any ascetic in other communities was.[294] The visible qualities first attracted people outside the community. Assaji, for example, was noticed by Sāriputta, who was at that time an ascetic in Sañjaya's school because of his proper decorum in walking, alms-begging, and eating. After observing the monk Sāriputta approached the monk to ask for his doctrine, which changed his religious life forever.[295]

The positive characteristics on his body, respectability shining from his modest lifestyle, reserving behaviour, and controlled manner significantly played an important role on the belief that led to a feeling of belief and trust. Applying this technique to attract people's religious interest, Buddha

291 The Book of the Gradual Sayings Vol. I, pp. 163 ff.

292 The Book of the Gradual Sayings Vol. II, pp. 22 ff.

293 Freiberger, Der Orden in der Lehre, pp. 118–119.

294 Ibid., pp. 134–135.

295 The Book of the Discipline Vol. IV, p. 52; cf. p. 127. According to the tradition, Sāriputta attained Sotāpanna at hearing the short doctrine. He persuaded his friend, Moggallāna, who was also an ascetic in the same school, to join the community of Sangha. They both became the chief disciples of the Buddha.

made up the respectable characteristics to his monastic followers by laying down the rules that prevented some undesirable behaviours, actions, and lifestyles and in tandem supported the respectable routine life, viz. appropriate manners of monastic follower in eating, walking, preaching etc. This resulted in the public positive image of the order in the society. However, the pattern of the discourse indicates that the visible image was merely the primary stage in the development of belief in Buddhism. People actually believed in the Buddha and became a Buddhist after they had heard the sermon and understood its meaning.

3.2 After Hearing the Sermon

The discourses portray the scene of conversation or instruction, in which Buddha delivered his doctrine, idea, opinion, etc. to the hearer. In the encounter with each other, the hearer could observe closely Buddha's visible qualities such as personality and manners in moving, speaking, etc. Besides, in the talk, the hearer knew more about the Buddha, particularly his insider aspects, and thus had more belief developed in the Buddha. Some householders were interested in the doctrine and liked to discuss on several topics with Buddha or monks. As householder, they were often curious about the reason behind the renunciation, viz. the doctrine and practice that the Buddha and his monastic follower devoted. The step was thus significant to the development of the right understanding about Buddha that led to the declaration of followership at the end.

At the end of some discourses, there are hearer's reflection of the dhamma and the Buddha in the sermon and conversation in the reaction to the Buddha's sermon, particularly after having learned the Buddha and his teaching for the first time. It is occasionally found in normal narrative, not the stock phrases, describing what the hearer thought and felt during the conversation. Due to the intention expressed in the message, the reflection can be categorized into two groups: compliment and apology. Both are not in form of the mnemonic passages, but in normal expression.

3.2.1 Compliment

Some hearers particularly remarked compliments to the Buddha and his doctrine in other ways, not only stock phrases (3) which "officially" reflect the impression on the sermon before the declaration of the belief.[296] In the 48 conversational discourses, eleven compliments are found in addition.[297] The subject matters of the compliments derive from the hearer's impression in the Buddha's answer, which the hearers considered reasonable, true, and beneficial to the human life. From the perspective of the speakers, the compliments were paid to address the characteristic qualities of the Buddha that he is "special," viz. more superior than other teachers. According to the theme of the compliment in the concluding part, the auhtor divides the compliments into 3 categories.

3.2.1.1 Compliment on Ability to Debate

Buddha received compliment about the given answer that he could clarify the issues, in which a hearer had raised a challenging question in the debate. The compliment with this theme is found in eight discourses.[298] Buddha was famous for his ability to give the right answer corresponding to the question, which satisfied the asker. King Ajātasattu (DN2) was satisfied with the Buddha's answer that the Buddha did not evade his question, unlike other teachers, whom the king compared with the man who, "*when asked what a mango was, should explain what a bread fruit is.*"[299] Likewise, the following compliment remarks on this quality.

> "We asked the honoured Gotama about the preservation of truth; the good Gotama explained the preservation of truth; and we approved of it and were pleased, and so we are delighted. We asked the honoured Gotama about awakening to truth; the good Gotama explained the awakening of truth; and we approved of it and were pleased, and so we are delighted. We asked the honoured Gotama about attainment of truth; the good Gotama explained the attainment of truth; and we approved of it and were pleased, and so we are delighted. We asked the honoured Gotama about a thing that is much service to the attainment of truth; the good Gotama explained the thing that is of much service to the attainment of truth; and we approved of it and were pleased, and so we are delighted. Whatever it was that we asked the honoured Gotama, that very thing the good Gotama explained; and we approved of it and were pleased, and so we are delighted. For, formerly, good Gotama, we used to know (a distinction) thus: 'And who are these

296 See detail in 2.3.2.
297 See Apendix II.
298 DN8, DN10, DN12, DN21, MN52, MN56, MN72, MN76.
299 DN I 53, 4–6; Dialogues of the Buddha Vol. I, p. 70.

little shaveling recluses, menials, black, off-scouring of our Kinsman's heels? And who are the knowers of *dhamma*? Indeed the good Gotama has aroused in me a recluse's regard for recluses, a recluse's satisfaction in recluses, a recluse's respect for recluses."[300] (MN95)

This compliment points to Buddha's ability in speech over that of other teachers. Debate on a doctrinal topic between the leaders or representatives of schools was depicted to be ordinary to the ascetics and mendicants in the scene.[301] Among them, it can be predicted that there were both good and bad debaters in comparison. The admiration implies the opposite characteristics of bad debaters. For example, evading answering a challenging issue or, despite not knowing the answer, responding ambiguously or unreasonably, just in order to save face. The debate as such was uninteresting and even annoying for the observers who attended the debate. It was also difficult for them to accept the points the debater had said and to trust others as teacher except for Buddha. As a result, the ability was admirable for the hearers and witnesses, who enjoyed the activity. As Upāli (MN56) confessed, he found it fascinating at the response given by the Buddha. And in order to keep the Buddha's response forward, he necessarily raised questions as if he was still Buddha's opponent in the debate, although the feeling of admiring the Buddha had developed in his mind.

"I, revered sir, was pleased and satisfied with the Lord's first illustration. But because I wanted to hear the Lord's diversified ways of putting questions, I judged that I must make myself his adversary..."[302] (MN56)

Likewise, the compliment by Kassapa, the naked ascetic

"And who, sir, on hearing the doctrine of the Exalted One, would not be well pleased, as if with a great joy. I also, who have now heard the doctrine of the Exalted One, am thus well pleased, even as if with a great joy."[303] (DN8)

As the examples raised above, we can imagine how the Buddha was raised by the tradition as a good debater with the opinion of the hearer or observers. From the thought and feelings in the compliment, the people

300 MN II 176, 25–34. – MN II 177, 1–11; The Collection of the Middle Length Sayings Vol. II, pp. 365–366.

301 Cf. Chakravarti, The Social Dimensions of Early Buddhism, p. 52.

302 MN I 378, 27–31; The Collection of the Middle Length Sayings Vol. II, p. 44.

303 DN I 176, 4–7; Dialogues of the Buddha Part I, p. 239.

seemed to be fascinated with the Buddha's ability and knowledge in his given answer and explanation, which was superior to other teachers. The compliments show that the debate as presented in discourse is not only the intellectual activity, in which people fight to one another for the victory and the defeat in the rational arguments, but also indicates the knowledge and wisdom. Some hearer appreciated the answers that the Buddha gave in response to their question. In this regard, the feeling is comparable to the satisfaction denoted by the stock phrase (1) in that the debate satisfactorily sustained the interest.[304]

3.2.1.2 Compliment on the Meaning of the Teaching

Some compliments mention the meaning of Buddha's answers and his teaching. The subject matter indicates that the hearer followed the Buddha's explanation, considered the arguments, and finally understood the message that Buddha presented. As followed, the hearer could estimate or judge on the value of what the Buddha had presented, as expressed in the compliment.

> "Good Gotama, it is like a great sāl tree not far from a village or market town whose branches and foliage might be dissolved because of their impermanence, whose bark and young shoots might be dissolved, whose softwood might be dissolved, so that after a time the branches and foliage gone, the bark and young shoots gone, the softwood gone, clear of them it would be established on the pith."[305] (MN72)

The estimation of Buddha's word was often made in comparison with other doctrines, which the hearers had learned or known before. The compliment clearly states the superiority of the Buddha's wisdom over that of other spiritual teacher.

> "Wonderful is this, Ānanda, and mysterious–both that this so noble group of conduct is well-rounded, not incomplete; and that I perceive no other, like unto it, among the other Samaṇas and Brāhamaṇas outside of this communion..."[306] (DN10)

304 Cf. 2.3.1.
305 MN II 488, 27–34; The Collection of the Middle Length Sayings Vol. II, pp. 166–167.
306 DN I 210, 1–7; Dialogues of the Buddha Part I, p. 269.

The value of the Buddha's word is also raised with hyperbole in the compliment. It illustrates how profoundly the hearer had considered and realised the significance of teaching to him that it saves him from falling down in the bad life and directs him to the better future.

> "Just, Gotama, as if a man had caught hold of a man, falling over the precipitous edge of purgatory, by the hair of his head, and lifted him up safe back on the firm land–just so have I, on the point of falling into purgatory, been lifted back on to the land by the venerable Gotama..."[307] (DN12)

From the example above, the hearer compared the Buddha's teaching with something that saves him from falling in the purgatory, which was known to the people at that time as the world after death of those who had behaved evil. The given compliment to the Buddha's teaching implies that he considered the teaching had saved him and thus precious for his life. The quality of the Buddha's teaching is also mentioned although his disciple passed on the teaching.

> "Revered Ānanda, it is as though a man who was seeking for one opening to (some hidden) treasure were to come at one and the same time on eleven openings to the treasure. Even so do I, revered sir, in seeking for one door to the deathless come to here at one and the same time of eleven doors to the deathless. And too, revered sir, it is like a man's house that has eleven doors; if his house were on fire he could make himself safe by any one of the doors. Even so can I, revered sir, make myself safe by any one of these eleven doors to the deathless..."[308] (MN52)

The admiring words were the outcome of evaluating the sermon. The hearer first considered the trueness of the teaching in relation to the facts. Then, he pondered the worth of learning the teaching to the understanding of life. In comparison to teachings of other schools, he mentioned the value of dhamma as well as the wisdom of the Buddha who had discovered and propagated the dhamma. The compliment on this theme shows the reflection about their impression and acceptance that the teaching of the Buddha is the truth.

---

307 DN I 234, 5–9; Dialogues of the Buddha Part I, pp. 296–297.

308 MN I 352, 35–36 – MN I 353, 1–8; The Collection of the Middle Length Sayings Vol. II, pp. 17–18.

3.2.1.3 Compliment on the Monastic Order

Some hearers may praise the order that the Buddha had established and headed. Seeing the teaching ability in the Buddha,[309] they could deduce that the community, of which the Buddha was the leader and the teacher, should offer the path to the true liberation and could bring the pupil to reach the aim successfully. Therefore, he finds the Buddha's community trustworthy.

> "Good Gotama, as the river Ganges, sliding towards the sea, tending towards the sea, inclining towards the sea, stands knocking at the sea, even so this company of the good Gotama, comprising householders and those that have gone forth, sliding towards Nibbāna, tending towards Nibbāna, inclining towards Nibbāna, stands knocking at Nibbāna..."[310] (MN73)

The wisdom of the Buddha can be also observed in the community of his pupils. The community as manifested to them is a place where one may get to know Buddha's wisdom in teaching and organizing the community. Some attitudes like tolerance and respect for other doctrines seemed to be little practiced in other ascetic communities. This attitude practiced in the Buddha's order thus fascinated the hearer.

> "Wonderful, good Ānanda, marvelous, good Ānanda; there can be no extolling of their own *dhamma* nor disparaging of the *dhamma* of others; but both the teaching of *dhamma* in its (whole) extent and so many great leaders can be seen. On the other hand, these Naked Ascetics are children of a childless mother, they both extol themselves and disparage others, and they show only three great leaders, namely Nada Vaccha, Kisa Saṅkicca, and Makkhali Gosāla."[311] (MN76)

In this way, as some hearer might deduce, as Buddha was a wise teacher, there should be only good monks who were wise to learn and practice for the liberation with him. Buddha's community of Sangha is thus admirable for the place, where good people assemble for the spiritual aim.

> "Good Gotama, as for those persons who, in want of a way of living, have gone forth from home into homelessness without faith, who are crafty, fraudulent, deceitful, who are unbalanced and puffed up, who are shifty, scurrilous and of

---

309 See detail in 3.2.1.1 and 3.2.1.2.

310 MN I 493, 24–28; The Collection of the Middle Length Sayings Vol. II, p. 172.

311 MN I 523, 34–36 – MN I 524, 1–4; The Collection of the Middle Length Sayings Vol. II, p. 202.

loose talk, the doors of whose sense-organs are not guarded, who do not know moderation in eating, who are not intent on vigilance, indifferent to recluseship, not of keen respect for the training, who are ones for abundance, lax, taking the lead in backsliding, shirking the burden of seclusion, who are indolent, of feeble energy, of confused mindfulness, not clearly conscious, not concentrated but of wondering minds, who are weak in wisdom, drivellers–the good Gotama is not in communion with them. But as for the young men of respectable families who have gone forth from home into homelessness from faith, who are not crafty, fraudulent or deceitful, who are not unbalanced or puffed up, who are not shifty, scurrilous or of loose talk, the doors of whose sense-organs are guarded, who know moderation in eating, who are intent on vigilance, longing for recluseship, of keen respect for the training, who are not ones for abundance, not lax shirking backsliding, taking the lead in seclusion, who are stirred up energy, self-resolute, with mindfulness aroused, clearly conscious, concentrated, their minds one-pointed, who have wisdom, are not drivellers–the good Gatama is in communion with *them*. As, good Gotama, black gum is pointed to as chief of root-scents, as red sandalwood is pointed to as chief of pith-scents, as jasmine is pointed to as chief of flower scents–even so is the exhortation of the good Gotama highest among the teachings of today." (MN107)[312]

In summary, the compliments on the different themes show the qualities of the Buddha that the hearers had observed. First is the quality of good debater and explainer, who gave an answer corresponding to the discussed issue. The comment reflects that the Buddha was a successful debater who offered convincing arguments even to the non-believers. Although some of them did not raise the Buddha as their teacher, they did mention his ability and intellect in the debate. Second is the quality of Buddha's wisdom that one may observe from the teaching. The admiration on this theme arose from the evaluation of the doctrine in comparison with other doctrines which they had learned and known. Third is the quality of Sangha, the order that the Buddha had established. From his wisdom and the ability in the explanation, it was deducible that the community must be successful in organizing and training people to the liberation. It must be the place, where good people with the determined intention come in order to learn and practice for the spiritual aim. The subject matters of the compliments interestingly indicate that Buddha was the spiritual teacher who possessed the ability to teach, the knowledge, and the community of wise pupils.

312 MN III 6, 10–29 – MN III 7, 1–3; The Collection of the Middle Length Sayings Vol. III, pp. 56–57.

The expression also implies a fact that the presented qualities of the Buddha are visible and observable during the conversation. The reflection did not concern magical or mysterious aspects of the Buddha. Having considered the goodness in the Buddha, some hearers sincerely gave him a compliment or an acknowledgment without declaring the followership,[313] while many of them decided to become a follower. The evaluation of Buddha and his doctrine was significantly related to the compliments, as in the stock phrase (3), which has a sense of compliment about Buddha's dhamma.[314] Tradition makes the stock phrase (3) stereotypical to represent the normality that the feeling leads to the decision for the declaration of the followership. In this way, it should signify that the positive attitude about the Buddha after the hearing of sermon was the factor to the declaration of belief in Buddhism.

3.2.2 Apology

Apology is found side by side with the admiration. In the discourse, there are four times of apology.[315] Apology is a social language in the society where people, who have mistaken to one another, treat to one another with respect. One apologizes when they realise they have done a mistake to the other one. Along these lines, some hearer who at first despised the Buddha apologized for the rudeness after demonstrating his ability and wisdom. Despite a small number of the passages, the utterance of apology clearly signifies how the hearers positively thought about the Buddha on the one hand and negatively about himself in the past on the other. Some hearers confessed the guilt, while admiring his ability and wisdom, to the Buddha simultaneously. The confession came out of a feeling of regret for a mistake in the Buddha.

> "An offence has overcome me, Lord, foolish and stupid and wrong that I am, who spoke thus about the Exalted One. May the Exalted One accept it of me, lord, that do so acknowledge it as an offence, to the end that in future I may restrain myself."[316] (DN25).

313 MN52, MN76.

314 See 2.3.2.

315 DN1, DN12, DN54, MN95. See Appendix II.

316 DN III 55, 5–8; Dialogues of the Buddha Part III, p. 50.

In psychology, the feeling is an emotional reaction to the thought of actions or behaviours in the past, which offers an unsatisfying outcome that we wish we could undo the action.[317] In this way, the feeling of guilt after the defeat is the consequence of remembering some bad behaviours of him to the Buddha in the past. Buddha's superiority was evident to him that he could not refuse and had to accept it. The utterance despite the sense of shame is rather favourable in psychology. It means the acceptance of the mistake in the past and the intention to refocus a corrective path in the future. The repentance will namely drive them into the direction that is opposite to the past, as it reveals in the speech.

> "For hitherto we, revered Sir, deemed wanderers belonging to other sects to be superior although they are inferior; although they are inferior we offered them food for superiors; although they are inferior we placed them in places for superiors. And we, revered sir, deemed monks to be inferior although they are superior; although they are superior we offered them food for inferiors; although they are superior we placed them in places for inferiors. But now we, revered sir, will know that wanderer belonging to other sects, being inferior, are inferior; because they are inferior we will offer them food for inferiors; because they are inferior, we will place them for inferiors. And we, revered sir, will know that monks, being superior, are superior; because they are superior we will offer them food for superiors; because they are superior we will place them for superiors. Indeed, revered sir, the Lord has inspired in me a recluse's regard for recluses, a recluse's satisfaction in recluses, a recluse's reverence for recluses..."[318] (MN54)

The expression of accepting mistake is found in this fashion. The hearer confessed that he had shown some bad attitudes and behaviours to the Buddha in the past that he felt now ashamed and apologetic about the benightedness. By now, he had known that the Buddha was more superior than other teachers were and thus deserved more superior treatment from him than the people deserved. This is the normal tendency of subject matter in the apology. However, there is also an apology that does not directly remark to the mistake, expressed instead by blaming stupidity of his own. Namely, it was his mistake that he should not have assailed the Buddha because he would never win him:

---

317 The Psychology of Regret http://www.psychologytoday.com/blog/the-mindful-self-express/201205/the-psychology-regret (last access 03.06.2013).

318 MN I 367, 30–36 – MN I 368, 1–9; The Collection of the Middle Length Sayings Vol. II, p. 32.

"Good Gotama, I was arrogant, I was presumptuous, in that I deemed I could assail the revered Gotama, speech by speech. Good Gotama, there might be safety for a man assailing a rutting elephant, but there could be no safety for a man assailing the revered Gotama. Good Gotama, there might be safety for a man assailing a blazing mass of fire, but there could be no safety for a man assailing the revered Gotama. Good Gotama, there might be safety for a man assailing a deadly poisonous snake, but there could be so safety for a man assailing the revered Gotama. Good Gotama, I was arrogant, I was presumptuous, in that I deemed I could assail the revered Gotama, speech by speech..."[319] (MN35)

Albeit indirectly expressed, the apology is considered more positive, as it shows that the people avoid the mistake and to pursue the corrective path.[320] It can be implied that the hearers would not be aggressive or challenging to the Buddha any longer, although he still remained in his religious community. The meaning of apology thus implies an acknowledgment of the Buddha's superiority.

Another form of apology, which is found in the discourses, is the confession of mistake in former time. This pertains to King Ajātasattu who confessed in front of the Buddha and his Sangha the guilt over killing his father that he suffered, after he vowed to take the Three Jewels for Refuges and asked the Buddha to be a lay follower.

"Sin has overcome me, Lord, weak and foolish and wrong that I am, in that, for the sake of sovranty [sic!], I put to death my father, that righteous man, that righteous king! May the Blessed One accept it of me, Lord, that do so acknowledge it as a sin, to the end that in future I may restrain myself."[321] (DN2)

In psychology, the confession is, according to Carl Jung, significant in two parts: the need to confess and the need to be forgiven and reconciled.[322] Human has naturally a religious instinct that makes a person feel guilty about what he has done in the past. The instinct powerfully drives him to a refuge to release the pressure. In the introductory story of DN2 King Ajātasattu is depicted to be obsessed on his own that he

319 MN I 236, 1–13; The Collection of the Middle Length Sayings Vol. I, pp. 289–290.

320 The Psychology of Regret http://www.psychologytoday.com/blog/the-mindful-selfexpress/201205/the-psychology-regret (last access 03.06.2013).

321 DN I 85, 15–19; Dialogues of the Buddha Part I, p. 94.

322 Todd, The Value of Confession and Forgiveness according to Jung, p. 41.

would like to meet a spiritual teacher for a talk. In this way, as Jung explained, he probably needed someone to hear his sin so that he felt forgiven and reconciled to the normal life. This leads to the crucial problem of who should have heard the sin and offered the forgiveness.[323] In the discourse, the king seemed to try to find the religious teacher, who could be the refuge for him and hear the sin. After having seen the Buddha and talked with him, the king was impressed with the Buddha's answer and sermon and finally converted to be a lay follower. He then made the confession at once, after he had become a follower. This implies *transference relationship*, the bond that he had to the Buddha whom he respected and trusted. Buddha's forgiveness was for him, as Jung said, "*not merely the intellectual recognition of the facts with the head, but their confirmation by the heart and the actual release of suppressed emotion.*"[324] The psychological explanation above indicates some *religious feelings* that the king had about the Buddha: the bonding between the Buddha as teacher and him as pupil, the trust in the Buddha as the enlightened that he had seen in the conversation and sermon, and the hope for the chance that he would receive from the Buddha after he had confessed the guilt. With the feelings, the king felt relieved to confess the sin in front of him.

3.2.3 Conclusion

The study above clearly reveals at least two points about the hearer's free expression about Buddha after hearing the sermon.

First, the statements were made to reveal the hearer's attitudes and feelings. The compliment contains an open admiration for Buddha's ability appreciated in his debate and explanation, his valuable teaching, and his community of Sangha; whereas, the apology implies, despite indirectly sometimes, the acceptance of their inferiority and mistake to the Buddha in the past. Existing in transition to the stock phrases, the free-style expression is supportive to the context, providing the continuity between

323 Ibid, p. 42.

324 Jung, Problems of Modern Psychotherapy, p. 59; referred in: Todd, The Value of Confession and Forgiveness according to Jung, p. 42.

the sermon and the meaning of stock phrase in the conclusion that the hearers admired to the Buddha and his sermon in some way before the declaration of belief.

Second, the compliment or the apology emphasizes the significance of stock phrase type II, which is the oral code denoting the development of belief and followership.[325] Some discourses, in which the hearers admired the Buddha and his sermon or apologized for the past, might not end with the stock phrase.[326] Therefore, it can be concluded that the stock phrase (3) which appeared every time in the declaration of followership is the true sign of followership that the tradition applied.

3.3 At the End: Levels of Belief in Buddhism in Reaction to Sermon

The study of expressions at the conclusion of discourse[327] has revealed that each stock phrase functions as a signifier of certain outcome in reaction to the Buddha's sermon. The stock phrases regularly appear together to convey a particular meaning. In this fashion, the combined stock phrases should be observed for a meaning communicated in the context. In the study of expressions above, the stock phrases (3)-(8) in the conclusion of discourse appear in two forms: the stock phrases (7) (8), (3) (4) (5) denoting the experience of *Dhammacakkhu* (type III) and declaration of belief (type II) and the stock phrases (3) (4) (5) denoting *only* the declaration of belief (type II). Apart from these, there are yet two groups representing that the hearer did not ask for the declaration of belief, i.e. no mention of (3) (4) (5). The two groups are necessarily divided from each other because they contain some features that signify a different degree of belief. In this way, the four groups denote *a different degree of the belief* expressed at the end of discourse. In the study, they are presented in order from the first level that represents a strong belief to the fourth level that represents no belief, in order to demonstrate from the meaning of stock phrase and the context that each group represents in the reaction.

325 See 2.3.2.
326 MN75, see 3.3.3.
327 See 2.3.

3.3.1 First Level: *Dhammacakkhu* Mentioned

The reaction in the first level is represented with the stock phrase type III, consisting of stock phrases (7) (8), and followed by the type II, consisting of stock phrases (3) (4) and (5)[328] respectively. This means, the hearer had heard a sermon, namely *Ānupubbikathā*, and attained the experience of *Dhammacakkhu* respectively before the hearer admired the teaching, took the Three Jewels for refuges and asked to become a follower. In some cases, the order may reverse.[329] The usage of stock phrases to represent the belief in this fashion does not often appear in the discourses. In Dīgha-nikāya and Majjhima-nikāya, there are only five people mentioned with the series of stock phrases: Pokkharasādi (DN3), Kūṭadanta (DN5), Upāli (MN56),[330] Dīgha-nakha (MN74) and Brahmāyu (MN95). The usage of stock phrase denoting the declaration of lay followership (5) indicates that the people despite the achievement of the unshakable belief in the Buddha remained in their householder life or in former religious life in case of Dīgha-nakha.[331] The question can be answered from perspective of the ascetic custom in the context. The men who lived the ascetic life

328 This means, the stock phrase (6) is not found together with (7) (8).

329 DN5, MN56.

330 Anālayo, A Comparative Study of Majjhima-nikāya Vol. 1, p. 326. The stock phrases are not applied in Chinese version.

331 Among the people mentioned with the experience of Dhammacakkhu, Dīgha-nakha seemed to be distinctive from other lay followers who passed on the development of belief, aroused by a strong motivation in their situation. In the discourse (MN74), he, like an ascetic, came to visit Buddha for a talk on a philosophical topic. The talk deals with Right View, a significant topic that inspires the understanding to the hearers. According to the text, Dīgha-nakha attained the Dhammacakkhu while Sāriputta who was beside the Buddha at the time attained Arahatship. It is questionable at this point: if Dīgha-nakha had really attained the Dammacakkhu and had a strong belief in the Buddha, he should have asked the Buddha to join his monastic order, not remained in his ascetic school. Moreover, the text does not appear the stock phrase (7), which is always followed by the stock phrase (8). Therefore, the author understands that tradition in doing this might intend to compare the attainment of the two persons: Dīgha-nakha as the representative of an ordinary man and Sāriputta as the person with great wisdom. On the other words, the discourse illustrates the great wisdom of Sāriputta by this comparative image.

were mostly still young, as they were able to develop spirituality better than the old one. The young men were thus more welcome while the old one was unwelcome and even denounced by the people in the monastic community.[332] In this connection, the people, particularly the Brahmins who were the teachers, should have been old and not appropriate to have the monastic life. This is also an implication that the lay followership is in some way not different from the monastic followership.

Between the two technical terms of the stock phrase type III: *Ānupubbikathā* and *Dhammacakkhu,* the latter receives more attention from scholars, as it can be understood in term of *religious experience* generally known in theistic religions. Peter Masefield considered it the subject to compare with experience of divine revelation in a theistic religion, which points to the role of some external components on *hearing* that effect to the arising of experience.[333] "*That is, the earliest practice was that of contacting the Dharma as inner, transcendental entity manifesting itself, through the medium of the Buddha, as sound.*"[334] Namely, it was a perception through eyes and ears of some elements in the Buddha while they were encountering him and hearing his sermonizing voice. Buddha's great characteristic voice, mentioned in Pāli and other traditions, played a particular role on the arising of explicit experience to the hearers in this case. The gained sensory perception was the 'holy experience,' that changed *puthujjana* the "normal person" into *ariyasāvaka* "noble disciple." The change was the hearer's attainment of *sotāpanna*, the primary stage of spiritual development in the Noble Path. In order to support his argument, Masefield cited to Andrew Rawlinson's study of the oldest layer of Lotus Sutta in that dhamma was originally conceived and experienced through words and sounds.[335] The outcome of this experience was the

332 Cf. Wijayaratna, Buddhist Monastic Life, pp. 3–4; Hinüber, Old Age and Old Monks in Pali Buddhism, pp. 65–78.

333 The seven people with the experience of Dhammacakkhu are mentioned in discourses in Dīgha-nikāya and Majjhima-nikāya. There are also other examples in Vinaya that Peter Masefield in his study of Divine Revelation of Pali Buddhism also observed.

334 Masefield, Devine Revelation in Pali Buddhism, p. 45.

335 Ibid.

acquisition of the right view,[336] which was accompanied by benefits for the spiritual development in Buddhism.[337] From the achievement of experience that related to some characteristic appearance and voice of the Buddha, Masefield concluded that Buddhist attainment was the religion of grace: namely, the spiritual attainment in Buddhism required the Buddha's grace in the process of spiritual development. This means that the experience was particularly achieved from Buddha's sermon. The finding in the study of concluding part also conforms with his conclusion: all of the five people in Dīgha-nikāya and Majjhima-nikāya are mentioned with the experience heard the sermon from the Buddha.[338]

However, the thesis on the experience as pointed out by Masefield is criticized. The main point is that the interpretation does not relate to the Buddha's teaching in general.[339] The fact about the experience is short and insignificant, while almost the whole canon focuses on wisdom and individual effort in the spiritual development, which has nothing to do with the experience. Masefield's interpretation thus reduced the religion of knowledge and practice into the graceful experience without considering other parts of the canon. The description points to the problem of language game in religious scriptures, as Harrison criticized Masefield's work, that the thesis may "*raise the question whether all religious traditions do indeed construct ontologies out of metaphor.*"[340] Moreover, there were some misunderstandings about the doctrines which Masefield link to the

---

336 Ibid, p. 54.

337 Ibid, p. 71. According to Masefield, the benefits are (1) acquaintance worth the path to be followed; (2) a desire for renunciation; (3) possession of faith; (4) possession of morality; (5) the guarantee of the generation of no fresh kamma; and (6) the annihilation of the majority of kamma hitherto generated.

338 Masefield focused only on the stock phrase (8), in which the hearer had the experience of Dhammacakkhu. He did not notice that the stock phrase (8) always follows the stock phrase (7), as the author interpreted that the experience of Dhammacakkhu (8) was the outcome of hearing the Buddha's sermon Anupubbīkathā (7).

339 Hallisay, Review on Divine Revelation in Pali Buddhism by Peter Masefield, p. 173.

340 Harrison, Buddhism: a Religion of Revelation after all, p. 259.

phenomenon to support his thesis.[341] The thesis was therefore implausible and disputed particularly among Buddhist and learners, who believe in the rationalism of the doctrine and spirituality.[342]

In spite of the critics, Masefield's study deserves a mention of pioneer work about the stock phrases. Besides, Masefield pointed to the role of hearing in the spiritual attainment or Sotāpanna, which is the primary stage of spiritual path in Buddhism.[343] He supported the idea that *hearing* the sermon in the discourses was the crucial path, along which householders reached a *complete understanding* in the religion, which was neglected by other scholars.[344] From the order of the stock phrases, it is irrefutable that the experience of *Dhammacakkhu* was the outcome of the *hearing*. The problem lies in what the *hearing* in the context meant and how the *hearing* operated in the spiritual attainment. Masefield interpreted the *hearing* in terms of perceiving an intrinsic power from the sermon. As a result, his interpretation was considered similar to the divine experience in theistic religions. The interpretation as such was too strict to the stock phrase (8) without considering other parts of the canon as well as the tradition. In this connection, he concluded his study that the Buddhist with this experience was not distinctive from the Brahmins in Vedic tradition.[345]

---

341 Main points as argued by Harrison are: 1) Masefield's misunderstanding about the role of right view in Buddhism; 2) Sotāpanna is originally translated as "one who has come into contact with the hearing," not "stream-enterer;" 3) referring to some terms like puthujjana "normal people" ariyasāvaka "noble disciple" which are problematic about its origin and relation to monk and nun.

342 See comments from the readers http://www.amazon.com/Divine-Revelation-Buddhism-Peter-Masefield/productreviews/9559028022/ref=dp_top_cm_cr_acr_txt? ie=UTF8&showViewpoints=1 (last access 02.06.2013).

343 Harrison, Buddhism: a Religion of Revelation after all, p. 262. Here, the interpretation lay on the word *sota*, which may mean "stream" or "hearing." Harrison proposed, the term originally means "One who has come into contact with (or undergone) hearing," while he found the meaning "stream-enterer" proposed by Masefield as incorrect. However, considering the meaning of the term based on the context of stock phrase (7), which obviously referred to the experience, Masefield's translation should be more sensible.

344 Harrison, Buddhism: a Religion of Revelation after all, p. 257. Harrison rather considered 'hearing' in Buddhism in light of hearing some sacred text like Paritta.

345 Masefield, Divine Revelation in Pali Buddhism, p. 146 ff.

The result of the analysis was far from the core of Buddhism, which is against ritualism and theism.

The author considers the *hearing* different from Masefield in that it merely means *a way of learning and understanding a teaching*. The experience did not simply occur because of hearing a sermon of Buddha, but always his sermon *Ānupubbikathā*, the symbol of all basic knowledge to learn in the spiritual path.[346] Therefore, the experience was not the direct gaining from hearing the voice of the Buddha, but it was the symbol of the complete understanding by having learned the basic knowledge in *Ānupubbikathā*. It seems that Masefield did not pay attention on the declaration of belief without the experience of *Dhammacakkhu*, from which he would have seen the difference between the two stock phrases (7), (8) and (3), (4), (5) and only (3), (4), (5).

In this way, we have to distinguish the declaration of belief with the experience of *Dhammacakkhu*, which represents the followership with the trust in the Buddha and his doctrine as a result of hearing the sermon *Ānupubbikathā*.

3.3.2 Second Level: Understanding Described and Belief Declared

The reaction at the second level is described with the stock phases in (3) (4) (5) respectively, representing the process of asking to become a Buddha's follower. The appearance of stock phrases is common, viz. to 40 people in the discourses. As tradition has it, the stock phrase signifies that the hearer has understood the Buddha's doctrine thoroughly and attained Sotāpanna, as in 3.3.1. However, having the text (3) considered, the people merely admired the doctrine superfluously with metaphors. The clear understanding of the doctrine leads to the hearer's compliment on how the sermon is brilliant, thrilled, and exalting.

> Most excellent, Lord, most excellent! **(1) Just as if a man were to set up that which has been thrown down, (2) or were to reveal that which is hidden away, (3) or were to point out the right road to him who has gone astray, (4) or were to bring a lamp into the darkness so that those who have eyes could see external forms** – just even so, Lord, <u>has the truth been made known to me, in many figures, by the Exalted One</u>.

346 See the argument in 2.3.3.

The main idea of the quoted passage is the last sentence that shows how the Buddha had clearly explained and analysed the teaching to the hearer. The answer removed their doubt and offered a sensible answer. The understanding led to hearer's agreement with the Buddha and finally to the admiration of what he had said. In this way, the stock phrase is the marker of the hearer's acknowledgment which also 'symbolizes' the hearer's impression on the Buddha's sermon in a short form, which is essential to the declaration of belief in Buddhism.[347]

However, commentary explained this stage of reaction similarly to the 3.3.1 that the people mentioned with the stock phrases achieved the stage of Sotāpanna.[348] Jīvaka Komārabhacca in MN55, who is mentioned with the stock phrases (3) (4) (5) illustrates this point. In the commentary, it is explained that Jīvaka had achieved Sotāpanna, like followers in 3.3.1. because he had understood the dhamma thoroughly (3) and taken the Three Jewels for refuges (4) and thus became *ariyasāvaka* 'noble disciple.' This means, the commentary ascribed the passage (3) to the explicit experience of *Dhammacakkhu*. From the explanation, commentary considers every people mentioned with the stock phrases (3) (4) (5), have achieved *sotāpanna* and become *ariyasāvaka*. In this way, there is no distinction between the people in 3.3.1 and 3.3.2. Both are the pious followers in Buddhism.

There are some points to argue that the interpretation of the commentary is false, as the author relies on the principle of the formulaic language. Having considered components of the stock phrases (7) (8), (3) (4) (5), it is implausible that the stock phrase (3) (4) (5) or (6) would convey the identical meaning. The stock phrase (3) (4) (5) or (6) lacks of the stock phrase (7) (8) that denotes to the hearing of the so-called *Ānupubbikathā* and the experience of *Dhammacakkhu*. These two components are not found in the stock phrase (3); whereas the stock phrase (3) points only to the

347 The author is of the opinion that the stock phrase (3), which is the admiration of sermon, is not only based on rationality of the sermon, but also an irrational impression on some aspects about the Buddha and his teaching. This implies that the fundamental belief in Buddhism is often involved with the subjectivity.

348 Papañcasūdanī Part III, p. 51.

personal impression to the teaching. Besides, the stock phrases could not be interpreted into the *Dhammacakkhu* from the context in the conclusion of Sāmaññaphalasutta (DN2), which mentions King Ajātasattu with stock phrase type II. Buddha later said to his pupils that the king did not attain the experience of *dhammacakkhu* because he had put his father to death.[349] In this way, it is reasonable to interpret that the stock phrase simply represents the declaration of the belief and followership.

3.3.3 Third Level: Belief in the Buddha Undeclared

The belief at this level is very strange and can be grouped: neither in 3.3.2 nor in 3.3.4. That means it denotes neither declaration of followership nor absolute reject of the belief. The third level represents some belief in the Buddha that was perhaps not strong enough to motivate the declaration to be a Buddhist follower, but the hearer promised they would keep the belief in the Buddha with themselves. This reaction is found only in Pāṭikasutta (DN24), in which Buddha went to visit Bhaggava at his place. There, Buddha talked with the mendicant about his encounters with challenges of adversary, while the mendicant heard and intermittently expressed his approval to what the Buddha had uttered. However, Buddha seemed to notice that the mendicant might not ask him to become a follower because he had his own view and interest on doctrine and practice in a different way from what the Buddha had. He then suggests the mendicant to keep the belief in him instead of persuading him to be his pupil at the end of the discourse.

(Buddha said)

> "Hard is it, Bhaggava, for you, holding as you do different views, other things approving themselves to you, you setting different aims before yourself, striving after a different aim, trained in a different system, to attain to and abide in the deliverance that is beautiful. Look therefore to it, Bhaggava, that you foster well this faith of yours in me."[350]

(Bhaggava said)

> "If, Sir, it be hard for me, holding different views, other things approving themselves to me, I setting different aims before myself, striving after a different aim,

349 Dialogues of the Buddha Part I, p. 95.
350 DN III 35, 3–7; Dialogues of the Buddha Part III, p. 32.

trained in a different system, to attain to and abide in the deliverance that is beautiful, then will I, at least, foster well my faith in the Exalted One."[351]

After this answer, the mendicant was satisfied with the conversation, as indicated by stocks phrase (1)

Idam avoca Bhagavā. Attamano Bhaggava-gotto paribbājako Bhagavato bhāsitaṃ abhinandîti.[352]
These things spake the Exalted One. And Bhaggavagotta, the Wanderer, pleased in heart, took delight in his words.

Commentary explains the conclusion of the discourse in a negative way, i.e. the mendicant did not believe in the Buddha but pretended to behave well with the Buddha. As elaborated in the commentary, Buddha knew this fact well and did not wish the mendicant to be his follower, so he let the mendicant go by. [353]

The author surmises that this explanation should be false because the interpretation of Buddhist followership in commentary is based on the stock phrases (3) (4) (5), raised in 2.3.1, as the marker of the pious follower. In this way, as commentary concluded, the hearer who did not declare the belief and become a Buddhist did not sincerely believe in the Buddha. However, for the Buddha, the declaration of followership was rather flexible and voluntary than decisive and strictly, especially when the hearer was not ready. From the quotation above, it is clearly seen that the Buddha did not show any negative reaction to the hearer, which will be seen next in 3.3.4. Rather, the mendicant understood the teaching and accepted to follow the Buddha's suggestion to such an extent. He did not argue against or challenge the comments that the Buddha had made. In spite of *unofficial* follower, he promised to keep the belief in the Buddha with himself. Furthermore, the discourse ends with stock phrases type I that denote the hearer's satisfaction. This means, the mendicant understood the Buddha's doctrine partly, but he still remained in his old doctrine.

Here, the Buddha's *consent* to the mendicant's attitude in the discourse needs a little attention. In somewhere else,[354] a belief in the Buddha is

351 DN III 35, 8–12; ibid.
352 DN III 35, 13–14; ibid.
353 Sumaṅgalavilāsinī Part III, pp. 830–831.
354 The Collection of the Middle Length Sayings Vol. I, p. 182.

always positive, although it is not strong to utter and just kept in mind. Other discourses, in which Buddha gave a sermon to ascetics outside the community of Sangha, show a similar tendency.[355] The discourse in its conclusion mentions that the ascetics were satisfied with the answer but remained living in their community. The condition of the belief is acceptable in Buddhism because it means a possibility in the future that the people may announce the followership. The belief can be gradually developed after hearing more sermons and talking with Buddha and might motivate the ascetic to declare the belief officially.

3.3.4 Fourth Level: No Expression of Belief

In this category, the hearer did not utter any expression of his own belief or respecting the Buddha or a senior monk. Their non-verbal expression described in the discourses signifies that they knew and accepted in their mind that the Buddha was right and more superior than they were. But for some reason, they did not acknowledge it and did not ask for discipleship, denoted with stock phrases (3) (4) (5). They did not mention a belief in the Buddha, as in 3.3.3. To this reaction, the Buddha clearly expressed his disappointment that his teaching had nothing to do with the people. In Udumbarika-Sīhanādasutta (DN25), Nigrodha, after the debate with the Buddha, was in stunned silence and apologized for the Buddha for his benightedness. The Buddha then tried to persuade the mendicant to ask him for declaration of followership under him, but the mendicant was still silent in response. The reaction had upset the Buddha that he, as described in the discourse, instantly left the place and went away.

> Then the Exalted One thought: 'Every one of these foolish men is pervaded by the Evil One, so that to not even one of them will the thought occur: Come let us now live the holy life taught by the Samaṇa Gotama, that we may learn to know it. What does an interval of seven days matter?'[356] (DN25)

Likewise, the demon Māra (MN50) seems to resist Moggallāna's instruction. Although the monk had warned him not to harm a noble monk, the demon did not apologize for his guilt or acknowledge the monk's

355 DN7, MN36.
356 DN III 57, 15–18; Dialogues of the Buddha Part III, p. 52.

instruction. He disappeared from the place at once. In Sandakasutta (MN76), Sandaka talked with Ānanda about monastic life. The mendicant seemed to understand the principle of Buddha's order well that he admired some attitudes taken in the community, but he himself did not ask to be a follower. Instead, he allowed some pupils of him to join the community.

> "Wonderful, good Ānanda, marvelous, good Ānanda; there can be no extolling of their own *dhamma* nor disparaging of the dhamma of others; but both the teaching of *dhamma* in its (whole) extent and so many great leaders can be seen. On the other hand, these Naked Ascetics are children of a childless mother, they both extol themselves and disparage others, and they show only three great leaders, namely Nanda Vaccha, Kisa Saṅkicca and Makkhali Gosāla."

Then the wanderer Sandaka addressed his own company, saying:

> "Let the good sirs fare forth; the living of the Brahma-faring is under the recluse Gotama, although it is not easy for us now to give up gains, honours, fame."[357] *(MN76)*

From the quotation, Sandaka complimented the Sangha and he seemed to know that the life under Sangha is advantageous. He thus persuaded his pupils to join the Sangha, but he himself remained the teacher of his community. This means that he understood the advantage of Sangha well, but for some reason he decided not to leave his community for the Buddha's community.

In the discourses, the three persons clearly expressed no interest to learn the doctrine. The reaction as such should explain the significance of the presence of stock phrase that indicates the hearer's satisfaction, raised in 2.3.1. The absence of the stock phrase has an implication that the sermon or the debate was not successful because they did not motivate the hearer's belief or feeling. It is obvious from the reaction that they did not take the Buddha's doctrine, not fulfill an idea, or make a change, which could imply satisfaction. In this way, the stock phrases denoting satisfaction after a debate or an answer in a discourse, is meaningful because it yet represents the hearer's understanding and acknowledgment of the debate or the answer.

---

357 MN I 524, 6–7; The Collection of the Middle Length Sayings Vol. II, pp. 202–203.

3.3.5 Case Studies of the Four Levels of Belief in Comparison

In this part, the development of belief in Buddhism in each level will be presented in charts to compare the development of belief and motivation from the first hearing of the Buddha's reputation until the hearing of his sermon that the author categorized in levels according to the usage of stock phrases.

3.3.5.1 First Level

Kūṭadanta (DN5) vs. Brahmāyu (MN91)

In this level, the belief in the Buddha was developed at the highest degree: they both achieved the experience of Dhammacakkhu and asked to become a lay follower. But the course of the development is different in that Brahmāyu had his belief completely developed at seeing the Buddha's signs of Great Man, while Kūṭadanta had his belief gradually developed by debating with him. As tradition has it, Buddha delivered the sermon Ānupubbikathā when the Brahmins, having seeing the Buddha's great qualities, yielded to him and wholeheartedly received any teaching from him. In sum, the belief in the Buddha was finally developed on an intense belief based on the former belief that Buddha was the great spiritual teacher.

Figure 9: Belief in the First Level: Kūṭadanta - Brahmāyu

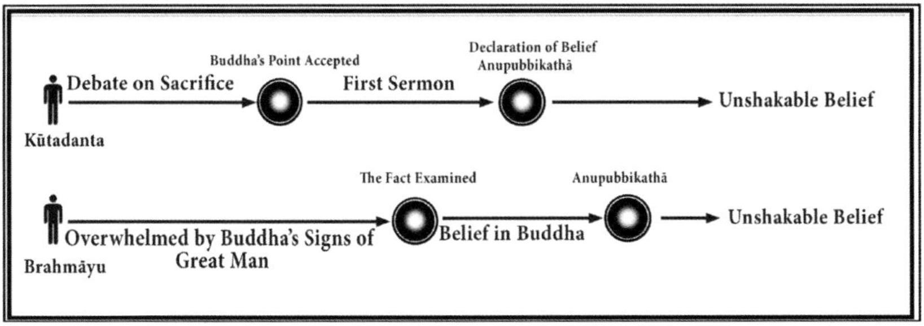

From the figure, the belief in the Buddha might be greatly and quickly developed with the trust in the physiognomic knowledge affirming that the person with the 32 signs of Great man was the Buddha, the great teacher. The consideration overwhelmed him that he went to visit the Buddha after he had received the report from his pupil. Seeing the Buddha in person, the Brahmin strengthened the belief in the Buddha and thus achieved the unshakable belief after hearing the sermon Ānupubbikathā that Buddha particularly gave him. At the end, the Brahmin declared the belief and asked to become a follower. In comparison to the case of Kūṭadanta, Kūṭadanta's belief grew slower because it started from the encounter between them and the debate on sacrifice. After the debate, the Brahmin acknowledged the Buddha and asked to become a follower. However, the Brahmin should have expressed his profound belief in the Buddha, so he heard another sermon Ānupubbikathā from the Buddha and thus had the unshakable belief.

3.3.5.2 Second Level

Soṇadaṇḍa (DN4) vs. Jīvaka Kōmārabhacca (MN55)

In this level, the belief in Buddha was developed from a conversation or a debate on a topic with the Buddha. It is noticeable that the hearer had realised some qualities of him such as his personality, his mentality, his ability to answer a question, etc. He thus came to visit the Buddha for a talk to experience his spiritual qualities closely. With an impression, the hearer had the belief in the Buddha developed that he accepted the Buddha as the spiritual teacher. The belief developed in the situation might have a limitation because the sermon that the hearer had heard was only about a topic which fulfilled his curiosity. He did not hear the sermon Ānupubbikathā and so did not have the experience of Dhammacakkhu. In this way, the feeling of worship for the Buddha can be limited in some degree.

Figure 10: Belief in the Second Level: Soṇadaṇḍa - Jīvaka Kōmārabhacca

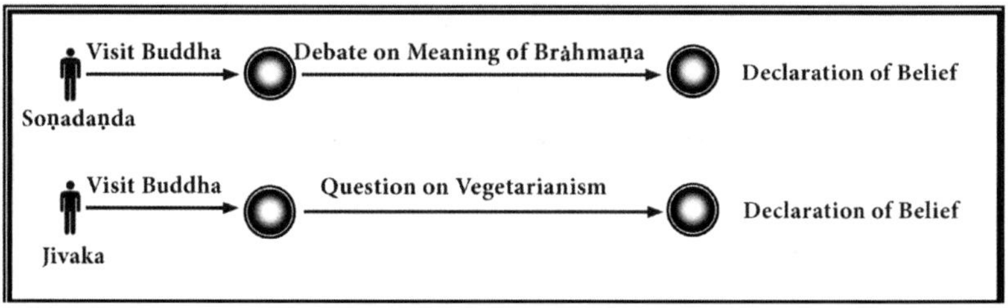

From the figure above, both Soṇadaṇḍa and Jīvaka conversed with the Buddha on a topic, in which they were interested. Soṇadaṇḍa chose the topic on the definition of Brāhmaṇa that he knew at best; whereas, Jīvaka chose the topic on vegetarianism which he found practiced in other religious communities, but not in Buddha's order. With satisfaction in the answer and perhaps other impressions, they declared the followership under the Buddha. However, the belief declared from the impression might be not so great that the hearer raised Buddha over himself. Soṇadaṇḍa in this way had an anxiety for a gesture of respect to the Buddha in public that might destroy his dignity in the society. Therefore, he requested the Buddha for the special gestures of respect representing his reverence in the Buddha, which the Buddha also accepted. In view of Taves's theory, the Brahmin considered the Buddha special, but not more special than his status of great teacher in the Brahmin community, and with the maintained dignity, he would not express the normal reverence for the Buddha as spiritual teacher in public. The behaviour is considered blameworthy in the tradition, as there is a critic about this request in the commentary.[358]

3.3.5.3 Third Level

Bhagavagotta (DN 24) vs. Jāliya and Maṇḍiya (DN7)

In this level, the belief in Buddha was developed after a conversation, but not much enough to become a follower. Hence, the hearer did not declare the belief in the formal fashion. It is noticeable that the hearer was an ascetic and acquainted with Buddha and his order to some extent that the Buddha went to them for a conversation. In so doing, Buddha seemed to expect that they might declare the followership. When it was not successful, Buddha did not react in a negative way. Instead, he supported the ascetic to keep the belief in him. The ascetics seemed to be satisfied with the conversation and have uttered a little impression.

Figure 11: Belief in the Third Level: Bhagavagotta, Jāliya- Maṇḍiya

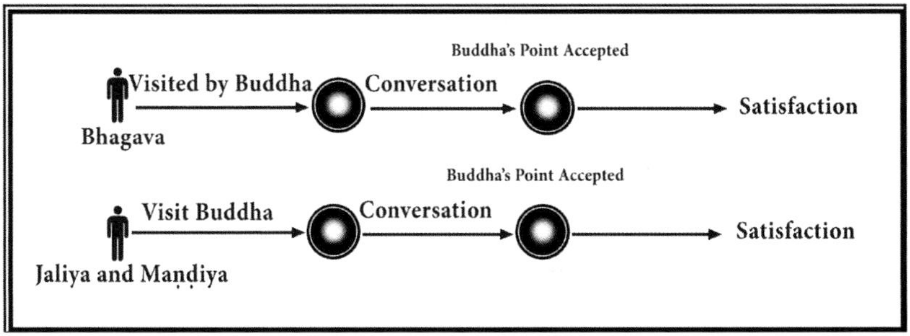

358 Cf. Malalasekera, Dictionary of Pāli Proper Name Vol. II, pp. 1297; see p. 81.

The belief in the third level is found merely in Bhaggava Paribbājaka, but the author shows in the diagram in comparison the conversation in DN7, in which the two ascetics, Jāliya and Maṇḍiya, went to the Buddha for a talk. The result is similar in that the ascetics were satisfied with the answer; they did not declare any belief. This implies that the ascetics were satisfied with the exchange of the religious idea and accepted Buddha's doctrine in some degree.

3.3.5.4 Fourth Level

Sandaka (MN76) vs. Nigrodha (DN25)

In this level, the hearer neither uttered a belief in the Buddha nor showed a sign signifying that he had the belief at the end of the conversation or the sermon. He debated the Buddha and realised the superiority shining from the answers or from the appearance during the conversation. He might pay the Buddha a compliment on the superiority, but he did not declare the followership. In the discourse, there is no use of any stock phrases revealing his personal belief in the Buddha or satisfaction in the sermon. Despite the fact that the hearers were familiar with the Buddha and his disciple to some extent, their reaction to the conversation and the sermon does not reveal a belief, trust, or satisfaction.

Figure 12: Belief in the Fourth Level: Sandaka - Nigrodha

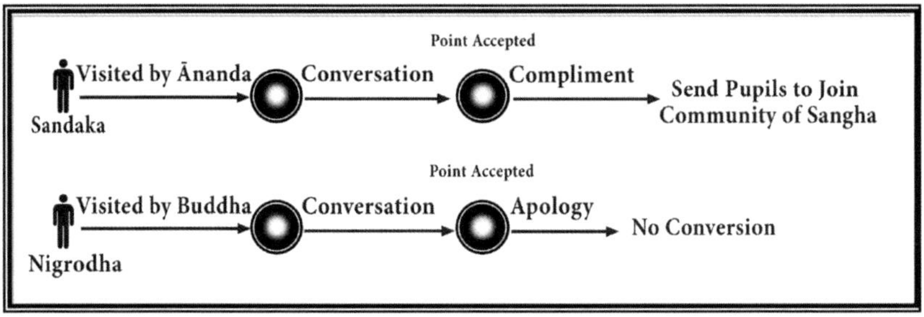

Figures 11 and 12, representing the third and fourth level of belief, clearly show that the use of the ending stock phrases is not common in the conclusion of every discourse. As concluded previously, not every hearer accepted the Buddha's teaching and showed his satisfaction with the exchange of the idea. Not every hearer acknowledged the sermon, gave him the compliment, and asked for the followership, which is the pattern generally seen in Nikāyas. In short, a mission is not always successful. However, the reactions of the hearer to the Buddha, which can be categorized in levels reflects the system of the oral text in the communication of some meaning to the audience, as one may observe from the appearance of stock phrases, that the belief is individual and dependent to the hearer's understanding, impression, interest on the Buddha, his order, sermon, etc. These factors result in the different degrees of the belief and the expression given to the Buddha.

3.3.6 Conclusion

As Lord found in his research, the complex is the core message of the tradition communicated in the oral text.

> These complex are held together internally both by the logic of the narrative and by the consequent force of habitual association. Logic are strong forces, particularly fortified by a balancing of elements in recognizable patterns such as those which we have just outlined. Habitual association of theme, however, need not merely linear, that is to say, theme a always follows theme b; theme b follows theme c. Sometimes, the presence of theme a in a song calls forth the presence of theme b somewhere in the song, but not necessarily in an a-b relationship, not necessarily following one another immediately. Where the association is linear, it is close to the logic of narrative, and the themes are generally of a kind that are included in a larger complex.[359]

Analysed in this principle, Nikāya discourse presents a complex concerning the development of belief in the Buddha until the declaration of the followership. In this complex, the declaration of lay followership can be seen from the logic regularly applied in the discourses with the usage of three groups of stock phrases: *Satisfaction, Declaration of Belief in Buddhism,* and *Attainment of Dhammacakkhu.*[360] The combination of the stock phrases in the conclusion of discourse can be categorized into four levels:

1. Stock phrases (7) (8) plus (3) (4) (5) represent experience of *Dhammacakkhu* and declaration of belief to become a lay follower. The request to

359 Lord, The Singer of Tales, pp. 96–97.
360 See 2.3.3.

become a monastic follower is not found at this level. The stock phrases (7) (8) signify to another kind of sermon and spiritual experience that the hearer received from the Buddha.
2. Stock phrases (3) (4) (5) or (6) represent declaration of belief to become a lay follower (5) or monastic follower (6)
3. Promise to keep the belief in the Buddha with himself and stock phrase (1) denoting satisfaction from a conversation with the Buddha
4. No stock phrase used in the conclusion of discourse. No effect of the sermon to the hearer

The outcome of hearing the sermon, as identified with certain stock phrases, significantly relates to the quantity and quality of dhamma. The hearer in the first level heard a particular sermon *Ānupubbikathā* from the Buddha, which symbolized the learning of every basic teaching. As a result, they had a complete understanding about the basic doctrines and thus had a stable belief in the Buddha and trust in what he teaches. In the second level, the hearer, having simply understood a teaching and been satisfied with the teaching, under the impression declared the followership. In the third group, the hearer, having carried out a conversation with Buddha, accepted the Buddha's answer but did not declare the belief, as in the first or the second level. In the last level, in which the hearer did not utter a word concerning the belief, the hearer had no belief in the Buddha and so remained passive to the Buddha's sermon.

At this point, it can be concluded, as the tradition tells with the usage of stock phrases, that belief in Buddhism is dependent on the amount of the teaching that one has learned on one hand and the personal impression on the other. Both relate to each other. From the meaning of the stock phrase (7) (8), it is irrefutable that the basic teachings are fundamental to the understanding of the doctrine and the unshakable belief in the Buddha, but the understanding also depends on a great trust in the teacher, which might be developed before hearing the sermon. With a great impression, the hearer may have the belief and the trust in the Buddha developed better while hearing the sermon.

The relation of the understanding during the sermon and declaration of belief at the end is the major point for next discussion. It is problematic as to how the logical and rational understanding in the hearing leads to the acceptance of the Buddha as the religious teacher, to a great respect and worship to him, and to the decision for the change of his life. Namely, it is improbable that the rationality at the understanding of debate and sermon would play the great role on the following religious behaviours as such. The thought lies in the view that Buddhism is the religion of pure rationality on which the intellectuality only influences a motivation on the belief and practice. Furthermore, the meaning of the stock phrases is downplayed in the reading. The discussion focuses on the relation between the rationality in the understanding of teaching and the feelings of admiration, adoration and worship for the Buddha as the religious teacher and the refuge, in order to clarify that the words in the stock phrases are meaningful in the context. This means, Buddhism as described in the Nikāya discourses, despite the claim of rational doctrine, has a sense of 'religiousness,' something concerning belief and feeling, which is not always reasonable or explainable.

3.4 First discussion

Religious Experience as Simple Ascription to Dhamma

This section discusses on *simple ascription* the individual's development of belief in Buddhism in response to Buddha's sermon, as stereotypically presented in the discourses of Dīgha- and Majjhima-nikāya. Religious experience in this context refers to a process of getting knowledge from an encounter with some *thing deemed special*, which gradually inspires feeling of motivation to approach more and closer the religious.[361] The purpose of the discussion aims at pointing to the connection between the *perception* (seeing and hearing the religious things: especially sermon) and *reaction* (religious expressions: emotion, words, and formal declaration of belief). The theory helps to understand the mechanism of the inner process in relation to the input and output expressed in the narrative. The problem to be seen at this point is that it cannot be imagined how the intellectual activity in the understanding of sermon is connected with the religious belief, expressed in the conclusion of discourse. The discussion then must demonstrate the relation between the two dichotomies: the understanding of the Buddha's teaching, which

361 See 1.3.3.

is logical and rational, and the arising belief in the teacher, which is generally sentimental.

The data required for the discussion has two parts: first, the texts describing the hearer's thought, behaviour, action, and speech, which exist in the introductory story and message of the discourse,[362] and second, the stock phrases denoting to different intentions in reaction to the Buddha's sermon, which exist in the conclusion of the discourse.[363] Formed in oral tradition, the texts are succinct for the oral transmission that the conveyed message is not descriptive and even stereotypical. In this way, some may consider the usage of this data unempirical, unnatural, and thus inappropriate for the discussion on religious experience. At this point, the author views that the succinct and stereotypical data suggest *pattern* of the development of belief and religious experience, established from the motives and stories in the discourse. On the other words, this is not an account of particularly religious experience, but rather the "doctrine of belief in Buddhism." The pattern of the development of the belief is never questioned in relation to the declaration of belief.[364] Instead, scholars often focused the topic in relation to the concept *saddhā* "belief," a doctrine of Buddhism, as a part of basic condition in the beginning and development of the spiritual path followed by the monastic followers.[365] In this way, the declaration of belief or the beginning of Buddhist path is rather conceived in term of *practice* than *starting motivator* into the practice, while the starting motivator into Buddhism is understood in terms of charisma of the leadership with which Buddha attracted people to join his community.

---

362 The data is surveyed and systematically presented in 3.1 and 3.2.

363 The data is systematically presented and discussed on the meaning in 2.3.

364 DN2, DN3, DN4, DN5, DN7, DN8, DN9, DN10, DN11, DN12, DN13, MN38, MN51, MN60, MN76, MN79, MN94, Jayatileke, Early Buddhist Theory of Knowledge, p. 398, in which he mentioned "story of faith of the monk having faith," which illustrates how fundamentally the faith or belief is grounded in the spiritual development of Buddhism, from renunciation of householder life until attainment of the liberation. In addition the study, the author proposes that the path in Buddhism is also suggested by the structure of the discourse in Nikāyas, which begins with seeing the Buddha and hearing the sermon.

365 Jayatileke, Early Buddhist Theory of Knowledge, p. 24.

The word *religious experience* can be applied to trace the process of the perception. As Taves pointed, religious experience should be discussed in terms of the perception of *a thing deemed (religiously) special* that results in an extraordinary 'experience,' which she called *experience deemed religious*. The word points to the subjectivity and individuality, which is the quality of perception and feeling. Indeed, religious experience is a private subject, which others cannot assess or judge whether it is correctly religious or merely hallucinatory, but it can be observed from the phenomenological aspect. "*...(E)xperience is better understood as embodied behaviour, where embodiment is understood at multiple levels from the neutral to the phenomenological and behaviour is broadly construed to include linguistic and mental events as well as overt actions. (...) Experience so conceived is typically expressed in a range of behaviours, some of which are public and provide data that can be queried and compared.*"[366] In other words, every physical and verbal expression is the proof that the claim of religious experience is real to the person.

Along these lines, religious experience in the discourse can be defined in term of *extraordinary* experience that somewhat influences a decision to do something involving the Buddha. To understand this phenomenon, first, it is to find how the extraordinary feelings mentioned at the end of discourse is related to the seeing and then hearing of the Buddha; second, to investigate the mental process how the understanding of the sermon inspires the belief in Buddhism.

Furthermore, the word *extraordinary* needs a new interpretation, which is more appropriate and guiding to the *patterned* development of belief and motivation behind religiosity. *Religious experience*, as the text implies, should indicate some behaviours, words, action, etc., which the text remarks unordinary or strange from their ordinary life and suggests the inclination to a special thing or person, as a result of perceiving a religious thing or person deemed special. As raised previously,[367] the development of the belief in the Buddha has two stages: first at hearing hearsay about Buddha's qualities and seeing him in person and second

366 Taves, Religious Experience Reconsidered, p. 64.
367 See 3.1 and 3.2.

at hearing the sermon delivered by him. As a result of the two incidents, attitude and words about the Buddha indicate a tendency to change. In the other words, the two incidents effect to a reaction which is unordinary to their everyday life. In the first stage, the hearer is motivated to approach and talk the Buddha closely, while in the second stage the hearer is claimed to declare a reverence for the Buddha and acknowledge him as the teacher.

3.4.1 At First Hearing Reputation and Seeing in Person

In 3.1 the author has presented the data on the image of the Buddha perceived in the hearsay, from which the hearer, who had never met the Buddha before, heard the description about him for the first time. Special qualities of the Buddha are divided into two categories: ideal qualities of spiritual teacher and 32 signs of Great Man. At first hearing the qualities, the hearer is depicted in the discourse to be silent and think through the superior characteristics, which he had to see with his eyes. The hearer was hence attracted to pay attention to the Buddha who was arriving at their community and had curiosity on seeing him in person. The question to deal with the discussion is the *mechanism that attracts the people*: what is behind the movement from this attraction.

Figure 13: Buddha Deemed Special in Hearsay

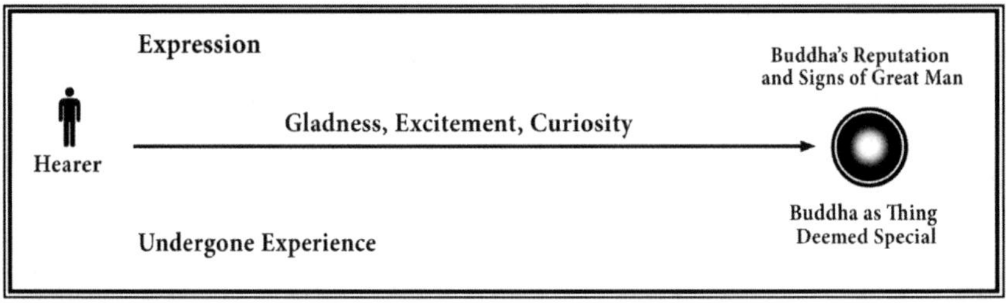

Despite no detail given about how the hearer and people in the background felt about the Buddha, their behaviours in reaction to the hearsay imply a message about the development of belief. The ideal qualities attracted the mass of people in the town or the village to visit the Buddha. Like other people, the hearer, who was the main character of discourse, was filled with wonder about the Buddha and felt 'moved' to go to the Buddha as well. Whereas, the special signs of the Great Man challenged the hearer who were well-learned in the treatise of Great Man to investigate the signs on the Buddha. To satisfy the curiosity, some of them sent their pupils to observe the Buddha closely for the signs, while some went to see the Buddha to observe the signs by themselves. Some of them recognized the Buddha as spiritual teacher, although they had not known anything about him. Clearly seen, the beliefs that the people had learned in their culture influenced on the imagination about the specialness of the Buddha and the evaluation that the Buddha should be the worthy spiritual teacher.

It is to notice that both ideal qualities of spiritual teacher and 32 signs of Great Man shared some characteristics about the 'specialness.' First, both qualities in the context are the social consensus on spiritual teacher. Both the Arahat and *mahāpurisa* the Great Man were the designation of "special" person, to whom the community particularly paid respect with the holiness in some way. People had learned in their traditions about the importance of the designation. The word *arahat*, as known in the householder's communities, was a significant term generally referring to the mendicant who reached the spiritual goal, while the *mahāpurisa* "the Great Man" was claimed to appertain to the Brahmin tradition.[368] Second, both Arahat and the Great Man were reckoned the religious person who could bring more happiness, merit, and other positive outcomes than other ordinary teachers could. In relation to the first point, Arahat was often attributed to be special, often without a clear conception.[369] The Great Man in the Brahmin's treatise was clearly defined in characteristics and prediction about the specialness, particularly, the Buddhahood

---

368 As *mahāpurisa* 'the great man' is not found in the Vedic tradition, the word might be invented to refer Buddha in Buddhist tradition particularly on the purpose of praising him. The belief about Arahat, Mahāpurisa, Buddha, etc. is rather the religious designation or concept made acquainted to the audience of the oral text. The focus here is the mechanism as to how the beliefs are developed to play a role regularly in the development of belief, which effects to the belief of the audience in the tradition.

369 See more detail in 3.1.1.1.

as a destiny of the Great Man. As the result, the Brahmins adhering to the treatise more quickly trusted in the spirituality of the Buddha and laid the belief in his doctrine than others who did not mention it. Third, both *arahat* and *mahāpurisa* were rarely found. The news of their coming in the community was very exciting for the villagers, householders, who had heard their reputation for a long time. In this perspective, description of people in both cases is attributed to the 'specialness'of the Buddha from the outset.

The belief about the Great Man clearly had a striking influence on the Brahmins. It can be seen from the background of the treatise as told in the introductory of discourses that the treatise was regarded as the elite science of Brahmins, which was restrictively known. The treatise had a long tradition and contained ideological beliefs which the Brahmin strongly adhered. The Great Man in this way was the perfect man in the legend, whose future was exactly predicted. Several Brahmins at hearing the news of Buddha's coming in their community assigned their pupils to observe the Buddha's signs as to whether they correspond to the descriptions in the treatise. Some of them were surprised by the word 'Buddha' denoting him because they did not realise the existence of the person as such in the reality. After being confirmed about the fact, the Brahmin went to the Buddha in order to observe the signs by himself. Buddha intentionally had some signs uncovered to the Brahmins so that they became faithful and unquestioning about the fact. This can be implied that the development of belief in Buddhism is necessarily based on the local belief or private belief.

The described situations point to the mechanism, which Max Weber mentioned in the term of *charisma*,[370] or Wijayaratna in terms of *hero-worship*,[371] that Buddha first attracted the followers with his charismatic features of leadership. Max Weber explained the phenomena that the local beliefs play a significant role as the support to the perpetuation of new legitimate authority for the succession of itself.[372] The former belief(s) is

370 Weber, The Religion of India, pp. 219–220.
371 Wijayaratna, Buddhist Monastic Life, p. 6.
372 Weber, Economy and Society, pp. 1146–1147.

the foundation of the newly developed belief. Corresponding to the social consensus on the ideal characteristics of spiritual teacher, Buddha was worthy of visit in the opinion of the people in the social context. From the beginning, he easily received a warm welcome and won a reverence for his goodness shining from his appearance.

Nevertheless, the structure of the discourse demonstrates that the reputation was only the first impact to the people to approach the Buddha. Buddha's *religion* according to the discourse does not lie in the reverence and support from the householder merely with the trust in the reputation. The valid belief in the Buddha acknowledged in the tradition is 'officially' generated in the next stage, at hearing the sermon.

3.4.2 At Hearing the Sermon

At this stage, the hearer heard a sermon from the Buddha or, in some discourse, a chief disciple. The conclusion of discourse presents the result of the sermon that the hearer achieved, denoted by one of three stock phrases. First, feeling of satisfaction,[373] which is interpreted as a positive feeling after hearing the given answer or explanation; second, the formal declaration of going to the Three Jewels for refuges and followership under the Buddha;[374] third, hearing Ānupubbikathā sermon leading to a spiritual attainment.[375] The three stock phrases are the sign of understanding the sermon and acknowledging the Buddha in different ways. Among the stock phrases, the declaration of the belief in the Buddha indicates the process of the development of belief in Buddhism.[376] It represents the *religious experience or* the mental process in the *perception* – knowledge acquired from the Buddha– with the thought and feeling, expressed in *reactions* – the admiration of the sermon and the declaration of the belief.[377]

373 See detail in 2.3.1.
374 See detail in 2.3.2.
375 See detail in 2.3.3.
376 See detail in 2.3.2.
377 The term *belief* is normally applied in Buddhism, while the term *faith* is avoided, in order to distinguish the characteristic of belief in Buddhism, which is based on use of reason and empirical experience, from the belief in acquainted theistic religions, which is based on the pure intuition and sensuality.

As the text implies, hearing the sermon was very significant to develop a correct understanding about religious conception, spirituality, and so on, which was connected with deeper understanding, knowledge, imagination, etc. of the individuals. Considering the continuation from the first stage, hearing the sermon supports the right understanding about the Buddha and his teaching because the people before hearing the sermon had had different beliefs and understandings about him, which could be true or false. At the visit, they came to the Buddha with their personal belief or with the rumour about him and his order. The meeting and the conversation with the Buddha thus opened the chance to ask for what they had doubted. In this way, several questions from householder may concern several topics on spiritual life and practice from the basic to the liberation despite the first visit. At the same time, Buddha had the chance to give the hearer a focus of intention to the doctrine that he would like to tell.

3.4.2.1 Development of Knowledge

As pointed by the name, Buddhism is the religion of enlightenment. The name of the founder, Buddha, means 'enlightened.' Buddhist is the person who follows the Buddha in his doctrine of enlightenment. The knowledge in the religious context is not to be learned and known, but to be enlightened by following the Buddha developing oneself to the fact that life is suffering and more to the reality for the liberation from the fetters that conceal the reality from their consciousness. The hearing of the sermon that inspires the declaration of followership indicates the first stage in the development of this knowledge.

Interestingly, the two origins of the first impression paved the different ways, at least two, to the aspects of hearer's interest and belief about the Buddha. The reputation about the ideal spiritual teacher and Arahat motivated the hearer's interest on the doctrine: what the Buddha had learned and practiced in the achievement of the spiritual goal. In the context, the hearer knew from the external characteristics the ascetic lifestyles and their spiritual aim, which was opposite to that of householder, but not exactly, the detail of the doctrine they were devoting. During the visit, they thus asked for the facts in relation to the external characteristics they had seen. However, the Brahmins' interest attracted by the treatise on the 32 signs of Great Man provided them another direction to the religion.

They particularly focused on the Buddha, who possessed the auspicious signs, with their traditional belief that the person was 'holy.' With the trust in their physiognomic doctrine, they believed that the man with the correctly observed 32 signs of the Great Man was the Great Man and thus the Buddha, the great teacher who was the Enlightened, according to the treatise. In this way, the Brahmins had no doubt in the Buddhahood and the truthfulness of his doctrine. They simply had an absolute trust in the person that any of his teaching must be the righteous and advantageous for the humankind, as it was the teaching of the Buddha. In this way, they wholeheartedly welcome a sermon that the Buddha preached and acknowledged it almost without a doubt.

The absolute trust in the Buddha affects to the success in the mission. Interestingly, among the five householders who achieved the spiritual attainment, mentioned with stock phrase type III, after hearing the sermon, two Brahmins, Pokkharasādi (DN3) and Brahmāyu (MN91) similarly became very faithful in the Buddha after knowing the fact about the signs on the Buddha that they acknowledged the Buddhahood without a challenging question.[378] Pokkharasādi went to see the Buddha in that evening in order to apologize for his pupil's benightedness and to observe the signs with his eyes once more. Brahmāyu after having known the fact about the signs from his pupil chose to sit in a lower seat near Buddha to observe the Buddha closely. The behaviours of the Brahmins indicate that both of them had acknowledged the superiority of the Buddha. They went to see the Buddha for his teaching with the trust that the teaching was truly the truth. With this mind, they were thus ready to hear the sermon. The situation is different in the case of householder who had various doubts about spiritual life in their mind. Jīvaka Komārachacca (MN55), for example, posed the Buddha the question on the vegetarianism, which was practiced by some ascetics but not by Buddha. Responding this question, Buddha then explained him the reason. At the end, Jīvaka, which had understood the points, accepted the answer and asked the Buddha to become a lay follower. Tradition denotes the acceptance with the stock phrase type I (1) and type II (3).

378 The five people are mentioned in the 3.3.1.

Figure 14: Development of Knowledge Traced from Stock Phrase Type I, II

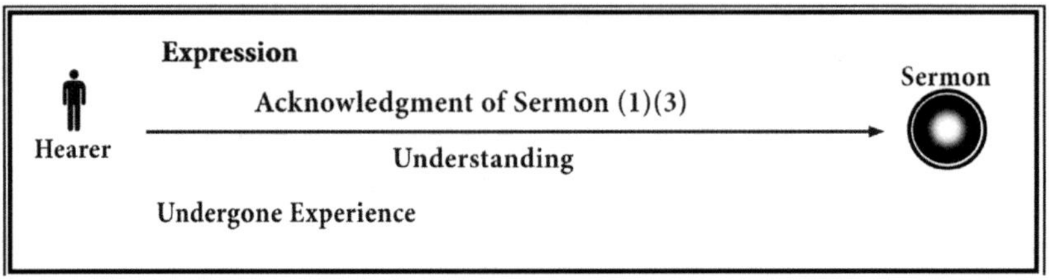

In this way, it is understandable about the role of the sermon on the understanding of the doctrine. In case of the Brahmins, who had the complete trust in the Buddha, the delivery of sermon tended to be more successful because the Brahmins completely concentrated their mind on the teaching without a bias or a question about the teacher and the doctrine. The knowledge from the physiognomic treatise provided the Brahmins a common sense that the spiritual teacher in front of him was the true Buddha whose teaching was the truth. Hence, the Buddha could easily direct the Brahmin to reach the answer he would like to present them. Tradition distinguishes this point with stock phrase type III, which denotse the Buddha's delivery of another special sermon *Ānupubbikathā* and the attainment of *Dhammacakkhu.* On the contrary, the householder who knew the Buddha from the external side mostly focused on the question that they had in their mind. The answer of the Buddha thus removed the doubts or simply corrected some misunderstanding about a single point and might not reach the core teaching of the Buddha. The outcome of hearing an ordinary sermon is thus not equal to that of the *Ānupubbikathā* sermon.

3.4.2.2 Evaluation of Dhamma and Buddha

Stock phrases type I and II which denote the understanding of the sermon imply an evaluation that Buddha's delivered sermon or given answer was accepted. The type II contains the part that implies an evaluation after the *understanding of the sermon* as a progress in the development of belief with the hearing of the sermon, viz. in stock phrase (3), denoting admiration of the sermon and the significance to his life and in stock phrase (4) in the worship to the Three Jewels. The former represents the positive judgment about the meaning of the sermon that Buddha had delivered, while the latter represents a trust, a feeling of certainty about the Buddhist institutions consisting of Buddha, his dhamma, and his community of followers.

Figure 15: Process of Belief in the Nikāya discourse

		Meaning of the Sermon Known
Understand	→	**To know the meaning offered in the sermon**
Evaluate	→	**To judge the value of the meaning offered in the sermon**
		Importance of the Meaning Realized

The stereotyped use of stock phrases denotes the doctrine about the development of belief in Buddhism as the result of understanding sermon.[379] The stock phrase (3) is the imagery of understanding the sermon thoroughly. The stock phrase (4) implies the positive evaluation and the acceptance of the main institutions, which are the pillars of the religion. In connection with the context, the Buddha and the dhamma only should be the subject to worship rather than the Sangha, which has nothing to do in the context. Relating to the previous understanding and admiration of the sermon, stated in stock phrase (3), the following process in (4) should be the action from the evaluation of the meaning of the sermon and the Buddha that they were superior and thus worthy of reverence for the hearer. The hearer therefore mentioned the Three Jewels.

Self-consideration and evaluation was an important activity in any decision to accept or assent a teaching, including the Buddha's teaching. As the text implies, the doctrines of the Buddha and other teachers, which are all claimed as dhamma, were a kind of *theory* on the knowledge and practice to attain the spiritual goal, proposed by the teacher who declared himself Arahat, Buddha, or the spiritual teacher who claimed the discovery of the truth. In this way, the knowledge and quality of teacher was

379 See 3.2.1.

firstly to observe for the reliability of the proposed theory. However, this is not easy for outsiders, especially the householder who was not familiar with the ascetic lifestyle and doctrine. A householder asked the Buddha about how to examine the spiritual person who preserved the truth.[380] Buddha's answer in response indicates the aspect of the truth that can be observed in a spiritual teacher. "*Bharadvāja, even though something may be thoroughly inclined towards ... well reported ... well considered ... well reflected upon, it may be empty, void, false, on the other hand, even although something is not well reflected upon, it may be fact, truth, not otherwise. Preserving a truth, Bharadvāja, is not enough for an intelligent man inevitably to come to the conclusion: 'This alone the truth, all else is falsehood.'*[381] In order to observe the quality of spiritual person, Buddha then suggested examining the spiritual teacher concerning three states: states of greed, state of aversion and state of confusion, each of which has a different characteristic. After that, the truth in him must be closely investigated:

> "After examining him and beholding that he is purified of states of confusion, then he reposes faith in him; with faith born he draws close; drawing close he sits down near by; sitting down near by he lends ear; lending ear he hears *dhamma*; having heard *dhamma* he remembers it; he tests the meaning of the things he remembers; while testing the meaning the things are approved of; if there is approval of the things desire is born; with desire born he makes an effort; having made an effort he weighs it up; having weighed it up he strives; being self-resolute he realises with his person the highest truth itself; and penetrating it by means of intuitive wisdom, he sees. It is to this extent, Bharadvāja, that there is an awakening to truth; it is to this extent that one awakens to truth; it is to this extent that we lay down an awakening to truth; but not yet is there attainment of truth."[382]

Kālāma- or Kesaputtasutta is another discourse that affirms individual discretion and judgment in a doctrine or teacher. In the discourse, Buddha taught, people should "*not be led by the proficiency in the collections,*

---

380 The Collection of the Middle Length Sayings Vol. II, p. 361. To preserve the truth signifies to the ascetic activity, in which the people carry out the Dhamma.

381 MN II 170, 30–32 – MN II 171, 1–7; The Collection of the Middle Length Sayings Vol. II, p. 361.

382 The Collection of the Middle Length Sayings Vol. II, p. 362–363.

nor by mere logic or inference, nor after considering reasons, nor after reflection on and approval of some theory, nor because it fits becoming, nor out of respect for a recluse (who hold it)." Instead, they should have discretion in considering them. "*But Kālāmas, when you know for yourselves: These things are unprofitable, these things are blameworthy, these things are censured by the intelligent; these things when performed and undertaken, conduce to loss and sorrow, – then indeed do ye reject them, Kālāmas.*"[383] Likewise, in response to the question of how an ordinary man without special insight distinguishes the Buddha from ordinary teachers, Buddha suggested to examine the person in the following ways: [384]

> Do those that are impure state which are cognizable through the eye and the ear do not exist in a Tathāgata or not?[385]
> Do those that are mixed states cognizable through the eye and the ear exist in a Tathāgata or not?[386]
> Do those that are absolutely pure states cognizable through the eye and the ear exist in a Tathāgata or not?[387]
> Has this venerable one been possessed of this skilled state for a long time or only for a short time?[388]
> Do there exist any perils for that venerable monk who has attained to fame and won renown?[389]
> Does this venerable one refrain out of fearlessness, does not he refrain out of fear? Is it because, through the destruction of attachment, that, being without attachment, he does not follow pleasures of the senses?[390]

The sermons clearly indicate that people must consider their spiritual teacher by themselves from the observable personality, behaviour, and doctrine. This means, *personal consideration and judgment* playing an important role in the decision to become a follower under the Buddha. The people may variously choose to follow whom and what they believe or *deem* to be true, sacred, or enlightened, etc. Some people preferred austere

383 The Book of the Gradual Sayings Vol. I, p. 72.
384 The Collection of the Middle Length Sayings Vol. I, pp. 379–380.
385 MN I 318, 5–6; The Collection of the Middle Length Sayings Vol. II, pp. 379 ff.
386 MN I 318, 11–12; ibid.
387 MN I 318, 17–18; ibid.
388 MN I 318, 23–24; ibid.
389 MN I 318, 29–31; ibid.
390 MN I 319, 2–4; ibid.

practices and believed that only the austere practitioner was Arahat, while some might prefer the ascetics with debater type. In this way, the reasons to join the community were myriad and not necessarily stick to the understanding or trust in the doctrine. Some Buddhists joined the order for learning more teaching after having heard a sermon. Some of them might wish to see miracles performed by the monks. Sunakkhatta Licchavi, for example, joined the Buddha's order in order to see the miracles that the Buddha might perform in his community.[391] Choosing a spiritual teacher is based on one's own consideration and interest. At the time of the decision, *it had occurred to him* that the spiritual teacher or the doctrine was *right.* He did not exactly know whether the understanding considered true was really true. He simply joined the community because of the thing seemed to be right at the time of consideration. As Taves pointed, he had the religious experience, inspired by the thing that he considered and thus felt special.

In this connection, the individual judgment also played the important role in the repudiation of the belief when the individual found the belief, the teacher, or the community they at first considered sacred or trustworthy opposite to their expectation. Sunakkhatta Licchavi, after having found that the Buddha did not perform a miracle, left the community merely because he did not see the miracle. Buddha's chief disciples, Sāriputta and Moggallāna, before becoming the Buddha's chief disciple, were ascetic within the ascetic school of Sañjaya. They left the old school for the community of Sangha at once after they had heard the summarized teaching of the Buddha from Assaji and had the experience of *Dhammacakkhu*.[392] In this way, the religious people as implied from the background could freely change their belief and practice from one teacher to another teacher. In Buddhism, a follower is allowed to leave the community easily by declaring before a witness that they do not want to be in the order any longer.

From this, it can be concluded that the personal knowledge, experience, and even interest about what deemed as sacred, important, right, etc. is influential to the view that a person or a thing is special and thus significant to the the decision. Behind the consideration is benefit and outcome hoped

391 Dialogues of the Buddha Part III, p. 8 ff.; cf. p. 83.
392 The Book of the Discipline Vol. IV, p. 52.

to receive after the involvement. The consideration is thus "the subjective weighing of anticipated rewards and costs when making choices."[393] At first seeing the Buddha or hearing his sermon, the hearer might declare the followership with the impression with the manner shining from him and the meaningful sermon. The decision is based on the certain knowledge, experience, ideas at the time. But after approaching closer to him, it is possible that he might follow the idea and reject the teacher and his doctrine, or remain his belief. This explanation points to the significance of *paññā* 'the wisdom' in Buddhist philosophy, as the basis of spiritual development.[394] Also, it can explain the inequality of the people in understanding a sermon and the degree of belief in the Buddha. Some people understood and achieved a spiritual attainment quickly while some people slowly. Tradition explained this in terms of karma, as one collected from the past lives the knowledge, experience, and skill in the learning and practicing the doctrine.

3.5 Summary

This chapter investigated the process of the belief developed in relation to the social and cultural context until the declaration of followership presented in the pattern of discourse. The development is found to occur at two stages.

First, the hearers were attracted to the Buddha with some characteristic feature, which the society valued as good or worthy to see, heard from hearsay. In the discourses, there are two motives mentioned about the Buddha's characteristic features. First, the hearsay concerned Buddha's spiritual qualities of religious teacher who was Arahat having spiritual knowledge, controlled manner, and good instructor of ascetic communities. Second, the hearsay concerned Buddha's thirty-two signs of Great Man that the Brahmins had known in a treatise of their tradition.

---

393 Stark; Finke, Acts of Faith, p. 85.

394 Gethin, The Buddhist Path to Awakening, p. 119. Paññā in some contexts is limited to the "wisdom concerning to the rise and the decay of things" and thus in this context ñāṇa may be more suitable as it denotes knowledge or awareness of the suitability of something for achieving the goal, the ceasing of suffering for both self and others.

The belief at first hearing and seeing was significant to the development of belief aroused by the sermon in the second stage. This belief attracted people to approach and talk with the Buddha, which led to the encounter and conversation in the next step. This indicates an aspect of Buddhist mission that the activity was not actively operated to target the people and convert them. Instead, Buddhism tended to attract people to visit the person or the community with a social consensus on some characteristics of worthy teacher. At the visit, some obstinacy against the Buddha had even decreased, as the people were partially convinced that Buddha and his community were good. Pāli tradition makes this part logically relating to the next part, which describes the scene of conversation.

Bhikkhu or monastic follower played the role of instructor and debater instead of Buddha, particularly after the Buddha had passed away. As the follower who has successfully learned and practiced the doctrine, they were in the position to explain the teaching when being asked. In DN23, the spiritual qualities of monastic follower and ability in the doctrine were mentioned in hearsay spreading in the community, attracting the main character to pay a visit. This indicates the scholarship in the doctrine as representative of the Buddha that the tradition emphasizes on the monastic follower. With the qualities, he was expected to represent the Buddha and manage to explain or defend the doctrine to people who came to them with questions and even turn them into a follower.

Second, the hearer, after having noticed the qualities, conversed with him about the topics. Some hearers had the trust in the Buddha before seeing him in person with their belief and evaluation that the Buddha must be a good spiritual teacher, so they followed the sermon without a doubt and easily had the belief developed. The expression in stock phrases shows four stages of belief in reaction to Buddha's sermon and his religion. It ranges from deep-seated belief unto non-belief:

1. First level: the hearer declared the Three Jewels for refuge and asked for followership, which was the official 'procedure' to become a follower under the Buddha. In the process, they attained the experience of *Dhammacakkhu,* by which the hearer completely understood the Buddhism and had a strong belief in the religion.
2. Second level: the hearer acknowledged the sermon, declared the Three Jewels for refuge and asked for followership

3. Third level: the hearer declared their belief, but *not* declared the Three Jewels for refuge and *not* asked for followership
4. Fourth level: the hearer did not declare anything and had no belief in Buddhism.

Detail about the acknowledgment and the declaration of the followership in the stock phrase is too little to investigate the true meaning. Nevertheless, it can be observed in some degree from the context of the discourses. Fortunately, in the conclusion of some discourses compliment and apology to the Buddha are found side by side. As surmised from the evidence, tradition ascribed the hearers to be *gladdened* by the sermon that motivates them to declare the belief and followership at the end while some of them accept the Buddha's superiority in the wisdom and the ability to debate the doctrine.

The first discussion analyses the expression of thought and feeling and the act of religious motivation. Despite little evidence given, it can be seen that religious belief and motivation came from the *evaluation* of the sermon and/or Buddha's ability in the delivery of the sermon. In the process, the evaluation was based on the hearer's understanding about the teaching and the degree of the significance of the teaching to his life. As a result, the belief in the Buddha declared could be in different levels. The understanding led to the feeling of admiring and respecting the Buddha as teacher who had discovered and spread the dhamma and his pupils who followed the Buddha's path. In this way, the belief in Buddhism as shown in the discourses suggested the importance ascribed to Buddha's dhamma as the universal truth that one could understand and see. Satisfied simply with some meaning in the teaching and declared it expressly, one becomes a Buddhist, follower under the Buddha.

The first encounter might further the next contacts. With the acquaintanceship and the realization of how the Buddha and his teaching was significant, some hearer regularly visited the Buddha and the Sangha for various reasons. This is the religiosity that connected the individual hearer with the order. The next chapter raises the religiosity of non-monastic follower as a result of the "religious experience" suggesting the meaning of the followership under the Buddha.

Chapter IV: Lay Religiosity in Relation to the Monastic Order

According to the structure of the discourse, after having heard sermon and understood its meaning, the hearer declared their belief in Buddha, took the 'Three Jewels' for refuge, and asked the Buddha to become a follower. Tradition regards the moment of the declaration as the beginning of spiritual path. This intention indicates the *composite ascription* in that the hearer accepted to follow in some way the goal that the Buddha had pointed. According to Taves, the ascription is a process, in which the individuals or the groups "*perpetuate an initial thing or event deemed special by agreeing on how it can be re-created.*" The re-creation the efficacy of practices relative to the goal may be freestyle for individuals or from a consensus of people in the group.[395]

This chapter investigates the religiosity and the intention behind as a result of the understanding and the evaluation of Buddha's teaching discussed in the last chapter. According to the last chapter, the experience with the Buddha following the understanding and the evaluation of the Buddha and his teachings, inspires the hearer to revere Three Jewels and to declare the Three Jewels for refuge. The procedure ends with the request to become a follower under the Buddha, which is the last component of the stock phrase type II, denoting the declaration of followership. In other words, this is a question on "composite ascription" after the "simple ascription." This chapter aims at observing "religiosity" in relation to the Buddha, his doctrine, and his community of monastic followers, viz. *the initiation* to the Buddhist path or 'conversion,' the announcement of praise to Buddha, and the devotions. Based on the theory of religious experience, the religiosity is viewed as the activity inspired by the knowledge and the realisation from the religious experience received in the hearing of sermon.

4.1 Conversion

The word "conversion" is generally perceived in terms of changing or turning of a person or a group of people from one belief into another belief,

395 Taves, Religious Experience Reconsidered, p. 53: See Table 1.3.

or from none of belief into one belief,[396] which is connected with socio-cultural complex: values, speech, norms, behaviours, beliefs, lifestyles, relations, and/or interests.[397] Applying the concept to Buddhism, in which one had requested the Buddha or one of his pupils for a permission to become a disciple or to remember them as a follower may be problematic because the activity does not signify to the process of *changing* individual belief, practice, and lifestyle into a commitment, which suggests *membership* of new religious life. However, conversion can be considered as *changing sides* from the unsuccessfulness of the former belief to overwhelm the believer, to the success of the new belief, which thus ably replaces the former belief.[398] In this way, the author insists on applying the word in context of the Nikāya discourse in that the convert acknowledged the teaching delivered by Buddha in place of or together with the former belief. At the same time, he was convinced that the Buddha was a true spiritual teacher who was worthy for compliment and praise. As implied in the declaration, the process of conversion in Buddhism officially means that the development of spiritual knowledge and practice on the spiritual path begins ever since.

The request is always represented with the group of stock phrases (3) (4) (5) or (6) respectively.[399] The stock phrases in this order imply a certain *pattern* in the declaration, starting with the admiration of the instruction or the debate, in which the Buddha had given to them, in stock phrase (3):

> Most excellent, Lord, most excellent! Just as if a man were to set up that which has been thrown down, or were to reveal that which is hidden away, or were to point out the right road to him who has gone astray, or were to bring a lamp into the darkness so that those who have eyes could see external forms – just even so, Lord, has the truth been made known to me, in many a figure, by the Exalted One.

As I have argued in the last chapter, the feeling of fascination in this regard *theoretically* occurred to everyone who would decide to become a follower. The stock phrase (3) is the admiration *symbolically* representing

396 Houlden, Article "Conversion", in: Oxford Concise Dictionary of World Religion, p. 109; Blasi, The Meaning of Conversion: Redirection of Foundational Trust, p. 11.

397 Giordian, Introduction: The Varieties of Conversion Experience, p. 1.

398 Pace, Convert, Revert, Pervert, pp. 189–190.

399 See 2.3.2.

that the hearer had understood and evaluated the value of the Buddha's sermon. In Taves's words, the teaching is deemed to be special and raised as the goal in the act of praising and worshipping the Buddha. As a result, the praise of the teaching shows that the hearer had realised the superiority of the Buddha: the hearer went for refuges to the Three Jewels, the symbolic institutions of Buddhism comprising the Buddha, his teaching, and his Sangha in stock phrase (4):

> Now, I betake myself, Lord, to the Exalted One as my refuge, to the Doctrine, and to the Brotherhood.

Finally, the hearer asks to be a follower, non-monastic (5) or monastic (6) that he is from now on a follower of the Buddha. The process is in presence of the Buddha or chief disciple.

> (5) May the Exalted One accept me as a disciple, as one who, from this day forth, as long as life endures, has taken his refuge in them.
> (6) I would fain, Lord, renounce the world under the Exalted One; I would fain be admitted to his Order.

In the conclusion of the discourses in Dīgha- and Majjhima-nikāya, it is found that there are 44 times, which indicate the requests at the end of discourse. In the 44 times of conversion, there are 37 times, in which people asked to be a lay follower and 7 times to be a monastic follower.[400] This means, only the people with the first and second levels of belief mentioned with the stock phrases (3) (4) (5) or (6) are Buddhist, Buddha's follower.

4.1.1 Conversion as the Following Act of Evaluation

Conversion and the religious experience generally take place side by side. "*The experience of believing often generates in or is accompanied by the experience of conversion, which is expressed in terms of radical change, a transformation that is almost always described in terms of 'before' and an 'after,' to the point of leading to a kind of 're-birth' and to the construction of a new identity.*"[401] From this standpoint, Torkel Brekke tried to understand with different aspects the phenomena that may imply the

400 See Figure 6, p. 58.
401 Giordan, Introduction: The Varieties of Conversion Experience, p. 1.

sense of Buddhist conversion in Pāli canon.[402] Relying on the theistic concept of conversion, he considered that the decision for a new belief should be essentially inspired by an "encountered experience," which in case of Buddhism is an experience of feeling impatient or unhappy to keep the householder's life that might motivate the sacrifice of householder's life.[403] For example, the awareness of suffering in human life: birth, ageing, sickness and death, as it had happened to Prince Siddhattha before his renunciation and enlightenment,[404] or to Sāriputta and Moggallāna before their decision to join the school of Sañjaya Velaṭṭhaputta.[405] From the awareness arises the feeling of *saṃvega,* a kind of fears that strives one to find the freedom from the life suffering.[406] The process of feelings and thought was exemplified to Yasa, a millionair's son in Banares who was aware of the disorder and disturbance in his mind while he was a householder.[407] His awareness became more intense that he left his family in one night for an opposite feeling - peacefulness. He then became a monastic follower of the Buddha after meeting him by accident and hearing his sermons. In this way, the conversion in the canon following the "religious experience," as Brekke concluded, merely inspired one to leave the family for the ascetic life. The movement from an ascetic school to another ascetic school is not reckoned to be 'conversion' in his opinion.

Brekke's framework for the analysis as mentioned above is too ideal in the context, where people were allowed to experience the right doctrine that inspired the monastic life. The feeling of *saṃvega*, as he regarded as

---

402 Brekke, Religious Motivation and the Origins of Buddhism. In the book, except the first article, which deals with Vinaya Khandaka, the other five articles concern the conversion and psychological factors playing a role on motivating the conversion or religious devotion. The subject matters of the article thus relate to one another.

403 Brekke, Religious Motivation and the Origins of Buddhism, p. 53.

404 In hagiographical literatures of the Buddha in the tradition, Buddha was described to be reminded to see this truth by himself that inspired him to leave his family for the solution.

405 Dhammapadaṭṭhakathā extended their story to cover this part in order to illustrate their inspiration to the ascetic life that they had been at first bored in the life and would like to find the solution before he met the Buddha.

406 Ibid., p. 78.

407 The Book of the Discipline Vol. IV, pp. 22 ff.

religious experience in Buddhism, was too much restrictive to the self-realization in the life suffering, while many people mentioned in Theragāthā and Therīgāthā joined the order with other different backgrounds, particularly problem in life and family.[408] Furthermore, it is not fit to the 'theme' presented in pattern of the discourse about how a belief in Buddhism is developed. As demonstrated in the last chapter, any thought and feeling about the superiority of the charismatic Buddha is also powerful to attract the followers to the community. Also, a sermon or a philosophical conservation, as the tradition created the discourses in this format, is influential to the belief of the hearer. In this way, the admiration of dhamma in stock phrase (3) is the crucial mark pointing to the impact to the hearer, which indicates the positive evaluation of the teaching and of the teacher, leading to the worship and the declaration of belief under the Buddha and the spiritual path.

'Conversion' as illustrated in Nikāya discourse is merely the declaration of the intention to follow the spiritual path 'deemed as special' after the experience with a part of the teaching and the spiritual teacher. [409] While hearing the sermon, Buddha seemed to be interesting, special, or respectable that they might like to know it more. The decision to become a monastic follower implied much more desire and curiosity than to become a lay follower because the ascetic life was more difficult.[410] But this lay life under the Buddha's teaching did not mean the "immoderate" life, as Buddha forbade the extreme happiness. Buddha taught householder to control his mind on sensual pleasure and to live sufficiently for the success and happiness in the family life, although he admired the renunciation.[411]

---

408 Blackstone, Women in the Footsteps of the Buddha, pp. 37–51.

409 It is noticeable that the declaration of belief, as processed in the stock phrases, was ritualized in the Buddhist 'conversion' nowadays. Some Buddhist schools view that the 'ritual' is the necessary expression before pursuing the path. However, the ritual was seriously criticized among the western newcomers, who had fled from the "blind faith" of Christianity and expected the opposite quality from Buddhism. This conflict clearly illustrates how the new follower's assent to the teaching is required before the declaration of belief as such. See Waterhouse, Buddhism in Bath, pp. 234–235.

410 Wijayaratna, Buddhist Monastic Life, p. 175.

411 Ibid., pp. 170–174; cf. Embree, Source of Indian Tradition, p. 125.

In this way, the lay life in Buddhism can be regarded as the primary step to Buddhist spirituality, as the Buddha remarked: "*Monks, in this Doctrine and in this Discipline, there is gradual training, gradual action, gradual teaching and gradual method.*"[412] As Buddhist householder, he could always follow the teachings. During the life, he could be *defeated,* like a monastic follower, by lack of effort to follow the Buddha or by a 'false view' which deviated him from the Buddha and his spiritual path to other teachers and their doctrine. In this way, despite merely an announcement, the request is thus meaningful for the membership in the community of those who follow the path.

4.1.2 Conversion into Non-Monastic Follower

The detail about the religiosity before and after the conversion is necessarily required in order to observe the change in the process of conversion.[413] In case of conversion into lay follower under the Buddha, the data is unfortunately limited and often vague because of a few mentions about the follower after the conversion.[414] Furthermore, the religiosity of lay follower was free from rule and discipline in opposite to that of monastic follower, which was controlled under certain rules and customs given in Vinaya. Hence, the life after the conversion into monastic follower is more predictable. To deal with this problem, the author observes the religious activities of the lay follower in relation to the Buddha, his teaching and his community of monastic followers under the impression that the lay followers did the activities with some acquaintance with the Three Jewels and realisation of their significance in some degree. The thoughts and behaviours in the discourse imply the 'Buddhist obligation' that the tradition ascribed to the lay follower. The stories provide the audience, or the reader, different images of the lay follower, what the lay follower is like, what they do, what they think, etc. Indeed, the images came from the perspective of the tradition as to how the lay follower should have behaved in the relations.

---

412 Ibid.

413 Giordan, Introduction: The Varieties of Conversion Experience, p. 1.

414 Nevertheless, we can observe the change of religious behaviour in some followers as exemplified in this chapter.

At first glance, the conversion for lay follower is distinguished from the conversion of monastic follower from the language in the declaring sentence, viz. the use of verb in the stock phrase denoting the request to be a follower: a monastic follower (5) and a lay follower (6). The sentences take distinctly different verbs that illuminate the aspect of followership under the Buddha. In the request to be a follower, the hearer *asked the Buddha or the witness to* ***bear*** *him* as a disciple. According to the grammar of the Pāli language, the verb of the sentence is conjugated in imperative mood from √dhṛ̥ or √dhar "to bear, to hold,"[415] while the verb denoting the hearer's asking to be a monastic follower is conjugated in optative mood from √labh "to get, to obtain."[416] In this way, the hearer who wished the monkhood *asked the Buddha or the witness to* **offer** *him* the ordination or the status of membership in his community. The use of verb clearly points to the different degree of concernment to the Buddha's community. The follower had to live under the instructions given by the Buddha and follow some customs of seniority within the community. Much more involved with the Buddha than the lay follower, the monastic follower was exclusively the member of the community. The request for permission from the leader for the membership is therefore necessary to join the community. On the contrary, lay follower does not directly involve with the Buddha and his community; the people only occasionally met the Buddha and his monastic followers. Nevertheless, it seems to be important that the declaration that they were the Buddha's follower was made in front of a witness, who was the Buddha or a member from the monastic community.

The meaning of the conversion for lay follower reminds us in some extent of the early rite of ordination or *Ehibhikkhu-upasampadā* "the ordination which is valid with the word 'Monk, come!,'" in which a man directly asked the Buddha to be a monastic follower.[417] They are similarly lack of certain ritual, which clearly corresponds to the Buddha's standpoint against ritualism.[418] In this kind of ordination, people who wanted to become a follower paid respect to the Buddha and simply asked him for it.

---

415 Buddhadatta, Concise Pāli-English Dictionary, p. 133.

416 Ibid., p. 221.

417 The Book of the Discipline Vol. IV, pp. 18–19, 26, 44, 56.

418 Kloppenborg, The Earliest Buddhist Ritual of Ordination, p. 164.

Then was the answer from the Buddha: "*Come, monks! Well taught is dhamma, fare the Brahma-faring for making an utter end of ill.*" The activity implies that the conversion in Buddhism is originally simple and meaningful that it simply emphasizes the intention of the new convert on the spiritual path. It thus expresses the acknowledgment in front of a witness that the new convert has the Buddha as his foremost spiritual teacher. Furthermore, it is clearly seen that the declaration of intention, which is a verbal statement, is significantly valid in the context.

The pattern of the declaration in the ordination of *Ehibhikkhu-upasampadā*, is similar to the conversion of lay follower. First, the declaration of belief is necessarily made before a witness from the monastic order. This points to the membership which must be known by a member of the community. Second, the declaration is clear and unambiguous. The scripture obviously has it that the sentence *maṃ dhārehi* "bear me" in the conversion of lay follower is conjugated in imperative form.[419] The sentence with the verb and structure shows a degree of strong intention. Third, the process emphasized on individualistic concern, on which one might ask the teacher for spiritual teaching and practice.[420] The person who wanted to join the community of the Buddha just declared the belief by going to the Three Jewels for refuges and asked the Buddha to bear them as a follower. The Buddha played the role as the teacher and the preceptor.[421] The sentence implies that the conversion for lay follower was recognized in the text in parallel to the simple rite of ordination, as the membership had not been appointed to play the role on the admission.[422] From this comparison, we can reckon with the chronology that, while the rite of ordination for monastic follower was far developed, the conversion of lay follower remained as simple as in former time because lay follower is always individual practitioner who concentrates only on the development of spirituality on his own. The conversion for them is merely an

419 Cf. a declaration to disavow the monastic life: (for example) *Gihīti maṃ dhārehi*. "Remember me as householder!" See more in The Book of the Discipline Vol. I, pp. 43–46.

420 Kloppenborg, The Earliest Buddhist Ritual of Ordination, p. 162.

421 Ibid., p. 164.

422 Ibid, p. 158.

official declaration of the intention to follow the Buddha and his teaching after having a trust in the teacher and the teaching.

4.2 Expression of Reverence to Buddha

The declaration is a kind of worship, which is usually directed to the sacred beings or objects, such as god, goddess, sacred person and sacred object, or something assumed to be more real and superior to the devotee.[423] In atheistic religion like Buddhism, the worship may be paid to Buddha or a spiritual teacher. The praise of the Three Jewels as in the stock phrase (4) is a form of worship in Buddhism, like the worship of the Buddha's image or pagoda, which is an activity of merit making.[424] Applying Taves to analyse the stock phrase, the follower reckoned the Buddha or the revered person or object to be 'special.'[425]

In the context of the discourse, expression of respect was a social language in the society that respected the value of hierarchy. The expression of respect was a social custom, in which a person particularly gave to those who possessed a higher birth, social status and virtuous value. Even religious teachers in an assembly were expected to pay respect to each other, in that the younger one paid to the older one or the lower status in a community (such as pupils) to the higher status (teacher or leader). The Buddha, as the tradition has it, was a religious leader who generally received a respect, not only from his followers, from people outside his community of follower. When he was present in an assembly with other religious leaders, he never paid a reverence to them, even to an older Brahmin, with the reason that nobody deserved a respect given by him.[426] This symbolizes the image of the Buddha established in the tradition that he was superior to other spiritual teachers in the society. In this way, tradition describes how the behaviour and attitude of the Buddha to other older Brahmins were unsatisfying and hence blamed by some of them who had not known him.[427] The conflict was finally solved when the Buddha proved in the

423 Ibid., p. 262.
424 Olson, Religious Studies, p. 263.
425 See detail in 2.3.2.
426 The Book of the Discipline Vol. I, pp. 2–3.
427 Dialogues of the Buddha Vol. I, p. 146.

assembly his superiority and worthiness for the respect. At least, the people accepted the superiority by paying him a compliment or behaving to him with respect.

The expression can be mainly divided into verbal and non-verbal expression. The verbal expression is the praise for the Buddha's qualities in public or before the Buddha while the non-verbal expression is the physical act of respecting the Buddha in different ways. Apart from surveying the acts of expression, this section also aims to investigate the presupposition in the last chapter that the people who had the experience of *Dhammacakkhu*, who had heard the *Ānupubbikathā* sermon and thus had more profound knowledge and understanding, could express the reverence to the Buddha more profoundly than the people without the experience of *Dhammacakkhu* did.

4.2.1 Verbal Expression

Praise is a significant expression of belief in Buddhism depicted in the discourses, as it demonstrates at best the understanding and the knowledge that the hearer had about the Buddha and his teaching. In Dīgha-nikāya and Majjhima-nikāya, there are some disciples who described in public their own knowledge and understanding about superiority of the Buddha and the teaching. Sāriputta, for example, expressed his personal belief in the Buddha and the teaching by elaborating the qualities of Buddha as well as his teaching several times.[428]

The expression of reverence has some element comparable to a kind of expression, called *Sīhanāda* "lion's roar," the utterance by the Buddha and chief disciples from the confidences in declaring or praising the qualities of himself or of the Buddha.[429] Manné studied the expression in particular as it implies the intention to issue a challenge.[430] Without the track found in the Vedic culture, she surmised, the expression should be inventive exclusively in the Buddhist culture, supposedly from the simile "lion's roar."[431]

428 Dialogues of the Buddha Vol. II, pp. 87–89; Dialogues of the Buddha Vol. III, pp. 95–110; The Book of the Kindred Sayings Vol. V, pp. 138–140.

429 Rhys Davids and Stede, Pāli-English Dictionary, p. 714.

430 Manné, Debates and Case Histories in the Pali Canon, p. 71.

431 Ibid., p. 81.

Seeing the expressions in context of debate in public,[432] she supported that the activity is not only the declaration of courage and confidence, but also the intention to express one's own position in public, the propaganda of his quality, challenging other teachers to debate.[433] It may also be the claim about relationship with their leader and co-practitioners.[434]

However, the author finds Manné's interpretation too specific to her thesis about debate and defense. In a similar way, followers may declare their belief in the Buddha in response to the questions, for instance, why they became Buddha's follower, why they believed him, how they find him and his teaching convincing etc. The response thus aims to demonstrate in public their religious knowledge about the Buddha or his teaching.[435] From the context, the question about the doctrine of the schools was always interesting for the outsiders. In the response, a follower was expected to demonstrate the reason from their perspective. In this way, the answer depended on the individual consideration and experience with the Buddha or his teaching. In the Nikāya discourses, there are two lay followers whose long utterance of revering the Buddha is collected, viz. Upāli (MN56) and King Pasenadi (MN89). In this section, the subject matters will be investigated and analysed in relation to the profile of the speaker and the context, where the speaker was while expressing the verbal respect to the Buddha.

4.2.1.1 Upāli

Upāli (MN56) was a former lay follower of Nigantha Nāṭaputta (or Mahāvīra, the founder of Jainism) who had been assigned to defend on the school's standpoint about the doctrine of karma with the Buddha. In the debate, he was defeated and impressed by the Buddha's argument, and even more fascinated by his attitude that the Buddha was modest and

432 Ibid., p. 71.
433 Ibid., p. 82.
434 Ibid., p. 72.
435 The Book of the Gradual Sayings Vol. II, p. 166–167; The Book of the Kindred Sayings Vol. II, pp. 38–41; The Book of the Gradual Sayings Vol. IV, pp. 248–252

careful about gaining a new follower who had been a famous follower of his competitant. Upāli thus gave these compliments to the Buddha[436]

Buddha said:

> "Now, Householder, make a proper investigation. Proper investigation is right in the case of well-known men like yourself."[437]

Upāli said:

> "I, revered sir, am even exceedingly pleased and satisfied with that which the Lord has said to me: "*Now, Householder, make a proper investigation. Proper investigation is right in the case of well-known men like yourself.*" For if, revered sir, members of other sects had secured me as a disciple, they would have paraded a banner all round Nāḷandā, saying: "The householder Upāli has joined our disciplehood." But then the Lord spoke to me thus: "*Now, Householder, make a proper investigation. Proper investigation is right in the case of a well-known man like yourself.*" So I, revered sir, for the second time, going to the Lord for refuge and to *dhamma* and to the Order of the monks. May the Lord accept me as a lay disciple going for refuge from today forth for as long as life lasts."[438]

Buddha said:

> "For a long time, householder, your family has been a well-spring to the Jains. You will bethink you to give alms to those that approach you?"[439]

Upāli said:

> "I, revered sir, am even exceedingly pleased and satisfied that the Lord speaks to me thus: "For a long time, householder, your family has been a well-spring to the Jains. You will bethink you to give alms to those that approach you?" I have heard, revered sir, that the recluse Gotama speaks thus: "Gift should be given to me only, not to others should gifts be given. Gifts should be given to my disciples only, not to the disciples of others should gifts be given. What is given to me is alone of great fruit, what is given to others is not of great fruit. What is given to my disciples is alone of great fruit. What is given to the disciples of others is not of great fruit." But then the Lord urged upon me giving to the Jains also. Indeed, revered sir, we shall know the right time for that. So I, revered sir, for the third time am going to the Lord for refuge and to *dhamma* and to the Order of the

---

436 Cf. The Book of the Gradual Sayings Vol. IV, pp. 127ff.

437 MN I 379, 3–4; The Collection of the Middle Length Sayings Vol. II, pp. 44–45.

438 MN I 379, 4–15; ibid.

439 MN I 379, 16–18; ibid.

monks. May the Lord accept me as a lay disciple going for refuge from today forth for as long as life lasts."[440]

From the dialog, it is clearly seen that Upāli's words repeated the Buddha's words before the utterance of second and third declaration of followership. The way the text mimicked can be interpreted that Upāli *considered* what the Buddha had commented as impressive that the Buddha was not a selfish teacher who exclusively aimed to gain more followers and supporters for his community. The impression inspired him to see the aspect of quality in the Buddha and hence to develop even greater belief in the Buddha. The repeated declaration shows how he demonstrated his understanding about the Buddha. On the other hand, from the perspective of the audience or the reader, the text aims to indoctrinate the audience or the reader in the personality of the Buddha as manifested to Upāli. In this connection, the audience or the reader can follow the thoughts of character that develop gradually from the beginning and understand why Upāli decided to become the Buddha's follower at the end.

Another occasion that Upāli expressed his belief in the Buddha took place when he met Nigantha Nāṭaputta, who visited him in order to see with his own eyes that his favourite follower had converted into the Buddha. By this time, Upāli had heard from the Buddha the *Ānupubbikathā* and became a stable follower who had 'complete' knowledge in the Buddha and his teaching. Upāli, who was asked about the Buddha his new teacher, declared the Buddha's qualities to Nigantha Nāṭaputta in the following ways:

"Of the wise, whose confusion is gone, whose mental barrenness is split asunder, who has won to victory,
Who is without ill, of very even mind, of grown moral habit, of lovely wisdom,
The 'All-within,' the stainless-of this Lord the disciple am I.
Of him who has no doubts, rejoicing, the material things of the world renounced, of joyful sympathy,
Who is a recluse, a human being, in his last body, a man,
The peerless, the dustless–of this Lord the disciple am I.
Of him who is sure, skilled, the leader away, the excellent charioteer,
The matchless, the shining, of no incertitude, bringing light,
Breaking pride, the hero–of this Lord the disciple am I.
Of the noblest of men, immeasurable, deep won to knowledge,

440 MN I 379, 18–32; ibid.

Bringer of security, a knower, on *dhamma* standing, self-controlled,
Who has gone beyond attachment, who is freed–of this Lord the disciple am I.
Of the supreme one, whose lodgings are remote, who has destroyed the fetters, who is freed,
Who speaks amiably, who is purified, the flag laid low, passionless,
Tamed, without impediments–of this Lord the disciple am I.
Of the seventh seer, trust gone, of threefold wisdom, Brahma-attained,
Washen, skilled in the lines, tranquil, who discovered knowledge.
Breaker of the citadel, Sakka–of this Lord the disciple am I.
Of the pure one, whose self is developed, who has attained the attainable, the expounder,
The one with recollection, whose vision is clear, not bent on passion, without hatred,
Impassible, attained to mastery–of this Lord the disciple am I.
Of him who has gone to the highest, the mediator, inwardly unobstructed, cleansed,
The unattached, the unaiming, the aloof, the attainer of the highest.
The crossed over, the helper across–of this Lord the disciple am I,
Of the calmed, the one of extensive wisdom, of great wisdom, without greed,
The Tathāgata, the well-farer, incomparable person, unequalled,
The confident, the accomplished–of this Lord the disciple am I.
Of the cutter of craving, the Awakened One, obscurity gone, unstained,
Worthy of offerings, the *yakkha*, the best of persons, beyond measure,
Great, attained to the height of glory–of this Lord the disciple am I."[441]

The description surprised Nigantha Nāṭaputta so much that he asked Upāli when (how) the description was made because it is wonderfully profound and elaborate. The given answer was despairing to him even harder. "*...This Lord has many splendours, many hundreds of splendours. And who, revered sir, would not give praise to one deserving praise?*"[442]

The answer shows how the verbal reverence of Buddha demonstrates the ability of the follower about the teacher and his teaching. In this case, Upāli who had the experience of *Dhammacakkhu* knew profoundly, why the Buddha was worthy for him to believe. Backwards to the stock phrases (7) (8) the follower had heard the *Ānupubbikathā* and understood thoroughly the teaching that he has no doubt about the teaching and the Buddha. This aspect of followership is comparable to that of Sāriputta,

441 MN I 386, 3–32; The Collection of the Middle Length Sayings Vol. II, pp. 50–53.

442 MN I 387, 2–4; The Collection of the Middle Length Sayings Vol. II, p. 53.

the chief disciple of the Buddha, who several times declared his belief in the Buddha in different ways.[443] In the discourses, Sāriputta described in detail how the Buddha was the best spiritual teacher by exaggerating his teachings into different points.[444] At another place,[445] having declared the belief in the Buddha, he was asked by the Buddha why and how he stated so. He then explained the Buddha with confidence what he understood. The ability to exaggerate the qualities or the teachings is the demonstration of 'knowledge' that the person has about the belief. The more he has acquired, the more he can demonstrate to others.

The ability to exaggerate Buddha's quality conforms to the meaning of stock phrases (3) denoting to the declaration of the belief, in which the hearer had understood and evaluated the Buddha's dhamma revealed from the sermon before the decision to go for refuge to the Three Jewels and to become a Buddhist. The praise is thus reasonably given from the quality of followership that the people decided to become Buddha's follower, as they had known and realised the significance of the Buddha and his teaching. In parallel, the respond is based on their personal impression that is reasonable and explainable. This shows that the "religious experience" in Buddhism is based on individual understanding of how the sermon and/or the teacher is worthy for him. The praise can be observed as the impression that the follower had for the teacher.

4.2.1.2 King Pasenadi

King Pasenadi (MN89) was another non-monastic follower[446] who described the Buddha's qualities in different ways. The king ruled the Kosala Empire, where the Buddha spent the majority of his lifetime in the propagation of his doctrine, as his empire is often mentioned in the background of Nikāya discourses. King Pasenadi's praises to the Buddha in several occasions are collected in the Pāli canon.[447] Significantly, one of his speeches

443 Cf. p. 154.
444 Dialogues of the Buddha Part III, pp. 95 ff.
445 Dialogues of the Buddha Vol. III, pp. 95–110; The Book of the Kindred Sayings. Vol. V, pp. 138–140.
446 The Book of the Kindred Sayings, Vol. I, p. 93–96.
447 MN87, MN88, MN89, MN90.

became the text of a discourse, which the Buddha called *dhammacetiya* "pagoda of dhamma" and assigned his community of monastic followers to learn by heart. In the discourse, the king, who was reminded to the Buddha by the peace of his garden, visited the Buddha at his place. At arrival, the king prostrated himself with his head on the Buddha's feet. The Buddha seemed surprised by the act, asked for the reason. The king then answered why he paid the Buddha with so high respect in form of praise, which concerns the eight following themes:[448]

1. The king was impressed by the ascetic practice of the Buddha's community in which the monastic followers remained in the ascetic vows through their life, while it was not always so in other ascetic communities;
2. He was impressed by the unity in the Buddha's community, in which the followers treated to one another as if they were brother, while it was not always so in some siblings;
3. He was impressed by the followers' appearance in that they looked physically and mentally healthy, while it was not so to some ascetics outside the Buddha's community;
4. He was impressed by the Buddhist assembly hearing a sermon from the Buddha that was very quiet, without any noise of cough and sneeze; whereas, he, who was the king of the Empire, was sometimes in his assembly interrupted by his people;
5. He was impressed by the Buddha's ability to tame some clever worriers into calamity, although they liked to attack other teachers in debate;
6. He was impressed by the ability to convert some clever worriers, Brahmins, merchants, and mendicants to be a follower in Buddha's order, who later became able followers, although they had attacked other teachers in debate;
7. He was impressed by the behaviour of two of his servants showing a great reverence to the Buddha: they talked to each other about the Buddha's dhamma and had their head to the Buddha's direction and their feet to him, although they worked and received money and property from him;
8. He was impressed by the Buddha's age of 80, which is similar to him.

448 The Collection of the Middle Length Sayings Vol. II, pp. 302–307.

The praise shows the qualities of the Buddha and his community, which were the reasons why the king believed in and respected to the Buddha with his head. As described by the king, he was surprised about the Buddha by the monastic community, which was distinctively stable, unbelievably quiet, respectable, etc. These were the impressing images of the Buddha and the community shining to the people outside the community like to the king. At the sight, the people were convinced that the community was virtuous and therefore worthy of reverence. It is noticeable that the *knowledge* manifested in the praising text clearly shows that it is an impression with the external aspects of the Buddha and his community in comparison with that of other spiritual teachers. The good image of community and personnel, shining wisdom in the ability to control people, etc. was all surprising for an observer like him. From this fact, it can be surmised that the king could declare the followership under the Buddha, although he had never heard a sermon from the Buddha.

There is a reason to think that King Pasenadi should not know very much about the Buddha and his teaching. In Kaṇṇakaṭṭhalasutta (MN90), the king asked some questions reflecting his interests, which do not concern the points in the Buddha's doctrine, viz. questions about people, deities, and/or Brahman. In Piyajātikasutta (MN87), the king was very surprised by the Buddha's doctrine about the suffering explained by his Queen Mallikā. The evidences clearly indicate that the king was the follower who despite revering the Buddha greatly did not know very much about his teaching. Moreover, his image in the Nikāya discourses rather shows that he was neutral about the belief and doctrine and therefore paid respect to every religious teacher equally. He treated the Buddha with a great respect as well as other religious teachers.[449] He was mentioned as the king who agreed with the companionship of wise and good men.[450] However, his attitudes and behaviours with respect to the Buddha were significant to the Buddha's community that his verbal reverence was transmitted in the tradition until nowadays.

449 The Book of the Discipline Vol. I, p. 69. King Pasenadi of Kosala Empire probably held the politics of religious tolerance like King Bimbisāra of Magadha Empire did. See the royal declaration at his coronation, which a monk claimed in asking for royal wood to build his living place.

450 Malalasekera, Dictionary of Pāli Proper Name. Vol. II, p. 169.

The comparison between the praise of the king and Upāli clearly points to the two different levels of profoundness in knowing the Buddha and his teaching that tradition presented through the two characters. Upāli, as example of the Buddhist in the first category, when asked why he believed in the Buddha, profoundly demonstrated his knowledge in the purity of the Buddhahood and the preciousness of his teaching. King Pasenadi, as example of the second category, believed in the Buddha because of the external characters shining distinctively from the Buddha, his teaching and his followers.

4.2.2 Non-Verbal Expression

Together with the verbal expression of respect, there was non-verbal expression, a social manner paid to virtuous people. It is said that the non-verbal expression is the performative language connected with religious action or ritual.[451] The gesture as communicated between religious people are the aggregation of symbols implying some meaning about the attitude, respect, and thought of the person who performs it in interaction to another person.[452] The gesture of respect may be a symbol of acceptance in the society. Especially, from those who are from other religious communities.

As the text implies, Buddha received the respects from his followers as well as other people who were not the followers. They ordinarily gave to the Buddha different gestures such as *añjali*, a gesture of hands with respect, declaration of name and family name, prostration, etc. while some people may not pay any respect to the Buddha.[453] The respect may be expressed by giving the highest seat. The Buddha was normally invited by his followers

---

451 Olson, Religious Studies, p. 240.

452 Ibid., p. 208.

453 The scene, in which a group of Brahmins visited the Buddha, was described with a stock phrase: "Some of them bowed to the Blessed One and took their seats on one side; some of them exchanged with him the greetings and compliments of politeness and courtesy, and then took their seat on one side; some of them called out their name and family, and then took their seats on one side; and some of them took their seats on one side in silence." From the description, some Bramins paid respect to the Buddha while some of them did not. DN4, DN5, DN23, DN32, MN35, MN41, MN42, MN150.

as well as ascetics outside the Sangha to take a higher seat, showing that he received a social acceptance in that he possessed a better or higher status in some way. One may assess the quality of themselves in comparison to others and behave appropriately due to it. As Upāli (MN56) was a follower of the Buddha who attained the experience of *Dhammacakkhu*, he regarded himself 'higher' than Nigantha Nāṭaputta, his former teacher. He thus took the high seat and did not care for the coming of his former teacher, Nigantha Nāṭaputta. The story shows that a gesture of respect in context of Nikāya discourse significantly relates to one's assessment as to whether the manner is appropriate to another person and in which extent they should do. Buddha as depicted in the text was the worthiest person for respect because of his superiority.

Along these lines, a challenge to the Buddha might take place when a person did not show an appropriate reverence to him. Ambaṭṭha (DN3), for example, did not realise how the Buddha was worthy of respect under the impression that the Buddha was not a Brahmin as he was. Therefore, he paid no respect to the Buddha appropriately, which showed the attention to challenge the Buddha. The Buddha then attacked him by blaming his knowledge of social manner that he did not behave appropriately in front of the religious leaders. The debate continued in a more serious way to reveal that the ancestor of the young Brahmin's family was originally not the true Brahmin but a servant of the king who was one of the Buddha's ancestors. The outcome shows the disadvantage of the inappropriate manner to the Buddha, ascribed to be the holy person in the context. Another example is Māgandiya, the mendicant, who said something impolite about Buddha, so the Buddha came to him for a debate.[454] To avoid a challenge with him, therefore, it seemed necessary for the people outside the Buddha's order to pay him a worthy respect. Behaviours and attitudes of the non-followers in this fashion imply the Buddha's superiority among the religious communities, as the tradition pictured the Buddha.

Like the verbal expression of respect, there is some significant difference in the degree of appreciation to the Buddha's qualities between the Buddhist in the first category and in the second category, as exemplified

454 The Collections of Middle Length Sayings Vol. II, pp. 181–182.

by Brahmāyu (MN91) and Soṇadaṇḍa (DN4) in comparison. Mentioned in the last chapter, with the trust in the treatise of signs of Great Man[455] Brahmāyu became quickly faithful and even more confident in the Buddhahood and the truthfulness of the sermon. Seeing the Buddha for the first time, the Brahmin paid a high reverence to the Buddha, even in front of his pupils. In contrast, Soṇadaṇḍa, who was at the end converted into Buddhist, paid the Buddha the respect in a limited way, especially in front of his pupil. With acceptance of the Buddha's wisdom from the answer, Soṇadaṇḍa became a follower and offered the Buddha and his community a meal at home. However, he asked the Buddha for an understanding that his respect given to him was necessarily limited to some extent so that the pupils still respected him as their teacher. [456] There, he explained the four gestures, which he symbolized his respect of the Buddha as pupil.

> "If then when I am seated in the assembly I stretch forth my joined palms in salutation, let the venerable Gotama accept that from me as a rising up from my seat. And if when I am seated in the assembly I take off my turban, let the venerable Gotama accept that from me as a salutation with my head. ... If then when mounted on my chariot, I bend down low the staff of my goad, let the venerable Gotama accept that from me as if I had got down, And if, when mounted on my chariot, I should wave my hand, let the venerable Gotama accept that from me as if I had bowed low in salutation."[457]

The Brahmin's request about the expression of respect shows that the expression of respect to spiritual teacher outside the Brahmin was dangerous to his status of teacher accepted in his Brahmin society. From the beginning of the conversation with the Buddha, he was worried about the defeat and losing face in the assembly.[458] The request to limit the expression of respect to the Buddha might imply the same worry. This is absolutely opposite to Brahmāyu, who paid a great respect to Buddha in front of his pupils.

The degree of reverence expressed to the Buddha is found relevant to the *process* in the development of belief in the Buddha. In case of Soṇadaṇḍa,

455 See detail in 3.1.1.2.
456 Sumaṅgalavilāsinī, Part 1, p. 293. Commentary explains that he was not sincere (kuhaka) to revere the Buddha.
457 Dialogues of the Buddha Part I, p. 158.
458 Manné, Debates and Case Histories in the Pali Canon, p. 25.

denoted by the stock phrases (3) (4) (6), he had the belief in the Buddha simply in some degree: he understood and realised the meaning of the teaching and acknowledged the Buddha's superiority in wisdom. However, Soṇadaṇḍa had not been convinced that the doctrine belonged to the Buddha, the legendary person in the treatise of Brahmins. Therefore, his belief in the Buddha was not emotionally strong and forceful to the extent that he would completely pay the respect to the Buddha with head. Another Brahmin teacher, Brahmāyu, dared to reveal his belief in the Buddha in public because he had no doubt about the Buddhahood and his doctrine.

This indicates a reflection from the discourse: the declaration of belief in the Buddha was more important than other 'expressions.' Buddha acknowledged the way that Soṇadaṇḍa revered him limitedly as such and seemed to understand his life conditions that he could not behave like other followers. His agreement indicates the emphasis on the development of the person's knowledge about his doctrine than the official and accurate expression of act, ritual, or symbols in public.[459] Buddha rather paid attention to the former rather than the latter, so he supported people, including householders and other ascetics, to hear his sermon, understand, and accept what he had pointed. In this way, the people significantly became Buddhist despite still living in their former community. They might visit the Buddha after the talk. In the communication between them, Buddha was treated with respect as the superior teacher, which points to the acknowledgment of the people from different communities.

It may be concluded that the respectful reverence of Buddha's followers is rooted in the knowledge a follower has about the 'Buddhahood,' the concept of spiritual teacher who have been enlightened. As this knowledge is based on the former belief and background of the follower, the degree in expressing the reverence at the encounter of Buddhahood can be variant. Brahmāyu as example of the follower who had a profound belief in the Buddha from his traditional treatise could show his reverence to Buddha more expressly than Soṇadaṇḍa, who both accepted the Buddha's superiority from his answer and feared that the reverence to Buddha in public destroy his fame. The difference lies in the development of the belief in the Buddha, grounded in the

459 Cf. 3.3.3.

impression, belief, imagination, etc. about what the Buddha is. Soṇadaṇḍa's behaviour can be compared with some European Buddhists, who do not feel 'moved' in the reverence to some oriental teachers,[460] because they simply respect the ability. Their belief in the teachers is not inspired from an inner impression about the particularity of the spiritual teachers.

4.3 Religious Devotions

Devotion is sometimes the synonym of the term *religion*, as it is the manifestation of inner thoughts and feelings: affection, zealous attachment, piety, reverence, and faithfulness, to an object, a person, spirit. It is thus connected with both theistic religions, in which the feelings of faith are the crucial motivation of the people in the religious activities,[461] and atheistic religions, in which the feelings of belief and trust center at a charismatic teacher and his teaching.[462] In latter case, religious devotion is carried out in form of revering the person, when they are still alive, or their remains or relic, when they passed away. Religious devotion can be perceived as the result of "religious experience," i.e. after the hearer has developed the belief by realizing the significance of the dhamma as the truth, the Buddha as the truth discoverer. This impression can be the push to continue the devotions in relation to the Buddha and his teaching. In this way, the religious devotion as mentioned here is motivated by the hearer's personal knowledge and realization of how the dhamma and the Buddha is special and significant to reach the spiritual goal. In Buddhism, religious devotion is emphasized on the Buddha and things attributed to the Buddha, viz. his teaching and his Sangha. Devoting to these institutions, as tradition has it, lay followers receive the merit, which causes the happiness and luck in the next life.[463]

---

460 Hayes, A Buddhist's Reflection on Religious Conversion, pp. 31–32.

461 Kinsley, David; Narayanan, Vasudha, "Devotion" in Encyclopedia of Religion, (2005) Kinsley refused the concept of devotion in atheistic religions. "… In many of these schools there is no ultimate gracious deity whose grace will give salvation or liberation. Thus in the nontheistic traditions, philosophically speaking, devotion has no ultimate value as a path to liberation, nirvāṇa, or the final goal…"

462 Ibid, p. 2317.

463 Harvey, An Introduction to Buddhist Ethics, p. 18.

In the context of Nikāya discourse, where the order was itinerant, meeting the Buddha and his community was not easy. After the three-month retreat, in which they stopped at a place for rainy time, they wandered from place to place, from town to town, and from empire to empire. The arrival of the Buddha and his community in a town was thus good news for the people in the town, as his fame on the qualities and wisdom was widely spread. Only in this chance, the followers visited him at his place and heard sermons from him.[464] The rare occasion to meet the Buddha can be perceived from a Brahmin's remark that King Pasenadi was fortunate that the Buddha spent most of his lifetime in his empire.[465] It may not be very convenient for the follower to carry out religious activities with the Buddha and his community, unlike Buddhist nowadays who can visit a monk at a temple located in their community.

In the text, it often occurred that some hearer gave food to the Buddha and the community of Sangha after the debate or the conversation. In this chance, talks and sermons might occur once more for the acquaintanceship.[466] Manné considered that the meal was a reward for the winner, as an alternative in case that the loser was not converted.[467] She cited the statement from the incident that a Jain ascetic who had lost the Buddha in a debate invited the Buddha for the meal, by giving the meal that he would receive from his followers to the Buddha and his community. Considering the debate in terms of competition for winner and loser, she was right at the point. However, the author thinks that the meal could not compensate the vow to become a follower of the competitant and it should be merely the chance for the loser to develop an acquaintanceship

464 I do not think that community of Sangha contacted the laity when they had settled down in monastery in a certain place. The contact could always take place, as long as the Buddha and his community were still in the social circle of Samaṇa-Brahmin and not only living in the thick forest. That the monks had to live on the alms from the people means a possibly following outcome that the monks and the householder might be familiar to each other and have some talks about the monk's doctrine and practice. This can lead to a debate or an exchange of understanding about the doctrine.

465 The Collection of the Middle Length Sayings Vol. II, pp. 397–398.

466 Dialogues of the Buddha Part I, p. 134.

467 Manné, Debates and Case Histories in the Pali canon, p. 26.

with the winner after the debate. The Jain ascetic did not show an act of embarrassment after the debate. Instead, he complimented the Buddha and apologized for the unsuitability that he had done to him. He told his lay follower to prepare the food, which would be given to him, to the Buddha. This fact points to his acceptance of Buddha's superiority. He was later familiar with the Buddha and debated with him some times,[468] which ends with satisfaction, although it appears that he was never the convert and became Buddhist. Therefore, giving a meal to the Buddha and the Sangha should be done rather with the willingness than obligation according to the rule that she claimed.

The author categorizes the devotion into two categories: the donation of food and materials to the Sangha and the religious education for the development of spiritual knowledge and practice.

4.3.1 Donation

Donation is a common religiosity that is often mentioned in Pāli discourses. As Buddha's monastic follower had to beg food to live, lay follower gave food and materials to them. In this relation, donation from lay follower is carried out with the realization of the virtues of the monastic life and the willingness to support the life.

Buddha and his monastic followers were wandering mendicants who had no certain settlement and no profession to earn an income. The only profession he often claimed, when he was asked, was his 'noble work' in developing the spiritual mind, which outcome is the liberation from the worldly sufferings.[469] No wonder, he had to live on the alms and donation offered by the householders, who saw the importance of his *work*. However, the Buddha had some limits on the acceptance of donation. The reaction from the Buddha that refused a food from a Brahmin who liked the Buddha's answer clearly indicates that the Buddha did not preach for food.[470] He would accept the offering only when the giver saw the *specialness* in the Buddha and in his sermon by himself. As the precept to

468 MN 35, MN 36.

469 The Group of Discourses Vol. I, pp. 4–6, 12.

470 Ibid., p. 13.

observe, the Buddha forbade his monastic follower to receive money and property from householders.[471] It is understandable that he distinguished his order from Brahmins, who earned money from an instruction. Along these lines, the meal after the debate should not be understood in terms of the reward that the Buddha would accept from the *loser*.[472] Rather, it was the loser's intention to offer the Buddha the meal for he had seen how able and important the Buddha was in the debate and the sermon.[473] It was also another chance to get to know the Buddha more.

Donation after hearing a sermon occasionally occured. It is mentioned in two discourses: DN3, in which Pokkharasādi invited the Buddha and his community to his home and MN56, in which Upāli stopped the contact and donation to the people in his former school in order to devote completely to the Buddha and his community. Pokkharasādi (DN3) was recognized in Brahmin's society as the follower of the Buddha.[474] He invited into his home Buddha and his followers and let his children become acquainted with them. From the decision it can be implied that the Brahmin had seen the advantage of a conversation with the Buddha. Therefore, he had the house open for the Buddha, so that his children might have the opportunity to know the Buddha, as he did. Upāli (MN56) particularly supported the Buddha and his community by having his home welcome for every follower. He kept giving the ascetics in his former school as the Buddha had suggested him, but he did not invite them into his house any longer. The expression shows the intention that the Brahmin and Upāli had their devotion specific to the Buddha, as tradition communicated the idea in the discourse that the followers had achieved the experience of *Dhammacakkhu* and had unshakable belief in the Three Jewels. Hence, they were not interested to make merit outside the Buddha's order. The decision is mentioned as a good quality of upāsaka/upāsikā.[475]

---

471 The Book of the Discipline Vol. II, pp. 53–70; Dialogues of the Buddha Vol. I, pp. 3–13.

472 Manné, Debates and Case Histories in the Pali canon, p. 156.

473 Ibid., p. 26.

474 Dialogues of the Buddha Part I, p. 147.

475 The Book of the Gradual Sayings, pp. 151–152.

Apart from the two lay followers, there are other cases that the hearers were satisfied with the Buddha's teaching and offered materials to the monastic followers who had delivered them the sermon: Ānanda (MN52, MN88) and Udena (MN94). In the first discourse (MN52), Ānanda while living in Pāṭaliputta, was visited by Dasama, a householder from Aṭṭhaka, Vesāli, to ask a question about a doctrine.[476] Similarly in the second discourse (MN88), Ānanda was visited by King Pasenadi of Kosala Empire to ask him for a confirmation on Buddha's decorum that he had heard.[477] Both hearers were satisfied very much by the answer and thus gave a precious gift to Ānanda. The householder invited Ānanda and his pupils in Pāṭaliputta and in Vesāli for a meal and gave them the clothes, gave Ānanda the clothes and built him five hundred of pavilions, while the king gave him a precious cloth that he had received from King Ajātasattu. In the third discourse, the incident occurred long after the Buddha's death. Udena, walking contemplating in a garden in Banaras, was met by accident in the garden by Ghoṭamukha Brahmin, who was in town for a business. The Brahmin asked him about the right ordination.[478] The answer given by Udena seemed to satisfy him very much that he declared of going to the monk for refuge. The monk refused at once and introduced him that the Buddha was their teacher. The Brahmin then declared the belief in the Three Jewels for refuge as well as offered a portion of his income to the monks. The Brahmin, whose offer was refused, then built for the monastic community with the money a canteen in Pāṭaliputta.

The great donation as such was not regular in every discourse. It is noticeable that the two householders Dasama and Ghoṭamukha who offered the order a great gift were visitors who did a business in another town and met a famous disciple of the Buddha for a conversation there. The great donation in a special meeting might be the reason why the tradition mentions the activity in a discourse. In comparison, a great donation of some Buddhists in the towns was not particularly mentioned in Nikāya discourses, perhaps because giving food daily was regular. In the towns, some Buddhist millionaires should have regularly donated

476 The Collection of the Middle Length Sayings Vol. II, p. 14.
477 Ibid., p. 297.
478 Ibid., p. 350.

the monastic community food and requisites. The pavilions and gardens under their names in the towns revealed that people in the town also supported the community.[479]

Understood in terms of Taves, the donation in context is the donation given to the thing and person considered *special*, viz. good and wise. First, the giver had seen from the sermon the meaning and significance of the teaching that the monastic followers learned, practiced, and transmitted to him. Second, he had seen the advantage and the necessity of the sermon to transmit to the people in the next generations, so he donated to support the succession of the people who carry out this activity. There may be other reasons concerning the *specialness* considered by the giver. At this point, the remark on compliment to Ānanda given by the householder Dasama is interesting: "*Now, revered sir, members of other sects will look about for a fee for the teacher, but why should not I pay honour to the venerable Ānanda?*"[480] This shows that the donation was the worship given to the teacher, just like the *dakkhiṇā* (or *dakṣiṇā* in Sanskrit) given to Brahmin his instruction or ritual. Buddhist order finally seemed to live on the gifts as the exchange of dhamma that they had learned and practiced from the Buddha, in spite of the fact that the Buddha had originally rejected this intention.

However, there is a difference between donation in the Brahmin culture and donation in the Buddhist culture. Theoretically, the donation occurs only from the hearer's arbitrariness. There is no statement or rule in the Nikāya discourse that gift must be returned for the sermon.[481] Instead, Buddha rejected that clearly and even hoped that his pupils lived on the gift from the belief and trust in their learning and practice for the spiritual aim. Monks *by chance* teach, explain, or give a sermon to people. Therefore, the image that monks received the donation in return is unavoidable.

479 King Bimbisāra built Veḷuvana in Rājagaha, Subhadda or Anāthapiṇḍika built Jetavana inSāvatthī, Visākhā Migāramātā built Pubbārāma in Sāvatthī, Ambapāli built Ambapālivana in Vesāli, as well as some millionaires built pavilions and gardens in Kosambi for monks.

480 The Collection of the Middle Length Sayings Vol. II, p. 18.

481 Dakkhiṇāvibhaṅgasutta (MN142), in which the outcome of giving to different people and in different ways is exaggerated, does not recognise giving as the duty of the lay follower.

This is found in the relation between the monastic and the non-monastic followers in that monastic plays the role of learner and practitioner while the non-monastic the role of supporter.

4.3.2 Religious Education

Religious education is a kind of religious devotion to the learning and practice of religious doctrine such as meditation.[482] The term may be perceived in terms of religious activity or educational activity. In the former case, it is the process of nurture for faith development; whereas, in the latter case, it is an activity designed to increase understanding of an important dimension of human existence and to encourage cross-cultural understanding.[483] In Buddhism, religious education is significant both in terms of religious activity and educational activity. Tradition first ascribed the teaching of the Buddha to the *thing deemed special* that made the follower in the process of conversion.[484] With the specialness of the teaching, people are attracted to join the community and to learn and practice more for their own spiritual development on the path. The religious education thus preserves the first experience and develops it further on. To carry out the activity, lay follower depends on Buddha and his disciples for the knowledge and experience about the teaching. Most basic 'education' in Buddhism is the attempt to control actions under some rules called *sīla* 'precepts' until the ideal actions are finally usual. *Sīla* in this way, like education, is not commandment, but rather a promise or vow to oneself to develop himself better, more spiritual, due to the Buddha's teaching.[485]

In this perspective, the community consists of two components: teacher(s) and follower(s), ranging from the Buddha to the senior teachers and the 'chief disciples' to the ordinary followers. Buddha is the great teacher of the community, leading the followers and playing the main role of *satthā* the spiritual teacher, as he had discovered the truth by himself and brought

482 Kinsley and Narayanan, "Devotion" in: Encyclopedia of Religion, p. 2320.
483 Halstead, "Religious Education" in: Encyclopedia of Religion, p. 7731.
484 See detail in 4.1.
485 Cf. Harvey, an Introduction to Buddhist Ethics, p. 80.

others to see the same truth.[486] His followers are called *sāvaka/sāvikā* 'hearer' denoting to bhikkhu, bhikkhunī, upāsaka, and upāsikā in terms of Buddha's four groups of followers.[487] As a result, the followership under the Buddha points to the knowledge about Buddha's doctrine that a follower, including a non-monastic follower, should have. King Pasenadi was angry with Queen Mallikā because she as a lay follower of the Buddha could not explain him a teaching of the Buddha. At once, she ordered a servant to visit the Buddha for the explanation of the requested teaching to tell the king, which finally satisfied him.[488] The status of lay follower 'upāsaka/upāsikā' as implied from the text may relate in some way to the religious knowledge, as the name upāsaka/upāsikā, which parallels the Upaniṣad with the literal meaning 'sitting in the nearby,' may imply that they are near the community for 'the Buddha's teaching.'[489]

In Dīgha- and Majjhima-nikāya, there are sixteen discourses, describing a conversation, in which another participant is an ascetic or practitioner from other religious communities. As Buddha and his community were itinerant, a visit to the Buddha and his community took place when they arrived at a town, but in some occasion, the Buddha and his monastic followers might visit their acquaintances for a conversation.[490] In visiting other ascetic schools, for example, the Buddha and his chief disciples received a warm welcome and then exchanged views about a doctrine. Occasionally, they visited some familiar lay follower, who was old or on sickbed, at home. Anāthapiṇḍika (MN143), for example, received a visit from Sāriputta and Ānanda at home. There, he was sermonized by Sāriputta to relieve from the physical suffering. The visits indicate the familiarity and good relationship between the people.

As depicted in the discourses, a visitor outside the order often had a purpose to ask a question, which one got from others and they wanted to get a direct answer from the Buddha. Oṭṭhaddha Licchavi (DN6), for example, paid the Buddha a visit because he had received news from

486 Stoesz, The Buddha as Teacher, p. 140.
487 See detail in 1.4.1.
488 The Middle Length Sayings Vol. II, p. 293. Cf. 3.2.1.2.
489 See detail in 1.4.1.
490 For example, MN76, MN143.

Sunakkhatta Licchavi about some experience in the contemplation during his ascetic life in Buddha's community and wanted to find out the facts from the Buddha. In the conversation, Oṭṭhaddha Licchavi told the Buddha what he had heard and asked the Buddha whether the experience is true. The Buddha then removed his doubt and clarified in detail the contemplation in his doctrine, which was more profound. Another example, Pañcakaṅga (MN78) heard from a mendicant a doctrine about goodness. With a doubt about the doctrine, he went to the Buddha and told the doctrine to him. The Buddha then explained why the doctrine should be rejected and gave him another answer. The raised examples show that the Buddha explained the problem that the people had asked him. But still, he ordinarily preached to his monastic community. To the individual hearer, monastic and lay alike, the topic of the delivered sermon is mostly determined by the interest of the follower who came to him for a question.

With the interest and activeness to visit the Buddha for the talks, householder could learn advance doctrines, which the Buddha ordinarily preached in his community. Pañcakaṅga was a lay follower who was interested in the doctrine. He appeared in several discourses in a conversation with the Buddha, chief disciples, and other mendicants.[491] In the discourses, he heard an advance teaching such on *kusala-akusala* "wholesome and unwholesome (action)" and *cetovimutti* "liberation with mind." With the interest, he was known among the heterodoxy ascetics that he was a Buddha's follower. His story signifies his acquaintanceship with the order as well as his interest on the doctrine and practice as if he was a monastic follower. Similarly, Ghaṭikāra (MN81), who had to take care of his blind parents, was in the era of Kassapa Buddha a lay follower who supported the Buddha and his community closely. The people exemplify the pious follower who had no chance to join the ascetic life because of some responsibility and therefore often went to the community for the spiritual knowledge.

At this point, it is not accurate to conclude that Buddha forbade his follower to teach the householder the spiritual doctrine.[492] In the conversation

491 The Collection of the Middle Length Sayings Vol. II, MN 78 pp. 222–228; Vol. III, MN 127 pp. 190–197.

492 Conze, A Short History of Buddhism, p. 53.

with Anāthapiṇḍika, Sāriputta and Ānanda tried to console Anāthapiṇḍika, who was very ill, not to regret the missing chance of hearing a sermon when he had been healthy.[493] Relating to the answer, the statement was considered to be supported with the monastic discipline that they are forbidden to instruct word by word to a person who is not an order member and to tell the person about the offences committed by them.[494] The author thinks that this is a misunderstanding about the dhamma, which has several meanings.[495] Despite the same designation 'dhamma', it may denote the spiritual teaching or mistakes in living monastic life. The latter dhamma was forbidden to any people outside the order because it could disgrace the order and the image of other followers. Upāsaka/upāsikā may hear the teaching if he *actively put a question* to the Buddha or to a monastic follower.[496] In case of Anāthapiṇḍika, it should be that the man did not ask for a teaching or an explanation about the doctrine. Unlike Pañcakaṅga the carpenter or others who often visited the Buddha for a talk, he involved in the donation, as mentioned in Etadaggapāli.[497]

Some of the followers in the order were successful in the education of the spiritual path, and therefore able to give a suggestion to nuns or householders. Several chief disciples were good representative for the Buddha in giving explanation or removing a doubt with personality and competency

493 Na kho gahapati gihīnaṃ odātavasanānaṃ evarūpī dhammikathā paṭibhāti pabbajitānaṃ, evarūpī dhammikathā dhammikathā paṭibhātīti: "Reasoned Talk such as this, householder, does not usually occur for householders clad in white. It is for those that have gone forth, householder, that reasoned talk such as this (usually) occurred." The Collection of the Middle Length Sayings Vol. III, p. 313.

494 Conze, A Short History of Buddhism, p. 20.

495 Cf. Gethin, He Who Sees Dhamma Sees Dhammas, pp. 516–521: Dhamma in the canon has several meanings: (i) teaching, (ii) good conduct or behaviour, (iii) truth, (iv) nature, (v) mental or physical state or thing. In this context, however, Dhamma represents the nature, which occurs under some conditions. An unsuitable behaviour is also regarded a kind of 'Dhamma,' as it simply occurs under the conditions.

496 Discourses on householder's talk about the spiritual life point to the permission granted for the lay follower to learn the doctrine.

497 The Book of the Gradual Sayings, Vol. I., p. 23.

in teaching.[498] However, it appears sometimes that they were not successfully able to deliver a lay follower a suitable sermon. Ānanda could not satisfy Gopakamoggallāna with his answer.[499] Sāriputta visited Dhanañjāni and preached him for a rebirth in Brahman world with the understanding that a Brahmin should have preferred the world to the noble path in the Buddha's doctrine. The Buddha's question to Sāriputta at the end of the discourse indicates that the Brahmin might have reached the noble path if he had been directed with an appropriate sermon.[500] The mistake in the instruction emphasizes the significance of *Ānusāsanīyapāṭihāriya* "miracle of education" that the Buddha had.[501] Buddha is thus regarded as *satthā devamanussānaṃ* "teacher of gods and humans."

The conversation between the followers may concern a suggestion on giving some advantageous tip for the benefit of the community. Vesavaṇṇa (DN32), the leader of the demon,[502] went to the Buddha to give him a mantra for the practitioners in the Buddha's doctrine, so that they were saved from some evil demons who were not the followers and might disturb their practice. Kevaḍḍha (DN11), as another example, who was a lay follower in Nālanda, suggested the Buddha to perform a miracle for the gaining of more followers as well as more belief from the people in the town. Responding to him, Buddha refused it and explained why he did not accept the idea. The intention of the people implied in the discourse manifests that they wanted to support the learning and practice of the doctrine including the propagation. The leader of the demons wished the Buddhist practitioners could practice the doctrine without disturbance from his subordinates, so he suggested the Buddha the protective mantra against the demons. Likewise, Kevaḍḍha, the Buddhist householder, wanted to see the Buddha's community established more firmly in his

498 Langer, Sermon Studies and Buddhism, p. 1: footnote no. 2.

499 The Collection of the Middle Length Sayings Vol. III, p. 65. The Brahmin did not seem to understand Ānanda's explanation and thus asked the monk again. At the end, there is no statement showing the Brahmin's satisfaction with the answer.

500 The Collection of the Middle Length Sayings Vol. II, pp. 378–379.

501 See 4.3.2.

502 Although Vessavaṇṇa was not a human, his case exemplifies the role of lay follower in the Buddha's community.

town. This clearly points to their supportive mind to the community: although they did not play a direct role on this, i.e. they were not a member of the order.

The relationship between the lay and the monastic followers about the religious education clearly shows that the monastic order was fundamentally the center where any follower, especially those who were actively interested in the Buddha's doctrine, freely came for the development of the knowledge and the exchange of ideas. The 'conversion' was simply the declaration of accepting Buddha as the teacher and his teaching as the truth. It symbolically means the intention to get to know and achieve more on the spiritual path. After that, the people who had declared the followership might be inactive or active to foster the path. If they did by paying visit to the Buddha or his disciple for knowledge and practice, they would make the progress on the path. Buddha and the Sangha were regarded as the *Kalyāṇamitta* "good friend," suggesting the beneficial things to the people.[503] Conversation was the way to exchange the thoughts that lead to one's better understanding on the topic and even to more interest to join the community. The finding illuminates the word *sāvaka* 'hearer' in that the follower began with and fostered the spiritual path with the hearing of the sermon. This is *paratoghosa* "voice from others" playing a significant role in the development of spirituality.[504]

4.4 Second Discussion

Religiosity in Relation to Monastic Order as the Composite Ascription to Dhamma

In this part, the discussion deals with the religious activities as the result of composite ascription. The theme to consider is the direction and the aim of the religious belief and activity. As Buddhism analysed into three pillars under the name, "Three Jewels" – Buddha, Dhamma, and Sangha– the discussion is made in relation to the Three Jewels.

The stock phrases (3) (4) (5) or (6) denoting the "conversion" in Buddhism clearly indicate the symbolic meaning of simple ascription

503 The Book of the Kindred Sayings, Part V, 29 ff.
504 The Collections of the Middle Length Sayings Vol. I, p. 353.

that the hearer, after having understood and evaluated the teaching and the Buddha in (3), greatly appreciated the meaning of the teaching and the significance of Buddha. Realizing these facts, the hearer revered to Buddhist institutions by declaring to go to the Three Jewels for refuges (4) and asking the Buddha to become a follower (5) or (6). The two activities imply the Buddhist's mind that he trusted in the Buddha and agreed to the consensus on the spiritual path that the Buddha had pointed. The mental process represented in the stock phrases after the hearing of the Buddha's sermon may be shortly deemed special that the intention to follow the Buddhist life was canceled with other reasons. The arising religious experience as implied in the discourse is not a determined experience in that the following life after the experience must continue on this religious path. The hearer self may derogate from it. The religious experience is therefore uncertain, seemingly temporary, and perhaps true for the hearer at a certain time. Several hearers became a monastic follower living the ascetic life for a while and decided to leave the life when they had found that the experience they had deemed special at first and inspired the religious life was not special for them any longer.[505]

4.4.1 The Three Jewels

Following the religious experience in hearing the Buddha's sermon, the hearer was connected with the main pillars of the 'religion': Buddha, Dhamma, and Sangha. First, he evaluated the body of knowledge achieved from the conversation or sermon. In this process, the hearer could assume and acknowledge the Buddha's superiority in his wisdom in that the Buddha had discovered the truth by himself. The hearer, comparing to himself, should realise that he was much inferior to the Buddha in this respect. Thus, he bowed to the superiority. This may manifest in worship and devotion in various forms. People might offer a praise describing the wisdom in front of the Buddha or to other people while many of them may visit the Buddha to prove the fact. These behaviours suggest the acknowledgment of Buddha's

---

505 The Collection of the Middle Length Sayings Vol. II, p. 236. See 4.1.1.

superior ability and wisdom, demonstrated in the text. The model of the unfolding development from the religious experience to the worship can be constructed in this way.

Figure 16: From Understanding of Dhamma to the Conversion

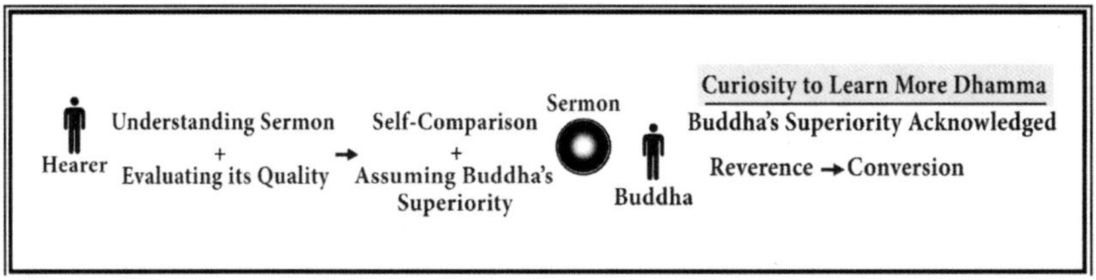

From the figure, during hearing the sermon the hearer followed the meaning of the sermon and at the same time evaluated the qualities implied from the sermon. Considering the qualities led to self-comparison and realization of the spiritual qualities of the Buddha and his teaching that the Buddha was the great teacher and his teaching was the truth. In this way, the hearer acknowledged the Buddha as spiritual teacher and had the reverent feelings for him and his teaching as expressed primarily in the admiration (3), followed by the declaration of going to the Three Jewels for refuges (4) and of followership under the Buddha (5) or (6) respectively. The acknowledgment that Buddha was the teacher implied an admiring feeling in (3) for the teaching (dhamma) and the teacher (Buddha), and a sense of curiosity to learn more the teaching and to get to know more the teacher. The declaration of followership is thus the thoughts expressed after engaging with the thing and the person deemed special for the re-engagement.

4.4.1.1 Buddha

In the development of the belief, Buddha was the ***first thing deemed special*** that attracted the hearer's interest to pay Buddha a visit in order to see and talk with him. The hearer might give admiration to the Buddha in several ways in relation to his dhamma, as seen in stock phrase (3) and compliments.[506]

506 Detail on the discussion, see 2.3.2.1.

Figure 17: Acknowledgment and Non-acknowledgment after sermon

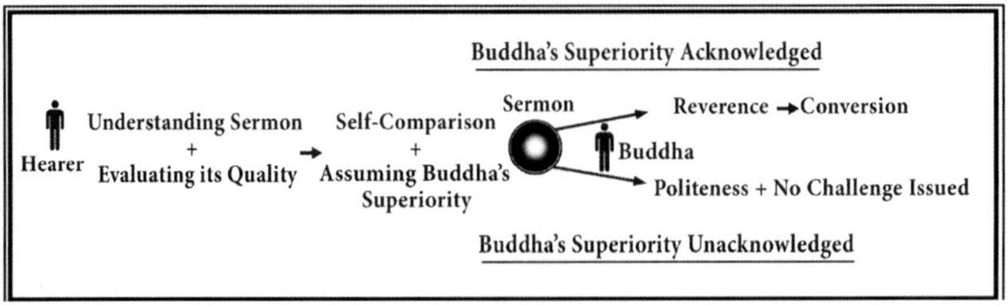

From the figure above, the acknowledgment of Buddha's significance and superiority found expression in the declaration of belief in the Three Jewels and conversion. Having seen the value of dhamma in relation to himself and to humankind, the hearer might think about the dhamma and Buddha in several ways from their background and understanding. Buddha was depicted in the text to be the enlightened teacher who taught the truthful dhamma; he had discovered the dhamma by himself and became a spiritual teacher; he was the person to whom the treatise mentioned that he was the real Buddha, etc. In this way, the Buddhists who had passed the process of conversion, which involved the understanding, evaluation, self-comparison, consideration of Buddha superiority, etc., expressed the feelings of respect to the Buddha and his teaching in different degrees, which can be found from their opinion about the Buddha and his dhamma.[507]

In case of the non-convert, the expression of acknowledging the Buddha's significance and superiority as the great teacher was not given. Buddha and his dhamma might not be considered important enough for them. This may come from the fact that the hearer might not completely understand the meaning of the sermon delivered by the Buddha. As followed, the hearer did not see the significance of the Buddha and so did not appreciate him. Some hearer might understand the meaning of the sermon that Buddha had delivered and realise the significance or superiority of the Buddha, but he decided not to become a follower with some reasons. For example, he still adhered to their old doctrine or old community. The discourse illustrates at this point with the picture that the hearer did not declare the followership

507 See 4.2.1.

and remained in the old community in spite of giving Buddha a compliment. They simply behaved polite and did no challenge to him.

4.4.1.2 Dhamma

Tradition presented the sermon text, the core message of the discourse, as the symbolic form of dhamma that Buddha presented to the hearer. In this relation, dhamma is viewed as the factor that affects to the belief of the hearer, to build up or strengthen the trust in the Buddha and to lessen or lose the trust in the former belief. At the moment of hearing the sermon, the hearer considers the teaching as the *thing deemed special* and had the *experience deemed special.* The more the hearer considered the teaching special, viz. the deep meaning in relation to himself and humankind, the more he realised the significance and the necessity that he had to become Buddha's follower in order to learn and practice the teaching.

Figure 18: Understanding of Dhamma in Relation to the Three Jewels

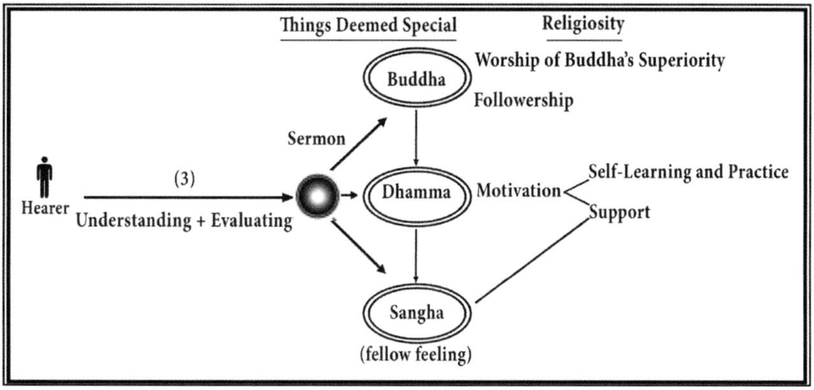

From the figure, the realization of the meaning and significance of the teaching finds expression in the conduct of religious activities concerning to the Buddha and the Sangha. Dhamma as the thing deemed special can be understood in terms of religious motivation to the decision to conversion in that it interests the hearer to learn and practice more. Having realised the significance of teaching, the hearer might become learner, practitioner, bearer, and transmitter of the dhamma and the representative of the Buddha in the delivery of sermon, as the dhamma was significant to be carried out further.

4.4.1.3 *Sangha*

As stated in the stock phrase (4) referring to homage to the three Jewels, Sangha is one of three pillars of Buddhism that the person to be a follower revered. Although in context of discourses, where Buddha delivered a sermon to a hearer Sangha did not involve with the religious experience and realization of the values, the stock phrase mentioned it as one of the Three Jewels. This may be an ascription in the later time, in which the monastic community became more significant and played an important role as representative of the Buddha in the propagation of the dhamma.[508] In order to develop the spiritual knowledge, followers must contact the monastic order and its members for the source of teachings—teacher of dhamma and practice. The importance of the monastic community is viewed from perspective of the followers.

Monastic order was significant to the followers even in Buddha's lifetime, as it was the community of Buddha's followers, where the followers shared the same goal and the same path. In the community, the followers could learn and share the knowledge and the experience in the practice with one another. Some of the members had been successful in reaching the spiritual goal and were in the position to give an explanation to others who were striving for the goal. In this way, the hierarchy was established within the community due to the person's level of spiritual success. Following the tradition of seniority, they paid the respect to a person with the higher spiritual quality. Along these lines, the *puthujjana* 'ordinary' people respected the *ariya* 'noble' people, and the noble people respected the higher noble people. Indeed, the status of monastic and non-monastic follower was a kind of hierarchical relationship, in which the non-monastic follower respected the other one for the sake of ascetic ideal, lifestyle, and the 'noble work.'[509] For these people, "*the attachment and confusion that they tend to breed must be overcome to achieve*

---

508 Oldenberg, Buddha, sein Leben, seine Lehre, seine Gemeinde, p. 112. In the footnote of the page, he remarked that the Buddhist refuges should be originally Buddha and Dhamma. Referring to Härtel (1956), p. 50, however, the third refuge is already mentioned in the Ashoka's edict of Bairat.

509 The act of respect that non-monastic follower makes for monastic follower shows the acceptance of superiority in social status and virtue.

spiritual liberation." Therefore, it is challenging to people who normally stick to the pleasure and thus admirable for those who defeat the desire to pleasure.[510] Furthermore, the realization of the significance of Buddha's teaching and practice might inspire the lay followers to follow the community and contribute to the order materially, so that the members of the order could completely devote on their noble work.[511]

Figure 19: From Hearing Sermon to Religiosity in Relation to the Order

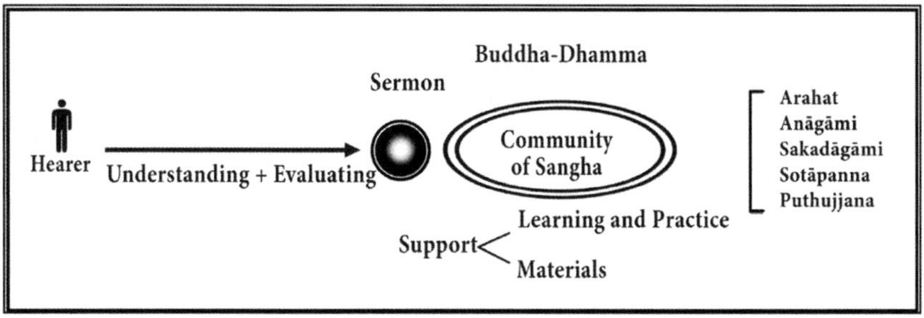

After the death of the Buddha, Sangha as representative of the Buddha should be the *thing deemed special* that the hearer could connect with the Buddha. First, monastic followers were the Buddha's devout followers who lived on the lifestyle once lived by the Buddha. Controlled by the discipline regulated for the community and the instruction from teacher, the disciplined followers behaved with decorum that impressed the people outside the community and attracted them to come to the community. Second, a monasic follower, having learned and practiced the Buddha's teaching, ably delivered a meaningful and impressive sermon. In this way, bhikkhu could be ascribed to be *person deemed special* in relation to the Buddha and his teaching. For example, he may be considered Arahat or skilful in some ways about the knowledge of dhamma and meditation. He was thus particularly revered by his pupils.[512]

---

510 Gross, Buddhism after Patriarchy, p. 31.

511 See 4.3.1.

512 Several monks nowadays in Thailand are ascribed by their pupils as Arahat with their knowledge about Dhamma, meditation, and decorum. Actually, nobody could know this fact.

Along these lines, the doctrine of merit in relation to the monastic order can be considered in term of the *goal deemed special* set for the happiness of the supporter, instead of Nibbāna. This is connected with the consideration of how the monastic followers were worthy in relation to the Buddha and the dhamma. Sangha was claimed as "*unsurpassed merit-field for the world*" which was worthy of sacrifice, hospitality, offerings, and veneration.[513] In this ideology, it is found that the Brahmanic notion was redirected and reinterpreted in accordance with the Buddhist values and goals.[514] The author is of the opinion that, if the finding is true, the monastic follower's earning of alms must have originally been based on householder's consideration and assessment that the group of mendicants was a good community and worthy of donation, before the claim of the fruit was 'propagandized' in the scripture.[515] The reason: Buddha's monastic follower is not in the position to call for or propagandize for any material support from householders. If we believe that the discourses were the result after composing and collecting the teachings through generations, it is possible that the 'propaganda' was the trace of the indoctrination after the redirection of the idea in an ancient context, in which the donation or *dakkhinā* was considered worthy for any good spiritual people. In response to this, they regarded themselves as a good practitioner for the deserving devotion from the householder. Finally, the monastic followers successfully indoctrinated householders in the new redirected idea of merit for the promotion of lay contribution to the order by committing the lay follower to this duty. The goal, as the hearer believed and imagined about the *dakkhinā*, was established in this religiosity. The donation devoted for the order has become an important doctrine in Theravada Buddhism, as stated in the Dānavibhaṅgasutta (MN142) and more emphasized in later tradition.

In summary, the donation and the idea of merit possibly relates to the idea of composite ascription in the context of Brahmanic culture, which could happen in two stages:

---

513 Harvey, An Introduction to Buddhist Ethics, pp. 21–22.

514 Amore, The Concept and Practice of Doing Merit in Early Theravāda Buddhism, p. 6: See chapter I. Puñña in Early Canonical Writings.

515 Cf. Freiberger, Der Orden in der Lehre, pp. 185–186.

First, the cult of merit to the order could theoretically happen as a result of having considered its significance in relation to the dhamma and the Buddha.[516] The monastic order was the community of spiritual people that the Buddha had established for the learning and succession of his doctrine about the appropriate lifestyle and spiritual practice for the liberation. In this way, people should be aware of the importance of the community if they see the importance of the dhamma and the Buddha. As the people saw the connection between the Buddha and the dhamma and the Sangha, they should try to support the community, in order to preserve the dhamma as long as possible. In sum, the follower ascribing the Buddha and his teaching for the specialness and therefore realised the importance of the monastic community and the necessity of supporting and preserving it.

Second, following the first stage, the activity in the first stage was assessed by the followers and the tradition as 'good,' and thus furthered for the goodness. In this way, the cult of merit to the order could gradually develop themselves without the *experience or* the right understanding about the Three Jewels and the connections. The people ascribed the specialness to the Three Jewels from their own understanding or personal belief. This means, the Buddha, the dhamma, and the Sangha, all were deemed as good, holy, spiritual, sacred etc. and thus appropriate and worthy of the donation or support. In this way, *the goal deemed special* set for the donation was changed into a desirable achievement that the donators might imagine from their world view. Benefit and happiness, which were often claimed as the goal of householder's life, could be ascribed to the goal headed in the donation and support of the Sangha. As a result, the donator without any knowledge about the Three Jewels might agree to worship and support the Three Jewels with the hope for desirable outcomes from the donation to the thing that they deem special.

The conclusion reminds us of the significance of understanding and realizing the meaning of teaching, which tradition symbolically presented in structure and pattern of discourse. It indicates that the truly *special thing* in the 'religion' is the *dhamma* that a discourse conveys for followers to learn and practice for their own spiritual development and liberation. Tracing the process of conversion, the hearing of the sermon is stereotypically connected

516 See 4.4.1.3.

with the Buddha and the Sangha. The Sangha is the community of fellows who share the same ideology and the same teacher. It has become more important, as the people pay attention and respect to the old generations who taught the teaching to them. The senior followers who had reached the spiritual attainment became the teachers of the monks in the next generation. The respect to the people finds expression in raising the community as another main institute of Buddhism, to which the Buddhists also worship like the Buddha. In this way, the Three Jewels are the social consensus connecting people together with the belief and activities that the people do alone or together. They are the instrument to check up the followership.[517]

The Three Jewels have become an object to worship in the tradition as appear in Kuddakapāṭha.[518] The commentary, Paramaṭṭhajotikā, attributes them to the gist of Buddhism, which the Buddha uttered before going forth at Isipatana in Banares *as the process of his ordination.*[519] The utterance significantly means "the pathway of entry into the Dispensation." This means, the Three Jewels are symbolically perceived as 'dhamma' the natural rule of the world that combats, dispels, carries off and stops the fear, anguish, suffering, unhappiness, etc. To speak clearly, going to the Three Jewels for refuge means "the arising of cognisance with confidence therein and giving preponderance thereto, from which defilement is eliminated and eradicated and which occurs in the mode of taking that as the highest value, whether or not someone else is a condition for so doing."[520] And the people who took the refuges have the impression, "this is my refuge, this is my highest value."[521] The understanding about the Three Jewels

517 Cf. Dialogues of the Buddha Part II., pp. 99–100.: The Teaching of Mirror of the Truth: This, Ānanda, is the way, the Mirror of Truth, which if a disciple of the noble ones possesses he may, if he should so desire, himself predict of himself: –'Purgatory is destroyed for me; and rebirth as an animal, or a ghost, or in any place of woe. I am converted; I am no longer liable to be reborn in a state of suffering, and am assured of finally attaining to the enlightenment [of Arahatship].'

518 The Minor Readings, p. 1. In addition, the name Three Jewels is referred as the object to worship, which is considered superior to others in Ratanasutta, ibid., pp. 4–6.

519 Ibid., p. 5.

520 Ibid., pp. 8–9.

521 Ibid., p. 9.

in the commentary should have a connection with the meaning of stock phrases in the conclusion of discourses in Dīgha- and Majjhima-nikāya in the extent that the acceptance of Three Jewels is a wisdom in Buddhism.

4.4.2 Development of Wisdom on the Spiritual Path

Tracing how the simple ascription and composite ascription played the role in the development of belief and the process of conversion, non-monastic follower is *theoretically* a group of Buddha's followers who have understood the meaning of dhamma and therefore realised the significance of the Three Jewels. They might have the belief in the Buddha in different degrees and fashions.[522] Hence, not every one of them had the interest to learn and practice more teaching from the Buddha or one of his the monastic followers. If they did, it was likely that they might be skillful and successful in the doctrine.[523] The outcome of learning and practice after the conversion can be compared with the outcome of hearing *Ānupubbikathā* sermon that Buddha delivered to some hearer. Dealing with the learning more often with great effort, the hearer could develop a general understanding about the Buddha's teaching and might finally reach the point that he has unshakable belief in the doctrine or reach a stage of spiritual attainment. This can be compared with the attainment of the spiritual experience, the *Dhammacakkhu*.

Figure 20: Spiritual Path with and without Ānupubbikathā in Comparison

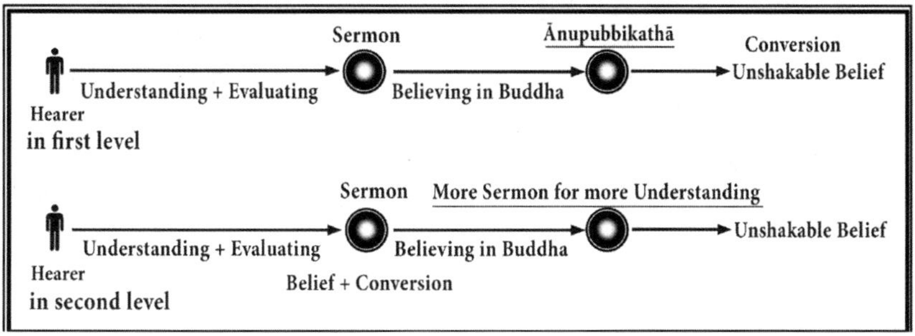

522 Cf. 3.3.
523 Cf. 4.3.2.

Learning and practicing is the way that Buddhist keeps going on the spiritual path. The effort concerns the two aspects. First aspect is to lessen gradually or stop the bad deeds, and the second aspect is to enhance the skill of good deeds, knowledge, and understanding in the spiritual path.[524] In this fashion, non-monastic follower is suggested to observe the precepts and respect some social customs, which leads to the peaceful household life, and in tandem, to develop the quality of mind by understanding the problem of life, which gradually leads to the sacrifice of adherence to the household life. The activity is difficult to achieve because it depends on one's wisdom and his effort to control himself. Despite no organization developed for the people to learn the doctrine and practice, the Buddha seemed to be open for them to come and ask a question. With the knowledge learned from the community, lay follower may be a practitioner at home. In the Nikāya discourses, there are some householders who could rehearse some liturgy by heart and had the spiritual mind developed.[525] Some of them were able to represent the community to defend the doctrine with other schools.[526] The ability claimed in the text indicates the chance of the householder to learn and practice under the guidance of the Buddha and his monastic followers. Lay followers were not forbidden to achieve the knowledge because of their lay lifestyle. In opposite, they could develop this knowledge with their own interest, wisdom, and effort, and with the knowledge collected constantly, they may reach the stage of having unshakable belief one day.

In this way, the follower who realised the importance of teaching might keep going on the spiritual path by learning Buddha's teaching and practicing more. In doing so, he had to keep in contact with the Buddha and his order because the community was the place of the people, who had the same goal. In the Nikāya discourse, bhikkhu and upāsaka, the followers of the Buddha, were described to be acquainted with each other. Lay follower

524 Cf. The Book of the Gradual Sayings, Vol. II, p. 15.

525 The Book of Gradual Sayings Vol. IV, pp. 35–36; The Book of the Kindred Sayings Part IV., pp. 190ff.

526 This seems to be common. Upāli, before declaration of belief into Buddhist, was representative and defendant of Nigantha Nāṭaputta, but not found in Buddha's community.

might come to visit monastic follower at the living place, or in vice versa, the monastic follower might visit the lay at home. In the relationship, monastic followers, particularly the chief disciple, were advisors of the other followers who had a doubt about doctrine or a problem in a practice. They discussed with one another about a topic of doctrine and asked a senior follower for the answer. The images indicate that the followers were united with the aim to develop the spiritual knowledge for their own achievement. Both monastic and non-monastic followers were the fellows who had the same spiritual teacher, acknowledged his doctrine by sharing the same ideology and goal. On this path, they helped one another in learning and solving the problem. The senior followers who successfully achieved the goal were the advisors of the others who were on the spiritual path, including the householders who had the interest in this path.

In this relation, it is noticeable here that bhikkhu played a distinguished role on the instruction of doctrine and experience than bhikkhunī, and upāsaka/upāsikā do. With this image, the status of monastic follower was raised due to the social custom in the Buddhist community that the disciplined follower is 'higher.' For instance, despite having achieved a higher spiritual attainment, the bhikkhunī, and upāsaka/upāsikā made a gesture of respect to the bhikkhu.[527] This shows that the hierarchy of a person in community was not counted merely from the stage of spirituality. The differentiation between monastic and non-monastic follower and even sexism was still significant to the social agreement within the religious community of the patriarchic society. Ascetic lifestyle was still important to the community in that the monastic follower is unconditionally 'higher' than the householder. Apart from the individual mission to follow the spiritual path for the spiritual goal, bhikkhu by duty transmitted the teaching to the followers in the other groups for the extension of the doctrine in other followers. Through the succession, the community survived and remained the place for generations of followers who learned and practiced the dhamma, to keep all the fetters gradually dropped. The end of the path was the Nibbāna and the

527 The reverence of bhikkhunī to bhikkhu is regulated with a rule of Garudhamma, while in case of lay follower the reverence to bhikkhu is based on the social custom that the householder always pays respect to the non-householder who devotes themselves for the spiritual aim.

person who reached the destination was called *asekha* 'not to learn,' which denotes the Arahat in Buddhist doctrine who had liberated from the fetters.

Figure 21: Learning and Practicing Dhamma after Conversion until Liberation

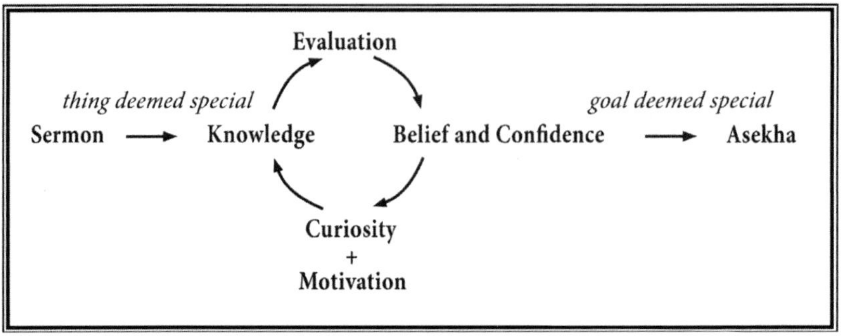

In sum, Sangha can be conceptualized here as the ideal community organized for Buddha's followers who ascribe teaching as the *thing deemed special* and the Nibbāna, which the Buddha pointed them as the *goal deemed special* that they should achieve. It is the place where people carried out the learning and practice for the development of the spiritual mind, which was gradually free from the fetters. As long as the people had not absolutely sacrificed the fetters, they were expected to keep this cycle of learning and practicing. Having heard the sermon that they considered special and trustworthy, they developed the understanding in the sermon, contemplated and evaluated the knowledge, adopted the knowledge to purify the action and the mind, and developed more profound knowledge. In the other word, the spiritual development in Buddhism is the process of considering and experiencing things according to the Buddha's teachings. As long as he considered the teaching special or true, they learned, considered, and realised it even more, until he was free from the fetters, i.e. the person became Arahat in Buddhism. In the cycle, the monastic follower was the person who devoted his life to this learning to reach the aim in this life while the non-monastic follower devoted his life partly on this learning. [528]

528 Cf. Harvey, An Introduction to Buddhist Ethics, p. 41. "...Influenced and inspired by good examples, a person's first commitment will be to develop virtue, a generous and self-controlled way of life for the benefit of life of self

With the cycle of learning and developing spirituality in the community, it is not surprising that the lay follower is a part of the community. Realizing the significance of monastic order in this relation thoroughly, they, developing the spiritual knowledge in this community, feel required to support the activities of the community with materials for the more convenience in the learning, practice, and transmission of the teaching. He also finds the life admirable and thus pays respect to the monastic life with this understanding and tries to promote good image to the order so that it is respectable for other people. Lay follower in this way supports the continuity of the religious ideology in the community.

4.5 Summary

This chapter has focused on lay religiosity as the spiritual path that lay follower set for the goal deemed special after he had found out the significance of teaching or 'dhamma' in the sermon and the superiority of the Buddha as the spiritual teacher who found out the dhamma. The dhamma in the development of belief and the process of conversion was the first thing that the follower deemed special, linked to the other two Buddhist institutions: Buddha and Sangha. This realisation inspired to the religious activities devoting for the dhamma: the declaration of belief in Buddhism (or lay Buddhist conversion), expression of reverence to Buddha, and religious devotion that comprises donation and religious education.

The declaration of the belief in the Three Jewels and followership is the process to state the follower's intention to start the life on the spiritual path to reach the aim that the Buddha has shown the followers. In this connection, lay follower had realised the significance of dhamma and superiority of the Buddha. He felt defeated and inferior and thus accepted to respect the Buddha and his teaching, which is traditionally defined in terms of "going to the Three Jewels for refuge." In tandem, he developed the trust in the Buddha and the path that the Buddha had pointed. That means, the lay follower had considered the meaning and significance of dhamma

---

and others. To motivate this, he or she will have some degree of preliminary wisdom, in the form of some acquaintance with the Buddhist outlook and aspiration to apply it, expressed as *saddhā*, trustful confidence on faith..."

and followed the teaching of the Buddha in that the spiritual goal was the true goal that people should achieve and the spiritual path is the true path to achieve the goal. As followed, the lay follower devoted to the dhamma by contributing to the community of monastic follower, the community of those who devoted to learning and practicing the dhamma. Some lay follower who was interested in the dhamma may come to visit the Buddha or a chief disciple for a conversation or an explanation about the doctrine and practice. The image about the followership seems to be naïve, but this is an interpretation in connection with the meaning communicated to the audience through the repetition of situations in discourses from the perspective of oral tradition.

Sangha was, as the text implies, the community of Buddha's dhamma, by which two groups of the follower: monastic and non-monastic shared the same ideology and followed on the same path. On one hand, the community was the place where the people learned and practiced for their own development of spirituality. Monastic followers, viz. bhikkhu and bhikkhunī, carried out this activity by duty in this regard, but the chance to access the knowledge was not close for the lay follower who had the interest and effort. They might visit the monastic followers for a discussion on the spiritual knowledge or a question about the doctrine, and might therefore reach a stage of spiritual attainment, as the text claims. On the other hand, the lay follower might contribute to the community of monastic followers with material supports for the continuity of the people and their activities. Considering the pattern of the lay followership, lay follower was *theoretically* reckoned the Buddhist, the Buddha's follower who aimed at reaching the goal of liberation, like monastic follower, and supports the order for the convenience in the spiritual development of the individual and the succession of the dhamma and the community in the future.

The spiritual goal of lay follower, which is not Nibbāna, can be explained from Taves's theory that the Three Jewels, ascribed by the people as special, are influenced by cultural contexts. In this connection, the Three Jewels were set for new goal and new path: the luck and happiness of the donator. This means, the *theoretical goal* in Buddhism, viz. the Nibbāna, to which the spiritual path pointed by the Buddha leads, was replaced by the new ascribed goals at wish: richness, happiness, good rebirth, etc. The devotions along the spiritual path were carried out to achieve the goals that the people have wished. In this way, the doctrine of merit was developed based on the doctrine of karma "cause to effect" and more emphasized when the context of the community was changed into the context in which the monastic order needed the stability of the support for its existence. The ascription of the Three Jewels as the highly supreme might be merely a form of evaluating the support of dhamma and Sangha, which is considered virtuous, worthy, and meritful to do. This should have become the popular goal in the later time for the householders, and even some monastic followers, who think that the Three Jewels are the superior power over any being. In Thailand, for example, monastic life or "life in the monastery"[529] is regarded as auspicious life which can decrease or stop some misfortune or bad karma or increase luck or merit of the person who is ordained into a monk or "Mae Chee" for a short time. The ascription of the Three Jewels with different goals can be observed further in different contexts of Theravada Buddhism nowadays.

529 In case of a man, the "monastic life" is to become a monk, while in case of a woman, the "monastic life" is to become "Mae Chee" the nun with shaved head or "Chee Phram" the nun without shaved head. Both of them are regarded as similarly 'Buad' "ordained" in that they live in a temple and under the monastic rules or the Eight precepts and the daily life determined by the monastery.

Chapter V: Conclusion

The study deals with the meaning *upāsaka/upāsikā* or "lay follower" in Dīgha- and Majjhima-nikāya with the aim to apply methods that are suitable for the analysis of a religious scripture developed in oral tradition. As religious scripture, the two Nikāyas are accounts of teaching containing belief, activity, organization, and authority over the Buddhist in some way; the approach to grasp any concept about the people should be to achieve the ideas and the relation between the elements reflected in the story. As the text originally formed and served in the context of oral tradition, Pāli discourse should be studied with an appropriate method in line with the characteristic of the orality and formulaic language to approach the meaning intended to communicate to the audience. The text may be approached, with more carefulness, with the philological study, which generally emphasizes a historical question, the authoritative aspect of religious scripture, the linguistic forms implying the relation to other literatures developed in the same era, etc. Oral literature, once developed, primarily concentrates on the function and meaning communicated to the audience in community with the device conveying the meaning that is typical for vocal performance. The question to crack here is how to achieve and systematically explain this *conceptual* idea in the text, which is communicated to us nowadays in scripts.

The author uses the discourses in Dīgha- and Majjhima-nikāya as source for the analysis, for they as old source of Buddhist tradition portray the development of Buddhist followership and the religiousness of the people. The study traced the process, through which one passes in order to become a Buddhist, as an oral text offers an abstract concept presented in certain pattern. Focusing on the process to become a lay follower and his religious activity, the author considers the concept of lay follower formulated in the structure stringed regularly with stock phrases representing meanings. Construed in this way, the Nikāya discourse is the *image of* the Buddhists and their "religion," learned and transmitted in the tradition.

5.1 Result of the Study

The concept of upāsaka/upāsikā is analysed in two sections: first "simple ascription," the religious experience in Buddhism implied in the stock phrases in conclusion of discourse; second, "composite ascription" the lay follower in relation to the monastic order.

5.1.1 Lay Follower and Religious Experience

The aim of this section is to analyse the meanings established by the use of stock phrases as to how the hearer is described to think, feel, and do in the decision to become a follower. In doing this, the author applied the theory of religious experience to understand the relation between the hearer and the agents, which are obviously influential to the development of belief and the decision to become a follower. The study consists of two parts: philological study of the stock phrases and an interpretation to understand the relation.

"Religious experience" in general signifies to an extraordinary experience as a result of the encounter with a manifestation of the "holy," something which is supernatural and unusual for the perceiver. Applying the concept to the study of religious phenomenon, the experience is viewed as the religious *meaning,* inspiring the person to yield and devote to this holiness that the person raises its significance to his life. As a result, the method is typical to the analysis of theistic religions or any religion dealing with the transcendental vision. However, the author saw the possibility to apply the concept to the study of lay followers in the discourse from the comparative perspective that religious people in any belief always deem as 'holy' a person or a thing that they follow. The phenomenon regularly occurs in the discourse in the description about the Buddha and his teaching with regular use of stock phrases. With the theory of religious experience that Ann Taves has developed the process in the discourse can be compared in this way.

Figure 22: Taves's Theory and its Application to Pāli Discourse

	Encounter and Perception		Religious Experience		Expression
Ann Taves	Some Things Deemed Special	→	Experience Deemed Religious	→	Faith and Religiosity
The Study	Buddha's Sermon	→	(Not Described)	→	Satisfaction Declaration of Belief

From the figure, Buddha's sermon is comparable to the thing deemed special that inspires a religious faith and religiosity. In hearing the sermon, the hearer may *gain satisfaction* with the sermon or *develop the belief in the Buddha* that he declares the belief and asks to become a follower. In this regard, the question of the study is posed to the idea behind the outcomes: what has happened in the mental process and how the expressions mentioned in the stock phrases reasonably relate to the sermon that the hearer has heard. This is the concept that the oral tradition presents the ideal followership of the Buddha, monastic and non-monastic alike.

5.1.1.1 Result of Philological Study

The stock phrases regularly found in the conclusion of discourse have three types.

Type I: expressing *satisfaction*. The stock phrase can be perceived in terms of a positive feeling of the hearer in reaction to the given answer that fulfills his interest or removes his doubt. In the study, the stock phrase was represented with (1) and as alternative (2).

Type II: *formal declaration of belief in Buddha*. The stock phrase consists of three elements: admiration of Buddha's sermon (3), declaration of going for refuge to the Three Jewels (4), and request to become a monastic follower (5) or a lay follower (6). The total meaning denotes the announcement of the intention to become a follower of the Buddha, or "conversion," representing the acceptance of the teaching and the teacher who gave the teaching.

Type III: *achievement of a spiritual attainment*. The stock phrase consists of two elements: the hearing of *Ānupubbikathā* sermon (7); and the experience of *Dhammacakkhu* (8), denoting an extraordinary experience achieved in the hearing of the *Ānupubbikathā* sermon. The stock phrase coexists with the stock phrase of the second type.

It is noticeable that the usage of the stock phrases implies the degree of acquaintanceship of the hearer with the 'religion' in some extent. The type I usually appears in the context, where the hearer was acquainted with the Buddha, his teaching, his monastic order, or a monastic follower to some extent that the talk satisfied him. The type II usually appears in the context, where the hearer was 'new' to the Buddha's doctrine in the sense that the delivered sermon could surprise him and strengthen his belief in the Buddha and the teaching. The type III, which is usually with the stock phrase II, appears in the context, where the hearer is 'new' and thus wonderful that the belief in the Buddha was fast developed before seeing him in person.

The usage and combination of the stock phrases assign four different levels of expression in response to the Buddha's sermon in the Pāli discourses:

1. First level: the hearer admired the meaning of the teaching in the sermon, declared the Three Jewels for refuge, and vowed to be a follower, which is the official 'process' to become a Buddha's follower, as tradition has it. They have also attained *Dhammacakkhu*, signifying the understanding of the basic teaching and unshakable belief in the Buddha.
2. Second level: the hearer went through the process of becoming a follower: he admired the teaching in the sermon, declared the Three Jewels for refuge and vowed to be a follower.
3. Third level: the hearers declared their belief, but *not* declared the Three Jewels for refuge and *not* vowed to be a follower, as in the first or second level.
4. Fourth level: the hearer did not declare anything and had no belief in Buddha.

With the regular use of stock phrases in certain ways representing the hearer's expression in response to the dhamma in the sermon, tradition implies that the hearers might *differently* understand the meaning of sermon, realise the significance of dhamma and have the reverent feelings for the Buddha and dhamma, i.e. in different degree and fashion. Compatible with the meaning offered by the tradition, the followership is reckoned on the use of the stock phrase type II, viz. the declaration of the followership under the Buddha. In other words, the first level represents the followership with a complete understanding of doctrine and thus unshakable belief in the Buddha and his teaching while the second level represents the followership and the belief in the Buddha in some extent.

5.1.1.2 Interpretation of the Meaning

The meaning of the stock phrases is significant to understand the concept of upāsaka/upāsikā, which can be in good agreement with the theory of religious experience provided by Ann Taves. With the usage of the stock phrases, tradition assigns the idea in every word of the short sentences, i.e. they represent the process of *simple ascription*, in which the hearer deemed the sermon as *special* and therefore had the experience deemed special with the sermon. The experience finds expression in admiration of the teaching in different ways, represented in the stock phrase (3). Despite the fact that some hearer may have developed trust to some extent in the Buddha by hearing his reputation or seeing his signs of Great Man, with which the hearer recognized the spirituality of the Buddha, the pattern of discourse points to the importance of the sermon in that it symbolically makes the hearer the true follower. In the stock phrase type II, the admiration of the dhamma represents that the hearer understood the meaning and evaluated the value of the teaching by referring to the metaphors of its significance to him. Behind this, he accepted the authority of the Buddha after having contemplated the meaning of the teaching in the sermon he has heard. It can be surmised that the hearer compared himself with some superiority in the Buddha as he had experienced. He thus appreciated the Buddha as the great spiritual teacher who had told him the truth, the dhamma as the truth that was significant to his life, and the Sangha as the community of people who devoted to the Buddha and the dhamma. The reverence to the Three Jewels indicates the acceptance of the Buddha and his teaching, inspiring the intention to follow the Buddha's teaching, as implied in the request to become a follower. From the analysis, it can be concluded that Buddha's follower is *theoretically* the person who declared the followership under the Buddha with awareness of these facts.

5.1.2 Lay Follower as the Composite of Sangha

In the process of "religious experience" viewed in the simple ascription, the hearer of the sermon had learned the meaning of the sermon and realised the significance of the teaching. Then, he had trust in the Buddha and his teaching, implied from the expression in the process. With the image reinforced by the use of stock phrases in the discourse, Pāli tradition ascribes lay follower to be a group of Buddha's follower who devoted to the religion with the realization of Buddha's great wisdom on the teaching. Thus, it can be surmised at first that Nibbāna or the liberation from the worldly fetters was theoretically the spiritual goal that lay follower should have on this path. In Taves's term, the lay follower saw the spiritual goal or Nibbāna as the *goal deemed special* and the ascetic life and religious activities on the learning, practice, support of the dhamma that the Buddha had taught and the tradition had cherished as the *path deemed special*. Sharing thought and feeling of how the Three Jewels were significant and worthy of reverence, the lay follower understood the monastic follower in the order, why they decided to sacrifice the worldly life for the spiritual life, and thus respected their religious life. Therefore, the lay follower promoted the monastic people with the intention to support and preserve the teaching and the ideal life.

Tradition regarded the stock phrase type II, the declaration of lay followership under the Buddha, as the *conversion* in Buddhism, like the request for monkhood. This followership was not a commitment in the religious community because anyone might keep his former social status or stay in the religious community. The declaration was simply the announcement of acceptance in the significance of dhamma and Buddha's superiority for the discovery of this dhamma, and the intention to follow the Buddha's spiritual path. In this way, the people *merely declared the significance of the Three Jewels to them* in some degree due to their wisdom in the consideration. With the declaration, the people stated the intention to develop themselves in the spiritual path, as he had his mind opened for the Buddha and his doctrine, and would gladly carry out a conversation about the doctrine with the Buddha or a monastic follower. This indicates the beginning of developing the familiarity and connection between the individual, the Buddha, and the order. Through the encounter and conversation, lay follower should have developed the knowledge about the doctrine and practice. Projected as the result of the 'ideal' conversion, the lay follower in relation to the Buddha and monastic order might do any activity implying his wisdom about the Buddha, dhamma, and Sangha, like monastic follower. For instance, explaining the teaching, meditating, or even reaching a spiritual attainment.

The praise to the Buddha was the description of the qualities of the Buddha. In other words, it was exaggeration of why the Buddha was respectable for the singer. As implied from stock phrase type II, the lay follower was the person who had seen the significance of the Three Jewels with his own wisdom. From this view, the praise was a personal impression to the Buddha from his experience with the Buddha, his doctrine, and his order. As the author found out, the reflection is significantly different between that of the lay follower in the first and the second level. These are the different images of the lay followers who attained and not attained the experience of *Dhammacakkhu* that tradition distinguishes with the use of stock phrases type III. Whereas, the praise of the lay follower who attained the *Dhammacakkhu* focused on the inner qualities of the Buddha on his superior wisdoms in different ways, the latter concentrated on the external qualities, such as the respectability, the decorum, the modesty, etc., which the follower had observed the Buddha and his monastic followers. The image also emphasizes the finding that the people became a follower with an impression that they had considered Buddha 'holy.' The impression was the basis to develop more profoundly on the spiritual path, as the meaning of stock phrase type III, which symbolizes the learning of the doctrine and the achievement of the spiritual attainment from the learning. In this way, lay follower might develop the spiritual attainment and have the stable belief in the Buddha by learning and practicing the doctrine.

Sangha as structured from the religious experience of individuals was therefore the assembly of people who had experienced the 'dhamma,' sharing the same belief, the same goal, and the same path that the Buddha had taught. Lay follower had consensus on the agreements within the community, as he knew the Buddha, the teaching, the monastic order and their significance, thus followed the customs, which the Buddha had laid down for the community. He paid respect to the monkhood and the seniority within the order, as monastic followers respected to one another on the spiritual attainment, knowledge of doctrine, years of ordination. Under this impression, lay follower saw the benefit of donating to the order and supported the activities of the community, such as giving some particular things necessary for an individual member of Buddha's order, providing the community with something that the members could not find by themselves, etc. Not controlled by the monastic rule, lay follower had freedom to live his life. Nevertheless, with the knowledge about the teachings, he knew what he should do and should not do and tried to control himself under Buddha's instruction. In this way, lay follower had a sense of unity with the monastic order, on the thought, the path and the goal. He was also a follower with this *way of life*. Different was the status of the householder that allowed the people to earn money and have family.

In this regard, lay follower can be reckoned as the member of Sangha who intends to join the spiritual path and reach the spiritual aim that the Buddha has directed for his followers. And with the lay follower the community can successfully continue, as remarked in the following quotation.

> The strength of the order of monks (bhikkhusangha) both in quality and in quantity depends upon the decisions made by Buddhists, primary, those made by our young men who seek admission into the order, but also by a continuing process of considering the fundamental purposes of life on the part of laity. The relationship of the bhikkhu with the laity is, of course, integral; guidance by the former depends greatly upon the support received from the latter, The integral relation requires that all Buddhists endorse the fundamental norms provided by the Buddha for a purposeful and meaningful life. For the Buddhist community to thrive and develop as a religious community, there must be the Buddhist laity committed to following the teaching of the Buddha. And also, there must continue to be among us young men who are prepared to make the decision to commit their lives fully to the life of bhikkhu.[530]

In summary, the status upāsaka/upāsikā as found in the discourse is a vague status, simply denoting realisation of the significance of Three Jewels to the extent of having declared the realisation and the trust in the Buddha and his teaching. They may be householder in different professions, Brahmins, or ascetics from other religious communities. The boundary marked in '*initiation ritual,*' which distinguishes the Buddhist from the non-Buddhist is simply the intention, declared that the person accepts the Buddha as the spiritual teacher and intends to follow his path. In practical, the lay follower might have a few chances to develop the spiritual knowledge because of his busy life. They usually visited the Buddha and his monastic followers by chance, but with an interest in the teaching, they might more often pay them a visit. However, no matter the people had declared the followership, the chance for the non-follower to develop the understanding is not close because the community is open to everyone who has a doubt or curiosity about the teaching, ascetic lifestyle and practice, etc. After having approached the community, he may continue or cancel the followership. If he does, he may join the community by *gradually* learning the doctrine or the practice, or by being nearby and supporting the activities. Finally, he might successfully reach a higher spiritual development along the path. If he is not

530 Ratanasara, 'Reaching Out' as an Expression of 'Going Forth,' pp. 101–102.

in this direction, he may dissociate himself from the community and go on his spiritual way.

The definition of "Buddhist" and the community of Buddha's follower as found in the study is different from sociological perspective, which defines people in terms of social status, role, and commitment in relation to one another. Lay follower is non-monastic Buddhist, who is the indispensable composite of the Sangha because monastic followers essentially depend on a donation from the people they contacted. The contact with the external people to propagate the doctrine is very significant to the survival of the community because it is the way to announce their ideology to the outsider. First, it is for the gaining of new followers who strongly believe in the doctrine and want to learn more by themselves in the community, and further, for the material supports from those who agree with the ideology in some extent but not have a strong belief to devote their life to the doctrine. The thought to make the contact with the outsiders noticeably relates to the conflict image. On one hand, the regulation of the monastic rules and some ideas reminds the monastic followers to separate themselves from the people outside the order. On the other hand, the people still keep the conversation with the outsiders about the doctrine. This clearly points to a distinctive Buddhist idea in constructing their religious community, which is necessarily close for the favourable image of spiritual learning and practice, but at the same time, open to the outside people for the gaining of more followers, both "professional" and "amateur."

In this fashion, the religion "Buddhism" as analysed from the discourse is the assembly of Buddha's followers with two kinds of "obligation:" obligation of "Buddhist followership" and monastic obligation. Upāsaka and upāsikā, the lay followers who take on the follower's commitment on fostering the spiritual path, but observe the precepts and behave morally, e.g. vegetarianism, celibacy, etc., as they would like to; whereas, bhikkhu and bhikkhunī take on both commitment. As the Buddha's follower, they both share the same ideal and the same spiritual path for their pursuit of the same goal as long as they recognize the significance of the Buddha, his teaching, and the community. They may leave this Buddhist followership at once, when they do not recognize the significance because this commitment is the personal commitment that one takes on with willingness. In opposite, monastic commitment is an ideological commitment regulating the members of the monastic order. It fulfils an essential function as social contract, rather than to be the ethics of the Buddhist spirituality of the individuality. The rules and customs are the agreement among the members in the community. With the life controlled in the community, bhikkhu and bhikkhunī can devote the life to foster the spiritual aim better than the lay followers can. As Bluck has remarked, the difference between the two kinds of Buddhist follower lies in difference on the advantage of monastic life in the spiritual path, not the 'higher quality.'[531] Furthermore, their characteristics shining to the public which signify the ability of the Buddha in the instruction, the credibility of the doctrine, the potential to reach the spiritual aim, etc. is essential to the development of trust of the people outside the community. The function of the 'monastic commitment' plays the role in the gaining of impression in the missionary activity, which is comparable to the Buddha's visible image and quality that attracts the people to visit and converse with him.

The study has also demonstrated the abstract idea about the role of belief in Buddhist philosophy presented with situations of the discourse. As portrayed, "belief" is significantly fundamental to the spiritual development in Buddhism, as it attracts the first attention of the people to the Buddha and his doctrine and even motivates continuity to foster on the spiritual path. The development of Buddhist followership is the development of the insight in the consideration of the person or the thing believed based on personal value, reason, and own experience. In other words, the belief is gradually replaced by the experience based on the learned wisdom in judgment as to why the thing to follow should be continued to follow. The stage of the spiritual development generally starts with a faith or a belief, which the people may have, as the basis, on which the trust in the Buddha and his teaching is developed. Actually, there is the mention of *saddhā* "belief," specifically *tathāgatabodhisaddhā* "belief in the Buddha's Enlightenment"[532] in Pāli canon, which particularly concerns this point. The finding in the study indicates that the belief is basis of Buddhist spirituality, expected to develop gradually with the learning. Unfortunately, this aspect of Buddhism is neglected in Buddhist philosophy with the

531 See his argument p. 4.

532 The Book of the Gradual Sayings Vol. II, pp. 38–40.

understanding that Buddhism, especially in discourses of Suttapiṭaka, is a rational cult enjoying debates and philosophical talks. As the study has already demonstrated, the development of the followership in Buddhism patterned in the discourse presents the *doctrine of belief in Buddhism*.

The pattern in the discourse has shown that Buddhist theoretically has the belief in the Buddha and the doctrine developed with an impression, which may be based on their former belief. This belief inspires the first evaluation that the Buddha is great or the doctrine sounds great. This evaluation inspires in the second step to approach and 'learn' the Buddha or the doctrine. With the trust developed at first to some extent, the more trust can be easier and faster developed, which finally motivates the decision to convert and continue learning and practice. As observed in the discourse, the belief may not be developed with the inflicting sermon. Instead, it is stereotypically developed with the surprise about some supernatural power or some special quality that is not general to humankind. Buddhism is thus a 'religion' concerned with the "supernatural."[533] Different from other religions is that the supernatural in Buddhism is the result of self-thought and imagination of the hearer about how the Buddha and his teaching are *special*. In this connection, the religious education, which is a factor to strengthen the understanding and the belief in the Buddha and his teaching, is essential to the lay follower in Buddhism. Religious education, viz. homiletics, according to the discourse is the only way to develop the knowledge in the doctrine and not to remain stagnant with the *specialness* of the Buddha and the achievement of happiness and good rebirth, which is not the goal of the spiritual path. The lack of this knowledge should involve the role of the monastic order in the religious education, viz. in the selection of the themes for the instruction of the lay followers, as the doctrine of karma and moral life seem to be more suitable to the people who live in the worldly life than the teaching and practice for the spiritual development. This is *perhaps* a cause lying in the development into the present phenomenon of Buddhist mentality nowadays, in which the division of monastic and non-monastic follower is clearly distinguished in form, spiritual path, and spiritual goal.

533 Cf. Stark; Finke, Acts of Faith, pp. 89–90.

The idea about lay follower in relation to the Three Jewels reflects in two significant rituals of lay followers in the tradition. The emphasis on the knowledge of how the Buddha, his teaching, and the community are significant and superior has been lost in the common sense of the people, but still remains in form that may be connected in some way with the image of householder in the discourse, as found in the study. The first is the initiation *ritual*, or 'Buddhist conversion' in which one first declares himself a lay Buddhist. In the ritual, he has to declare going for refuge to the Three Jewels three times and announce the followership in front of a witness who is a monastic follower, often without an inspiration from the Three Jewels. Second, the basic liturgy, which the Buddhist ordinarily prays daily and in a religious ceremony, is the description of the qualities of the Buddha, dhamma, and Sangha, which is mentioned in Pāli discourse. The liturgy may originally signify the self-reflection about the significance of the Three Jewels, which helps the Buddhist feel more connected with the Three Jewels. It is difficult to reconstruct the origin and ideological development of the rituals, but they clearly reinforce the meaning of lay follower existing in the tradition that they are the Buddha's follower because they have realised the significance of the Buddha, his dhamma, and his community. This realization is symbolic of acceptance of the Buddha's path that the Buddha has pointed.

In relation to the oral tradition, in which the discourses are developed, the concept of non-monastic follower gained by the theme and formulaic language of the discourse may aim at promoting the significance of the sermon and homiletics as a way of spiritual development in Buddhism. Particularly, it demonstrates that sermon has the influential meaning to affect the thought and the belief that changes non-Buddhist into Buddhist, who recognizes the meaning of the Three Jewels, and the ordinary Buddhist into the true Buddhist, who has the unshakable belief in the Three Jewels. This implication may be an intention from the Pāli tradition to communicate that the spiritual mind in Buddhism can be developed by hearing the teaching or learning the scripture. From this perspective, the image of Buddhism projected in the Pāli canon is to promote the learning of scripture in the tradition. This is an aspect of Buddhism emphasized by the scripture. Likewise, the similar answer to the question of followership may be given from other aspects such as donation, observance of precepts, or meditation.

In this fashion, Buddhism can be variously described by people or scripture with emphasis on the aspects that they are dealing with.

5.2 Suggestion

The study has contributed to some understanding about the followership in the Nikāya discourses. Formerly, it was concluded that lay follower is another stage of the development in Mahāyāna Buddhism, in which the monastic life was downplayed for the raised ideal of the lay followership into Bodhisattva ideal.[534] In another theory, the lay follower began to play more roles especially in Mahāyāna from the cult of Buddha's Stūpa.[535] However, the author finds the lay followership intrinsically mentioned in Dīgha- and Majjhima-nikāya, like the monastic followership, in the unique way of oral text. This indicates that the Buddhist tradition does not downplay the spirituality of the lay follower.

The suggestion that the author particularly gives here is the ideas about the approaches to the study of Pāli scriptures and Inclusivism.

5.2.1 Methods in Studying Scripture

The author has learned the usage of methodological approaches in dealing with "Buddhism" described in Pāli canon.

First, religious experience, a systematic perspective in Religionswissenschaft, is applicable even to Theravada Buddhism. The reason: it focuses on the human's behaviours in relation to the thing, person, doctrine, etc. deemed special by them. Thanks to Ann Taves, the theory becomes more effective to the study of religions and other similar phenomena, in which people attracted by a thing/person which/whom they deem special behave in a way relating to the specially deemed. It is the perspective into any activity carried out in relation to the thing/person deemed special connected to a goal. In study of Buddhism, both in the scripture or in the fieldwork, the approach can be applied to observe the relation of the Three Jewels to religiosity. Despite the fact that the Three Jewels are not the divine,

534 Cf. Freiberger, Kleine, Buddhismus, pp. 208–209.

535 Vetter, On the Origin of Mahāyāna Buddhism and the Subsequent Introduction of Prajṇāpāramitā, p. 1253.

Buddha, his doctrine of the truth, and his community, symbolized under the name Three Jewels, can be considered as the things deemed special for the Buddhist. The Three Jewels in any Buddhist tradition are the object to worship, as seen in the daily prayer, the beginning of any Buddhist ritual, and even in a non-Buddhist ritual that the Buddhist doer wants to make *auspicious*. To deal with these phenomena, the approach is applied to concentrate on the goal and the path in relation to the Three Jewels to reconstruct the true meaning behind the activity.

Second, theories about the orality in the Pāli canon, or in the canon of other Buddhist traditions should be revised. Orality in Buddhist traditions needs more researches for basic knowledge about the form, structure, and language. As partially seen in the study, the disciplines in textual studies of written tradition may not always be applicable to understand the text, which is originally composed in the culture of oral transmission because an oral text has unique techniques in presenting the ideas to the audience. Dealing with a meaning in Pāli discourse, the author has learned that the discourse as recited to the audience contain some particular meanings and functions, which have never been noticed with a reading. Dealing with an oral text for the meaning accurately, it is a complicated work based on several aspects of linguistics and cultural study:

> The study of oral poetry presumes an acquaintance with its social environment and practical functions. In the case of Western literature we may, as readers, regard ourselves as the natural recipients of poetic messages and may expect our own aesthetic principles to apply in the reception of a literary work. By contrast, as we prepared to postpone our aesthetic judgment. Instead of trying to grasp immediately the meaning of a piece of oral poetry, we must look at the way it is performed, its 'reading' in its cultural context, the primarily producers of the piece of poetry in question and the primary readers of its message. We must first experience an anthropological translocation by setting aside, as far as possible, our highly automized preconceptions, norms, attitudes and values, and try to enter the realm of the 'other.' We must be prepared to question even basic truths of our own reality and experience and invite the continuous learning of new categories, forms of expression and process of meaning. To be able to counteract with the 'other,' we must be empty and alert, humble and inquisitive, silent and attentive.[536]

536 Honko, Problems of Oral and Semiliterary Epics, p. 26.

The present study is merely an example in applying the approach to the meanings of non-monastic follower communicated in the discourses. Despite imperfects and superficiality in the procedures, the author hopes that the result of the study will remind scholars to revise the orality, methods and thoughts in dealing with the Pāli canon as well as other Buddhist canons for contribution to research Buddhist traditions.

5.2.2 Inclusivism in Buddhism

The study has demonstrated that the relation between belief and religiosity in Buddhism can be considered from the perspective of ascription to the goal and the path *deemed special*. The phenomenon of the ascription may be perceived in terms of inclusivism, in which a major tradition accepts a minor tradition and places its doctrine over that of the minor tradition. "*Inclusivist are those who attempt to recognize the potentially valuable contribution of religious others and at the same time uphold a sense of superiority for their own tradition.*"[537] Buddhism is considered as a remarkably tolerant religion in this way that it may be risky of diluting the tradition.[538] As seen in the debate with a Brahmin particularly in Dīghanikāya, Brahmanic concepts can be interpreted in a new way, in the way that "*they* (the Buddhist) *can use from the other's concepts, do what they like with them, and then discard the essential things. In the process they thereby assert themselves.*" The concept of *dakkhiṇā* applied in Buddhism can be understood with the idea of inclusivism, in that the lay donation is the redirection of the Brahmin's *dakṣiṇā* in Buddhist tradition, from the donation to the Brahmin for the uttered Mantra or the performed ritual Therein to the donation to Sangha.

One of the forms frequently found in a local tradition of Theravada Buddhism is the tendency to absorb the primitive belief or animism, such as the belief in ghost, supernatural.[539] Three Jewels are worshipped by some Buddhists for their happiness and wishes. In this connection, the

537 Kiblinger, Buddhist Inclusivism, p. 9.

538 Ibid., p. 3.

539 The following examples are given from the author's experience with Thai Buddhism. For the academic study on this topic, see, for example, Swearer, The Buddhist World of Southeast Asia (1995).

Three Jewels is deemed as the ultimate power over the beings based on the belief that they can protect the worshipper from the harmful spirits, believed to be the origin of disaster, sickness, and other undesirable incidents. The inclusive tendency in this fashion can be understood as the Three Jewels ascribed in relation to other goal and path that they deem special. This means, the Buddhists revere the Three Jewels as the foremost reverent object, which they recognize their superiority over any being. Therefore, they in making objects symbolizing the Three Jewels imagine that the objects could protect them from the evils. As a result, the symbols of Three Jewels – Buddha's image, liturgy in Pāli language, palm-leaf manuscript, the holy tread from the robe, etc. – are reckoned to be the sacred thing. The worship and praise to the Three Jewels are applied in any Buddhist ritual and non-Buddhist ritual for the auspicious start and the success of the ritual. Considering the phenomena with Taves's theory, the people ascribe the Three Jewels in connection with the goal and the path that they desire because they do not know accurately how the Three Jewels are superior, and in respond to this question, how they should behave to the Three Jewels. This shows that some Buddhist may interpret the Three Jewels in another function, which has nothing to do with Buddha's teaching. They simply replace the Three Jewels to the spirits in the previous belief.

It is noticeable that these phenomena exclusively pertain to the people who are 'far' from a center of Buddhist education. They still call for the certainty in life and thus ask for this aspect from Buddhism, although Buddhism teaches to use wisdom and effort to attain an achievement. In Vinaya-piṭaka, Buddha suggested his pupils to follow some request of householder that is traditional and important for their feeling of certainty, for example, giving them blessings after they sneeze or cough,[540] or after a food giving.[541] This seems to be trivial, as the Buddha self had at first rejected the blessing from his disciples after a sneeze. However, for the Buddhist, who is still *sekha* 'the person to learn,' this is important. They do not understand the world "as it is" and may not be interested to understand the fact that nothing can help them, but one's own wisdom and effort. Hence, they are still dependent to the refuge that they trust.

540 The Book of Discipline Vol. V, p. 195.
541 Ibid., pp. 297–298.

In this way, the Three Jewels as refuge may be simply *upāya* 'method' that helps the Buddhists feel confident in their daily life. This is important because Buddhist is the people who merely declare the intention to follow the spiritual path. They have not had the complete trust in the teaching. They may have this belief shakeable with some fear and leave Buddhism for others. They thus need to feel confident in their life, in order to develop themselves successfully on the spiritual path. Without the religious education – learning of doctrine, having a talk with a well-learned follower, learning to meditate, etc. – the Buddhist may stick to the superiority of the Three Jewels as refuge and ascribe them in relation to the goal and path that they desire. In this way, they will never understand the meaning behind the symbol, which is the true path of their religion.

Appendix I: Progressive Talk and Sermon for an Understanding of Doctrine

No.	Name of Discourse	Position	Sermonizer	Hearer	Ending
1	Brahmajālasutta	DN1	Buddha	Sangha	Satisfaction
2	Mahālisutta	DN6	Buddha	Oṭṭhaddha Licchavi (H)	Satisfaction
3	Jāliyasutta	DN7	Buddha	Jāliya (H)	Satisfaction
				Maṇdiya (H)	Satisfaction
4	Kevaḍḍhasutta	DN11	Buddha	Kevaḍḍha(H)	Satisfaction
5	Mahāpadānasutta	DN14	Buddha	Sangha	Satisfaction
6	Mahānidānasutta	DN15	Buddha	Ānanda	Satisfaction
7	Mahāgovindasutta	DN19	Buddha	Pañcasikha Gandhabbaputta (H)	Satisfaction
8	Mahāsatipaṭṭhānasutta	DN22	Buddha	Sangha	Satisfaction
9	Cakkavatti-Sīhanādasutta	DN26	Buddha	Sangha	Satisfaction
10	Aggaññasutta	DN27	Buddha	Vaseṭṭha	Satisfaction
				Bharadavāja	
11	Pāsādikasutta	DN29	Buddha	Cunda	Satisfaction
				Upadāna	
12	Lakkhaṇasutta	DN30	Buddha	Sangha	Satisfaction
13	Āṭānāṭiyasutta	DN32	Buddha	Sangha	Satisfaction
14	Saṅgītisutta	DN33	Sāriputta	Sangha	Satisfaction
15	Dasuttarasutta	DN34	Sāriputta	Sangha	Satisfaction
16	Mūlapariyāyasutta	MN1	Buddha	Sangha	Unsatisfaction
17	Sabbāsavasutta	MN2	Buddha	Sangha	Satisfaction
18	Dhammadāyādasutta	MN3	Buddha	Sangha	Satisfaction
			Sāriputta		
19	Anaṅgaṇasutta	MN5	Sāriputta	Moggallāna	Satisfaction
20	Ākaṅkheyyasutta	MN6	Buddha	Sangha	Satisfaction
21	Sallekhasutta	MN8	Buddha	Mahācunda	Satisfaction
22	Sammādiṭṭhisutta	MN9	Sāriputta	Sangha	Satisfaction
23	Satipaṭṭhānasutta	MN10	Buddha	Sangha	Satisfaction
24	Cūḷasīhanādasutta	MN11	Buddha	Sangha	Satisfaction

No.	Name of Discourse	Position	Sermonizer	Hearer	Ending
25	Mahāsīhanādasutta	MN12	Buddha	Sāriputta	Satisfaction
26	Mahādukkhakkhandhasutta	MN13	Buddha	Sangha	Satisfaction
27	Cūḷadukkhakkhandhasutta	MN14	Buddha	Mahānāma(H)	Satisfaction
28	Anumānasutta	MN15	Moggallāna	Sangha	Satisfaction
29	Cetokhilasutta	MN16	Buddha	Sangha	Satisfaction
30	Vanapatthasutta	MN17	Buddha	Sangha	Satisfaction
31	Madhupiṇḍikasutta	MN18	Buddha	Ānanda	Satisfaction
32	Dvedhāvittakkasutta	MN19	Buddha	Sangha	Satisfaction
33	Vitakkasanthānasutta	MN20	Buddha	Sangha	Satisfaction
34	Kakacūpamasutta	MN21	Buddha	Sangha	Satisfaction
35	Alagaddūpamasutta	MN22	Buddha	Sangha	Satisfaction
36	VammīIkasutta	MN23	Buddha	Kumārakassapa	Satisfaction
37	Rathavinītasutta	MN24	Sāriputta	Puṇṇa Mantāniputta	Satisfaction
38	Nivāpasutta	MN25	Buddha	Sangha	Satisfaction
39	Ariyapariyesanasutta	MN26	Buddha	Sangha	Satisfaction
40	Mahāhatthipadopamasutta	MN28	Sāriputta	Sangha	Satisfaction
41	Mahāsāropamasutta	MN29	Buddha	Sangha	Satisfaction
42	Cūḷagosiṅgālasutta	MN31	Buddha, Anuruddha	Dīgha-parajana (H)	Satisfaction
43	Mahāgosiṅgālasutta	MN32	Sāriputta and others	Buddha	Satisfaction
44	Mahāgopālakasutta	MN33	Buddha	Sangha	Satisfaction
45	Mahāsaccakasutta	MN36	Buddha	Saccaka (H)	Satisfaction
46	Cūḷataṇhāsaṅkhayasutta	MN37	Buddha	Moggallāna	Satisfaction
47	Mahātaṇhāsaṅkhayasutta	MN38	Buddha	Sangha	Satisfaction
48	Mahā-assapurasutta	MN39	Buddha	Sangha	Satisfaction
49	Cūḷa-assapurasutta	MN40	Buddha	Sangha	Satisfaction
50	Mahāvedallasutta	MN43	Sāriputta	Mahākoṭṭhika	Satisfaction
51	Cūḷavedallasutta	MN44	Dhammadinnā Buddha	Visākha (H)	Satisfaction
52	Cūḷādhammasamādānasutta	MN45	Buddha	Sangha	Satisfaction
53	Mahādhammasamādānasutta	MN46	Buddha	Sangha	Satisfaction
54	Vīmaṃsakasutta	MN47	Buddha	Sangha	Satisfaction
55	Kosambiyasutta	MN48	Buddha	Sangha	Satisfaction
56	Kandarakasutta	MN51	Buddha	Sangha	Satisfaction

No.	Name of Discourse	Position	Sermonizer	Hearer	Ending
57	Sekhapaṭipadāsutta	MN53	Ānanda	Sākka Nobles(H)	Satisfaction
58	Bahuvedanīyasutta	MN59	Buddha	Ānanda	Satisfaction
59	Ambalaṭṭhikā-Rāhulovādasutta	MN61	Buddha	Rāhula	Satisfaction
60	Mahā-Rāhulovādasutta	MN62	Buddha	Rāhula	Satisfaction
61	Cūḷa-Māluṅkyasutta	MN63	Buddha	Māluṅkyaputta	Satisfaction
62	Mahā-Māluṅkyasutta	MN64	Buddha	Māluṅkyaputta/ Ānanda	Satisfaction
63	Bhaddālisutta	MN65	Buddha	Bhaddāli	Satisfaction
64	Laṭukikopamasutta	MN66	Buddha	Udāyī	Satisfaction
65	Cātumasutta	MN67	Buddha	Sangha	Satisfaction
66	Naḷakapānasutta	MN68	Buddha	Anuruddha	Satisfaction
67	Gulissānisutta	MN69	Buddha	Sangha	Q&A*
68	Kīṭāgirisutta	MN70	Buddha	Sangha	Satisfaction
69	Tevijja-Vacchagottasutta	MN71	Buddha	Vacchagotta (H)	Satisfaction
70	Mahāsakuludāyisutta	MN77	Buddha	Udāyi (H)	Satisfaction
71	Samaṇamuṇḍikasutta	MN78	Buddha	Pañcakaṅga(H)	Satisfaction
72	Ghaṭīkārasutta	MN81	Buddha	Ānanda	Satisfaction
73	Makhādevasutta	MN83	Buddha	Ānanda	Satisfaction
74	Piyajātikasutta	MN87	Buddha	People (H)	King respects to Buddha three times
			Queen Mallikā	King Pasenadi(H)	
75	Bāhitikasutta	MN88	Buddha	Sangha	Satisfaction
76	Dhammacetiyasutta	MN89	Buddha	Sangha	Satisfaction
77	Kaṇṇakatthalasutta	MN90	Buddha	King Pasendi(H)	Without stock
78	Devadahasutta	MN101	Buddha	Sangha	Satisfaction
79	Pañcattasutta	MN102	Buddha	Sangha	Satisfaction
80	Kintisutta	MN103	Buddha	Sangha	Satisfaction
81	Sāmagāmasutta	MN104	Buddha	Sangha	Satisfaction
82	Sunakkhattasutta	MN105	Buddha	Sunakkhatta(H)	Satisfaction
83	Āṇañjasappāyasutta	MN106	Buddha	Sangha	Satisfaction
84	Gopakamoggallānasutta	MN108	Buddha	Vassakāra (H)	Satisfaction
				Gopakamoggallāna (H)	-

No.	Name of Discourse	Position	Sermonizer	Hearer	Ending
85	Mahāpuṇṇamasutta	MN109	Buddha	Sangha	Satisfaction
				60 Monks	Arahantship
86	Cūḷapuṇṇamasutta	MN110	Buddha	Sangha	Satisfaction
87	Anupadasutta	MN111	Buddha	Sangha	Satisfaction
88	Chabbisodhanasutta	MN112	Buddha	Sangha	Satisfaction
89	Sappurisasutta	MN113	Buddha	Sangha	Satisfaction
90	Sevitabba-asevitabbasutta	MN114	Buddha	Sangha	Satisfaction
91	Bahudhātukasutta	MN115	Buddha	Ānanda	Satisfaction
92	Mahācattārīsakasutta	MN117	Buddha	Sangha	Satisfaction
93	Ānāpānasatisutta	MN118	Buddha	Sangha	Satisfaction
94	Kāyagatāsatisutta	MN119	Buddha	Sangha	Satisfaction
95	Saṃkhāruppattisutta	MN120	Buddha	Sangha	Satisfaction
96	Cūḷasuññatasutta	MN121	Buddha	Ānanda	Satisfaction
97	Mahāsuññatasutta	MN122	Buddha	Ānanda	Satisfaction
98	Acchariyabbhutadhamma-sutta	MN123	Ānanda	Sangha	Satisfaction
99	Dantabhūmisutta	MN125	Buddha	Aciravata	Satisfaction
100	Bhūmijasutta	MN126	Buddha	Bhūmija	Satisfaction
101	Anurudhasutta	MN127	Anurudha	Abhiyakaccāna	Comment
				Pañcakaṅga(H)	-
102	Uppakkilesasutta	MN128	Buddha	Sangha	Satisfaction
103	Bālapaṇḍitasutta	MN129	Buddha	Sangha	Satisfaction
104	Bhaddekarattasutta	MN131	Buddha	Sangha	Satisfaction
105	Ānandabhaddekarattasutta	MN132	Buddha	Ānanda	Satisfaction
106	Mahākaccānabhaddeka-rattasutta	MN133	Buddha	Sangha	Satisfaction
107	Lomasakaṅgiyabhadde-karattasutta	MN134	Buddha	Lomasakaṅgiya	Satisfaction
108	Mahākammavibhaṅgasutta	MN136	Buddha	Ānanda	Satisfaction
109	Saḷāyatanavibhaṅgasutta	MN137	Buddha	Sangha	Satisfaction
110	Uddesavibhaṅgasutta	MN138	Buddha	Sangha	Satisfaction
111	Araṇavibhaṇgasutta	MN139	Buddha	Sangha	Satisfaction
112	Dhātuvibhaṅgasutta	MN140	Buddha	Sangha	Satisfaction
113	Saccavibhaṅgasutta	MN141	Sāriputta	Sangha	Satisfaction

No.	Name of Discourse	Position	Sermonizer	Hearer	Ending
114	Aṇāthapiṇḍikovādasutta	MN143	Buddha	Ānanda	Satisfaction
115	Channovādasutta	MN143	Buddha	Sāriputta	Satisfaction
116	Puṇṇovādasutta	MN145	Buddha	Sangha	Satisfaction
117	Nandakovādasutta	MN146	Buddha	Sangha	Satisfaction
118	Cūḷarāhulovādasutta	MN147	Buddha	Rāhula	Satisfaction Arahantship
119	Chachakkasutta	MN148	Buddha	Sangha	Satisfaction
120	Mahāsāḷāyatanikasutta	MN149	Buddha	Sangha	Satisfaction
121	Piṇḍapātapārisuddhisutta	MN151	Buddha	Sāriputta	Satisfaction
122	Indriyabhāvanasutta	MN152	Buddha	Ānanda	Satisfaction

* The last question and answer
(H) householder or ascetics outside the Sangha

Legend (16 discourses)

Dīgha-nikāya (total sum 5): Mahāparinibbānasutta (DN16); Janavasabhasutta (DN18); Mahāsamayasutta (DN20); Pāyāsirājaññasutta (DN23); Sampasādanīyasutta (DN28)

Majjhima-nikāya (total sum 5): Raṭṭhapālasutta (MN82); Aṅgulimālasutta (MN86); Selasutta (MN92); Dhanañjānisutta (MN97); Bakkulasutta (MN124)

Discourse ending with verses or explanation on the name (total sum 6): Mahāsudassanasutta (DN17); Cūḷagopālakasutta(MN34); Brahmanimantikasutta(MN49); Isigilisutta(MN116); Devadūtasutta(MN130); Dakkhiṇavibhaṅgasutta(MN142)

Appendix II: Progressive Talk and Sermon Leading to Reactions to Buddha

No.	Name of Discourse	Position	Sermonizer	Hearer	Result: in Expression					Decision on Conversion		
					Stock phrases (3)	Other Compliment	Apology	Truth Realised	Jewel Refuges	Monastic Disciple	Non-monastic Disciple	No expression
1	Sāmaññaphalasutta	DN2	Buddha	King Ajātasattu	✓	✓	✓		✓		✓	
2	Ambaṭṭhasutta	DN3	Buddha	Pokkharasādī	✓			✓	✓		✓	
3	Soṇadaṇḍasutta	DN4	Buddha	Soṇadaṇḍa	✓				✓		✓	
4	Kūṭadantasutta	DN5	Buddha	Kūṭadanta	✓			✓	✓		✓	
5	Kassapa-Sīhanādasutta	DN8	Buddha	Acelakassapa	✓	✓			✓	✓		
6	Poṭṭhapādasutta	DN9	Buddha	Poṭṭhapāda	✓				✓		✓	
				Cittahattha Sāriputta	✓				✓	✓		
7	Subhasutta	DN10	Ānanda	Subha	✓	✓			✓		✓	
8	Lohiccasutta	DN12	Buddha	Lohicca	✓	✓			✓		✓	
9	Tevijjasutta	DN13	Buddha	Vāseṭṭha	✓				✓		✓	
				Bhāradvāja	✓				✓		✓	
10	Sakkapañhasutta	DN21	Buddha	Sakka		✓		✓*	✓			converted
11	Pāṭikasutta	DN24	Buddha	Bhagavagotta	✓							✓
12	Udumbarika-Sīhanādasutta	DN25	Buddha	Nigrodha	✓							✓
13	Sigākalovādasutta	DN31	Buddha	Siṅgala	✓				✓		✓	
14	Bhayabheravasutta	MN4	Buddha	Jāṇusoṇi	✓				✓		✓	

No.	Name of Discourse	Position	Sermonizer	Hearer	Result: in Expression					Decision on Conversion		
					Stock phrases (3)	Other Compliment	Apology	Truth Realised	Jewel Refuges	Monastic Disciple	Non-monastic Disciple	No expression
15	Vatthūpamasutta	MN7	Buddha	Sundarika-bharadvāja	✓				✓	✓		
16	Cūḷahatthipadopamasutta	MN27	Buddha	Jāṇusoṇi	✓				✓		✓	
17	Cūḷasāropamasutta	MN30	Buddha	Piṅgalakoccha	✓				✓		✓	
18	Cūḷasaccakasutta	MN35	Ānanda	Saccaka Niganthaputta	✓	✓						✓
19	Sāleyyakasutta	MN41	Buddha	People in Sāla Village	✓				✓		✓	
20	Verañjakasutta	MN42	Buddha	People in Verañja Town	✓				✓		✓	
21	Māratajjanīyasutta	MN50	Moggallāna	Māra								✓
22	Aṭṭhakanāgasutta	MN52	Ānanda	Dasama		✓						✓
23	Potaliyasutta	MN54	Buddha	Potaliya	✓		✓		✓		✓	
24	Jivakasutta	MN55	Buddha	Jīvaka	✓	✓			✓		✓	
25	Upālisutta	MN56	Buddha	Upāli	✓	✓		✓	✓		✓	
26	Kukkuravatikasutta	MN57	Buddha	Puṇṇa Koliyaputta	✓				✓		✓	
				Seniya	✓				✓	✓		
27	Abhayarājakumāra-sutta	MN58	Buddha	Prince Abhaya	✓				✓			
28	Apaṇṇakasutta	MN60	Buddha	People in Sāla Village	✓				✓		✓	
29	Aggi-Vacchagottasutta	MN72	Ānanda	Vacchagotta	✓				✓			

No.	Name of Discourse	Position	Sermonizer	Hearer	Result: in Expression					Decision on Conversion		
					Stock phrases (3)	Other Compliment	Apology	Truth Realised	Jewel Refuges	Monastic Disciple	Non-monastic Disciple	No expression
30	Mahā-Vacchagottasutta	MN73	Buddha	Vacchagotta	✓	✓			✓	✓	✓	
31	Dīgha-nakhasutta	MN74	Buddha	Dīgha-nakha	✓			✓	✓		✓	
				Sāriputta				✓*				converted
32	Māgandiyasutta	MN75	Buddha	Māgaṇḍiya	✓				✓	✓		
33	Sandakasutta	MN76	Ānanda	Sandaka		✓						✓
34	Cūḷa-Sakuludāyisutta	MN79	Buddha	Sakuludāyī	✓				✓	✓		✓
35	Vekhaṇasasutta	MN80	Buddha	Vakhaṇasa	✓				✓		✓	
36	Madhurasutta	MN84	Kaccāna	King Madhura	✓				✓		✓	
37	Bodhirājakumārasutta	MN85	Buddha	Prince Bodhi	✓				✓		✓	
38	Brahmāyusutta	MN91	Buddha	Brahmāyu	✓			✓	✓		✓	
39	Assalāyanasutta	MN93	Buddha	Assalāyana	✓				✓		✓	
40	Ghoṭamukhasutta	MN94	Udena	Ghoṭamukha	✓				✓		✓	
41	Caṅkīsutta	MN95	Buddha	Kāpadika	✓		✓		✓		✓	
42	Esukārīsutta	MN96	Buddha	Esukārī	✓						✓	
43	Vāseṭṭhasutta	MN98	Buddha	Vāseṭṭha	✓				✓		✓	
				Bharadvāja	✓				✓		✓	
44	Subhasutta	MN99	Buddha	Subha Todeyyaputta					✓		✓	
45	Sagāravasutta	MN100	Buddha	Sagārava	✓				✓		✓	

No.	Name of Discourse	Position	Sermonizer	Hearer	Result: in Expression					Decision on Conversion		
					Stock phrases (3)	Other Compliment	Apology	Truth Realised	Jewel Refuges	Monastic Disciple	Non-monastic Disciple	No expression
46	Gaṇakamoggallānasutta	MN107	Buddha	Gaṇaka-moggallāna	✓	✓			✓		✓	
47	Cūḷakammavibhaṅga-sutta	MN135	Buddha	Subha Todeyyaputta	✓				✓		✓	
48	Nagaravindeyyasutta	MN150	Buddha	People in Vinda Town	✓				✓		✓	

* The hearer attained a higher spiritual attainment after hearing the sermon.

Appendix III: Code Number of Stock Phrases

Number	Stock Phrase (Pāli with English Translation)	Type of Stock Phrase
(1)	Idam avoca [Bhagavā], attamanā [te bhikkhū] [Bhagavato] bhāsitaṃ abhinandun-ti Thus spoke [the Exalted One]. Delighted [these monks] rejoiced in what [the Exalted One] had said.	Type I: Hearer's Satisfaction
(2)	Itiha te ubho [mahānāgā] aññamaññassa subhāsitaṃ samanumodiṃsûti In this wise did each of these [great beings] rejoice together in what was well spoken by the other.	
(3)	Seyyathā pi bhante nikkujjitaṃ vā ukkujjeyya paṭicchannaṃ vā vivareyya mūḷhassa vā maggaṃ ācikkheyya andhakāre vā tela-pajjotaṃ dhāreyya: "cakkhumanto rūpāni dakkhintî" ti evam eva Bhagavatā aneka-pariyāyena dhammo pakāsito. Most excellent, Lord, most excellent! Just as if a man were to set up that which has been thrown down, or were to reveal that which is hidden away, or were to point out the right road to him who has gone astray, or were to bring a lamp into the darkness so that those who have eyes could see external forms – just even so, Lord, has the truth been made known to me, in many a figure, by the Exalted One.	Type II: Denoting Formal Declaration of Belief in Buddha
(4)	Esâhaṃ bhante Bhagavantaṃ saraṇaṃ gacchāmi dhammañ ca bhikkhu-saṅghañ ca. And I, even I, betake myself as my guide to the Exalted One, and to the Doctrine; and to the Brotherhood.	
(5)	Upāsakaṃ maṃ bhagavā dhāretu ajjatagge pāṇupetaṃ saraṇaṃ gataṃ May the Exalted One accept me as a disciple, as one who, from this day forth, as long as life endures, has taken his refuge in them.	
(6)	Labheyyāhaṃ bhante bhagavato santike pabbajjaṃ, labheyyaṃ upasampadan-ti. I would fain, Lord, renounce the world under the Exalted One; I would fain be admitted to his Order.	

Number	Stock Phrase (Pāli with English Translation)	Type of Stock Phrase
(7)	Ekamantaṃ nisinnassa kho [brāhmaṇassa Pokkharasādissa] Bhagavā ānupubbikathaṃ kathesi seyyathīdaṃ dānakathaṃ sīlakathaṃ saggakathaṃ kāmānaṃ ādinavaṃ okāraṃ saṃkilesaṃ nekkhamme ānisaṃsaṃ pakāsesi. Yadā bhagavā aññāsi [brāhmaṇaṃ Pokkharasādiṃ] kallacittaṃ mudu-cittaṃ vinīvaraṇa-cittaṃ udagga-cittaṃ pasanna-cittaṃ atha yā buddhānaṃ sāmukkaṃsikā dhammadesanā taṃ pakāsesi: dukkhaṃ samudayaṃ nirodhaṃ maggaṃ. Seyyathā pi nāma suddhaṃ vatthaṃ apagata-kāḷakaṃ sammad eva rajanaṃ patigaṇheyya. Then to him thus seated the Exalted One discoursed in due order; that is to say: he spake to him of generosity, of right conduct, of heaven, of the danger, the vanity, and the defilement of lusts, of the advantages of renunciation. And when the Exalted One saw that [Pokkharasādi, the Brahman,] had become prepared, softened, unprejudiced, upraised, and believing in heart, then he proclaimed the doctrine that Buddhas alone have won; that is to say: the doctrine of sorrow, of its origin, of its cessation, and of the Path. And as a clean cloth from which all stain has been washed away will readily take the dye.	Type III: Denoting a Spiritual Attainment
(8)	Evameva kho [brāhmaṇassa Pokkharasādissa] tasmiṃ yeva āsane virajaṃ vītamalaṃ Dhamma-cakkhuṃ udapādi: "yaṃ kiñci samudaya-dhammaṃ sabban taṃ nirodha-dhamman" ti. Atha kho [brāhmaṇo Pokkharasādi] diṭṭha-dhammo patta-dhammo vidita-dhammo pariyogaḷha-dhammo tiṇṇa-vikiccho vigata-kathaṃkatho vesārajjappatto aparapaccayo satthu sāsane. Just even so did [Pokkharasādi, the Brahman,] obtain, even while sitting there, the pure and spotless Eye for the Truth, and he knew: 'Whosoever has a beginning in that is inherent also the necessity of dissolution.' And then [Pokkharasādi the Brahman] as one who had seen the Truth, had mastered it, understood it, dived deep into it, who had passed beyond doubt and put away perplexity and gained full confidence, who had become dependent on no other man for his knowledge of the teaching of the Master, addressed the Exalted One, and said:	

Appendix IV: Religiosity of Non-Monastic Follower in Pāli Discourse

The author has categorised religiosity of the non-monastic followers in different levels of belief denoted by the usage of stock phrases with the aim to demonstrate that the strength of the belief in the Buddha can be observed in the behaviours and activities towards the Buddha, his teaching and his community. In parentheses is the author's reconstruction based on the data in other Nikāyas, in which the followers with the level of belief should concern.

Category		Expressions	I.	II.	III.	IV.
After conversation		Dumb and speechless		✓	(✓)	✓
		Make an apology to Buddha on his false belief and bad behaviour to the Buddha in the past		✓	(✓)	✓
On Conversion	Action	Take the Three Jewels for refuges	✓	✓		
		Ask to become a monastic follower	(✓)	✓		
		Ask to become a lay follower	✓	✓		
		Hesitate to become a monk in the second decision		✓		
	Expression of Respect	Announce with confidence his belief and show respect to Buddha in public	✓			
		Confirm the belief in Buddha and his order despite being challenged	✓			
		Show a greatly physical expression of respect to Buddha	✓	✓		
		Describe Buddha's qualities and goodness in detail	✓	✓		
		Keep the belief in Buddha for himself		✓	✓	✓
		Show a limited expression of respecting to Buddha		✓	✓	✓
		Take a lower seat than the Buddha's seat	✓	✓	✓	✓
		Compliment Buddha and his followers	✓	✓	✓	✓

Category		Expressions	I.	II.	III.	IV.
Religiosity to Buddha and the Order	Attitudes	Have the house open for Buddha and his followers every time	✓	✓		
		Stop contact with his former religious belief and community	(✓)	✓		
		Delight to see Buddha and his followers	✓	✓		
	Donation	Offer a precious gift	✓			
		Provide the order permanent structure	✓			
		Confide in Buddha and his followers and expect great merit from offering	✓	✓		
		Offer clothes to Buddha and his followers	✓	✓		
		Offer food to Buddha and his followers		✓	(✓)	✓
	On debate and discuss on doctrine	Learning and practice Buddha's teaching in private	✓	✓		
		Appreciate the Buddha's teaching for understanding of life	(✓)	✓		
		Remember and mention to Buddha when talking about his teaching	✓	✓		
		Agree with Buddha's argument against an activity and abolish the old activity		✓		
		Have interest in the Buddha's doctrine and discuss on it with Buddha	✓	✓	(✓)	

Bibliography

1 Primary Sources

Carpenter, J. Elstlin (Ed.) (1911), The Dīgha-nikāya. Dialogues of the Buddha. Volume III. London: Pali Text Society.

Chalmers, R. (Ed.) (1898), The Majjhima-nikāya Vol. II. London: Pali Text Society.

Chalmers, R. (Ed.) (1899), The Majjhima-nikāya Vol. III. London: Pali Text Society.

Hare, E. M. (Transl.) (1935), The Book of the Gradual Sayings. Volume IV. London: Pali Text Society.

Hare, E. M. (Transl.) (1943), The Book of the Gradual Sayings. Volume V. London: Pali Text Society.

Horner, I. B. (Ed.) (1933), Papañcasūdanī. Majjhima-nikāyatthakatha of Buddhaghosācariya Part III. London: Pali Text Society.

Horner, I. B. (Transl.) (1951), The Book of the Discipline. Volume IV. London: Pali Text Society.

Horner, I. B. (Transl.) (1952), The Book of the Discipline. Volume V. London: Pali Text Society.

Horner, I. B. (Transl.) (1954–1959), Majjhima-nikāya. The Collection of the Middle Length Sayings (Majjhima-nikāya). - Volume I–III. London: Pali Text Society.

Horner, I. B. (1933), Papañcasūdanī. Majjhima-nikāyaṭṭhakathā of Buddhaghosācariya. Vol. 3: Suttas 51–100. London: Pali Text Society.

Ñāṇamolī, Bikkhu (Transl.) (1956), The Path of Purification. (Visuddhimagga) Colombo: Lake House Bookshop.

Ñāṇamolī, Bikkhu (Transl.) (1978), The Minor Readings (Kuddakapāṭha). The First Book of the Minor Collection (Khuddakanikāya). London: Pali Text Society.

Norman, H. C. (Ed.) (1906), Dhammapadaṭṭhakathā. The Commentary on the Dhammapada. Vol. I. London: Pali Text Society.

Norman, K. R. (Ed.) (1984), The Book of Discourses. Volume I. London: Pali Text Society.

Rhys Davids, Caroline A.F.; Woodward, F.L. (Transl.) (1917–1930), The Book of the Kindred Sayings. - Volume I–V. London: Pali Text Society.

Rhys Davids, Thomas W. (Transl.) (1888/1977), Dialogues of the Buddha. - Volume I. London: Pali Text Society.

Rhys Davids, Thomas W. (Transl.) (1890), Dialogues of the Buddha. - Volume II. London: Pali Text Society.

Rhys Davids, Thomas W. (Transl.) (1903), Dīgha-nikāya. Dialogues - Volume III. London: Pali Text Society.

Rhys Davids, Thomas W.; Carpenter, J. Elstlin (Ed.) (1886), The Sumaṅgalavilāsinī, Buddhaghosa's Commentary on the Pāli-Nikāya Part I. London: Pali Text Society.

Rhys Davids, Thomas W.; Carpenter, J. Elstlin (Ed.) (1890), The Dīgha-nikāya. - Volume I. London: Pali Text Society.

Rhys Davids, Thomas W.; Carpenter, J. Elstlin (Ed.) (1903), The Dīgha-nikāya. Volume II. London: Pali Text Society.

Stede, W. (1931), Sumaṅgalavilāsinī, Buddhaghosa's commentary on the Dīgha-nikāya. Vol. II. London: Pali Text Society.

Stede, W. (Ed.) (1932), Sumaṅgalavilāsinī, Buddhaghosa's Commentary on the Dīgha-nikāya. Part III. London: Pali Text Society.

Trenckner, V. (Ed.) (1888), The Majjhima-nikāya Vol. I. London: Pali Text Society.

Woods, J. H. and Kosambi, D. (1922), Papañcasūdanī. Majjhima-nikāyaṭṭhakathā of Buddhaghosācariya. Vol. 1: Suttas 1–10. London: Pali Text Society.

Woods, J. H. and Kosambi, D. (1928), Papañcasūdanī. Majjhima-nikāyaṭṭhakathā of Buddhaghosācariya. Vol. 2: Suttas 11–50. London: Pali Text Society.

Woodward, F. L. (Transl.) (1972–1982), The Book of the Gradual Sayings. Volume I–V. With an introduction by Caroline A. F. Rhys Davids. London: Pali Text Society.

Woodward, F. L. (Transl.) (1979), The Book of the Kindred Sayings. Vol. I–V. With an introduction by Caroline A. F. Rhys Davids. London: Pali Text Society.

2 Secondary Sources

Agostini, Giulio (2002), Indian Views of the Buddhist Laity. Precepts and Upāsaka Status. Diss. phil. Berkeley: University of California.

Ahir, D. C. (1996), The Status of the Laity in Buddhism. Delhi: Sri Satguru Publications (Bibliotheca Indo-Buddhica series; 171).

Allon, Mark (1997), Style and Function. A Study of the Dominant Stylistic Features of the Prose Portions of Pāli Canonical Sutta Texts and their Mnemonic Function. Tokyo: International Institute for Buddhist Studies (Studia philologica Buddhica Monograph series; 12).

Amore, Roy (1970), The Concept and Practice of Doing Merit in Early Theravāda Buddhism. Diss. phil. New York: Columbia University.

Anālayo, Bikkhu (2007), Oral Dimensions of Pāli Discourses:. Pericopes, other Mnemonic Techniques and the Oral Performance Context. In: Canadian Journal of Buddhist Studies; 3, 2007: 5–33.

Anālayo, Bikkhu (2009), The Vicissitudes of Memory and Early Buddhist Oral Transmission. In: Canadian Journal of Buddhist Studies; 5, 2009: 5–19.

Anālayo, Bikkhu (2011), A Comparative Study of the Majjhima-nikāya. Volume 1–2. Taipei: Dharma Drum Publishing (Dharma Drum Buddhist College research series; 3).

Barua, Dipak K. (1971), An Analytical Study of Four Nikāyas. Calcutta: Rabindra Bharati University.

Berkwitz, Stephen C.; Schober, Juliane; Brown, Claudia (2009), Introduction to Buddhist Manuscript Cultures. In: Berkwitz, Stephen C. (Ed.): Buddhist Manuscript Cultures. London: Routledge: 1–15.

Blackstone, Kathryn R. (1998), Women in the Footsteps of the Buddha. Surrey, London: Curzon.

Blasi, Anthony J. (2009), The Meaning of Conversion: Redirection of Foundational Trust. In: Giordan, Guiseppe (Ed.): Conversion in the Age of Pluralism. Leiden, Boston: Brill: 11–31.

Bluck, Robert (2002), The Path of the Householder. Buddhist Lay Disciples in the Pāli Canon. In: Buddhist Studies Review; 19, Issue 1, 2002: 1–18.

Bodhi, Bhikkhu (2001), The Jhānas and the Lay Disciple According to the Pāli Suttas. In: Premasiri, P. D. (Ed.): Buddhist Studies:. Essay in Honour of Professor Lily de Silva. Peradeniya: University of Peradeniya: 36–64.

Brekke, Torkel (2002), Religious Motivation and the Origins of Buddhism. A social-psychological exploration of the origins of a world religion. London: Routledge Curzon (Routledge Curzon critical studies in Buddhism).

Bronkhorst, Johannes (1986), The Two Traditions of Meditation in Ancient India. Delhi: Motilal Banarsidass.

Bronkhorst, Johannes (2000), Die buddhistische Lehre. In: Bechert, Heinz et al. (Ed.): Der Buddhismus I. Der indische Buddhismus und seine Verzweigungen. Stuttgart: Kohlhammer: 23–213.

Bronkhorst, Johannes (2007), Greater Magadha. Studies in the Culture of Early India. Leiden: Brill (Handbook of Oriental Studies: Section 2 South Asia; 19).

Bronkhorst, Johannes (2011), Buddhism in the Shadow of Brahmanism. Leiden: Brill (Handbook of Oriental Studies: Section 2 South Asia; 24).

Buddhadatta Mahathera, A. P. (1994), A Concise Pāli-English Dictionary. Delhi: Motilal Banarsidass Publishers.

Carter, John R. (Ed.) (1979), Religiousness in Sri Lanka. Colombo: Marga Institute.

Chakravarti, Uma (1996), The Social Dimensions of Early Buddhism. New Delhi: Munshiram Manoharlal.

Collins, Steven (1992), Notes on some Oral Aspects of Pāli Literature. In: Indo-Iranian Journal; 35, 1992: 121–135.

Conze, Edward (1959), Buddhism. Its Essence and Development. New York: Harper & Row.

Cousins, L. S. (2005), Pāli Oral Literature. In: Buddhism. Critical Concepts in Religious Studies. London, New York: Routledge: 96–104.

Dutt, Nalinaksha (1945), Place of Laity in Early Buddhism. In: Indian Historical Quarterly; 163, 21, 1945: 121–145.

Foley, John M. (1988), The Theory of Oral Composition. History and Methodology. Bloomington, Indianapolis: Indiana University Press.

Foley, John M. (1992), Word-Power, Performance, and Tradition. In: Journal of American Folklore; 105, Issue 417, 1992: 275–301.

Foley, John M. (1996), Signs, Texts, and Oral Tradition. In: Journal of Folklore Research; 33, Issue 1, 1996: 21–29.

Foley, John M. (2007), "Reading" Homer through Oral Tradition. In: College Literature; 34, 2, 2007: 1–28.

Franke, R. Otto (1913), Das einheitliche Thema des Dīgha-nikāya. Gotama Buddha ist ein Tathagata. In: Wiener Zeitschrift für die Kunde des Morgenlandes; 27, 1913: 198–216; 276–304.

Franke, R. Otto (1913), Die Verknüpfung der Dighanikāya-Suttas untereinander. In: Zeitschrift der Deutschen Morgenländischen Gesellschaft; 67, 1913: 409–461.

Franke, R. Otto (1914), Der dogmatische Buddha nach dem Dighanikāya. In: Wiener Zeitschrift für die Kunde des Morgenlandes; 28, 1914: 331–355.

Franke, R. Otto (1914), Die Zusammenhänge der Majjhima-nikāya-Suttas. In: Zeitschrift der Deutschen Morgenländischen Gesellschaft; 68, 1914: 473–530.

Franke, R. Otto (1914), Majjhima-nikāya und Suttanipāta. In: Wiener Zeitschrift für die Kunde des Morgenlandes; 28, 1914: 261–276.

Franke, R. Otto (1915), Der einheitliche Grundgedanke des Majjhimanikaya. Die Erziehung gemäß der Lehre (dhamma-vinaya). In: Wiener Zeitschrift für die Kunde des Morgenlandes; 29, 1915: 134–171.

Freiberger, Oliver (1996), Zum Vergleich zwischen buddhistischem und christlichem Ordenswesen. In: Zeitschrift für Religionswissenschaft; 4, 1996: 83–104.

Freiberger, Oliver (1997), Anmerkungen zur Begriffsbildung in der Buddhismusforschung. In: Kieffer-Pülz, Petra; Hartmann, Jens-Uwe (Ed.): Bauddhavidyāsudhākaraḥ. Studies in honour of Heinz Bechert on the occasion of his 65th birthday. Swisttal-Odendorf: Indica et Tibetica Verlag (Indica et Tibetica; 30): 137–152.

Freiberger, Oliver (1997), Zur Verwendungsweise der Bezeichnung paribbājaka im Pāli-Kanon. In: Roth, Gustav; Bechert, Heinz; Bretfeld,

Sven; Kieffer-Pülz, Petra (Ed.): Untersuchungen zur buddhistischen Literatur. Göttingen: Vandenhoeck & Ruprecht: 121–130.

Freiberger, Oliver (2000), Der Orden in der Lehre. Wiesbaden: Harrassowitz (Studies in oriental religions; 47).

Freiberger, Oliver (2000), Profiling the Sangha. Institutional and Non-Institutional Tendencies in Early Buddhist Teachings. In: Marburg Journal of Religion; 5, Issue 1, 2000: 1–12.

Freiberger, Oliver (2001), Salvation for the Laity? Soteriological Concepts in Early and Modern Theravāda Buddhism. In: Studia Asiatica (Bukarest), 2, 2001: 29–38.

Freiberger, Oliver (2005), Ein „Vinaya für Hausbewohner"? Norm und Praxis der Laienanhänger im frühen Buddhismus. In: Schalk, Peter; Deeg, Max (Ed.): Im Dickicht der Gebote. Studien zur Dialektik von Norm und Praxis in der Buddhismusgeschichte Asiens. Upsala: Uppsala Universitet: 225–252.

Freiberger, Oliver; Kleine, Christoph (2011), Buddhismus. Handbuch und kritische Einführung. Göttingen: Vandenhoeck & Ruprecht.

Gethin, Rupert (2001), The Buddhist Path to Awakening. Oxford: Oneworld Publications.

Gethin, Rupert (2004), He who Sees Dhamma Sees Dhammas: Dhamma in Early Buddhism. In: Journal of Indian Philosophy; 32, Issue 5–6, 2004: 513–542.

Giordan, Guiseppe (Ed.) (2009), Conversion in the Age of Pluralism. Leiden, Boston: Brill (Religion and the Social Order; 17).

Gokhale, Balkrishna (1989), Āloko Udapādi. The Imagery of Illumination in Early Buddhist Literature. In: Samtani, N. M. (Ed.): Amalā Prajñā. Aspects of Buddhist Studies; Professor P. V. Bapat Felicitation Volume. Delhi: Sri Satguru Publications: 1–10.

Gombrich, Richard F. (1984), Introduction: The Buddhist Way. In: Bechert, Heinz; Gombrich, Richard F. (Ed.): The World of Buddhism. Buddhist Monks and Nuns in Society and Culture. London: Thames & Hudson: 9–14.

Gombrich, Richard F. (1984), The Evolution of the Sangha. In: Bechert, Heinz; Gombrich, Richard F. (Ed.): The World of Buddhism. Buddhist

Monks and Nuns in Society and Culture. London: Thames & Hudson: 77–89.

Gombrich, Richard F. (2004), Religious Experience in Early Buddhism. In: Sutcliffe, Steven (Ed.): Religion. Empirical Studies. Aldershot Hants England, Burlington VT: Ashgate: 123–148.

Gombrich, Richard F. (2005), Recovering the Buddha's Message. In: Buddhism. Critical Concepts in Religious Studies. London, New York: Routledge: 113–128.

Gombrich, Richard F. (2006), Theravāda Buddhism: A Social History from Ancient Benares to Modern Colombo. 2nd edition. London: Routledge (The library of religious beliefs and practices).

Gross, Rita M. (1993), Buddhism after Patriarchy. A Feminist History, Analysis, and Reconstruction of Buddhism. Albany: State University of New York Press.

Griffiths, Paul J. (1999), Religious Reading: The Place of Reading in the Practice of Religion. New York: Oxford University Press.

Hallisay, Charles (1988), Review Article: Divine Revelation in Pāli Buddhism, by Peter Masefield. In: Journal of International Association of Buddhist Studies; 11, Issue 1, 1988: 173–175.

Hallisay, Charles (1995), Road taken and not taken in the Study of Theravada Buddhism. In: Lopez, Donald S. (Ed.): Curators of the Buddha. The study of Buddhism under colonialism. Chicago, Ill: University of Chicago Press: 31–61.

Hallisay, Charles; Hansen, Anne (1996), Narrative, Sub-Ethics, and the Moral Life. Some Evidence from Theravāda Buddhism. In: Journal of Religious Ethics; 24, 2, 1996: 305–327.

Halstead, J. Mark (2005) "Religious Education". In: Jones, Lindsay (Ed.): Encyclopedia of Religion. Vol 11: Pius IX - rivers. Detroit: Thomson Gale (Encyclopedia of Religion; 11).

Harrison, Paul (1987), Buddhism: A Religion of Revelation after All ? À propos Peter Masefield's "Divine Revelation in Pali Buddhism" by Peter Masefield. Review Article. In: Numen; 34, 2, 1987: 256–264.

Harrison, Paul (1995), Searching for the Origins of the Mahayana. What are we looking for? In: The Eastern Buddhist; 28, 1995: 48–69.

Hauschild, Wolf-Dieter (2005), Article: “Laien”. In: Betz, Hans-Dieter (Ed.): Die Religion in Geschichte und Gegenwart. Handwörterbuch für Theologie und Religionswissenschaft. Volume 6: Sh-Z. Tübingen: Mohr Siebeck: 17–21.

Havelock, Eric A. (1963), Preface to Plato. Oxford: Basil Blackwell.

Harvey, Peter (2000), An Introduction to Buddhist Ethics. Foundation, Values, and Issues. Cambridge: Cambridge University Press.

Henaut, Barry (1993), Oral Tradition and the Gospels. The Problem of Mark 4. London: Continuum International Publishing (The Library of New Testament Studies; Supplement series; 82).

Hinüber, Oskar von (1994), Untersuchungen zur Mündlichkeit früher mittelindischer Texte der Buddhisten. Mainz: Akademie der Wissenschaften und der Literatur.

Hinüber, Oskar von (1996), A Handbook of Pāli Literature. Berlin; New York: De Gruyter. (Indian philology and South Asian studies; 2).

Hinüber, Oskar von (1997), Old Age and Old Monk in Pāli Buddhism. In: Formanek, Susanne; Linhart, Sepp (Ed.): Aging: Asian Concepts and Experiences Past and Present. Vienna: Verlag der Österreichischen Akademie der Wissenschaften.

Hoens, Dirk Jan; Kloppenborg, Ria (Ed.) (1983), Selected Studies on Ritual in the Indian Religions. Essays to D. J. Hoens. Leiden: E. J. Brill.

Holder, John J. (2000), Review Article: How Buddhism Began: The Conditioned Genesis of the Early Teachings by Richard F.Gombrich. In: Philosophy East and West; 50, 2, 2000: 297–299.

Honko, Lauri (1995), Problems of Oral and Semiliterary Epics. In: Heissig, Walther (Ed.): Formen und Funktion mündlicher Tradition. Vorträge eines Akademiesymposiums in Bonn Juli 1993. Opladen: Westdeutscher Verlag: 26–40.

Humphreys, Christmas (1976), A Popular Dictionary of Buddhism. 2nd edition. London: Curzon Press.

James, William (1902), The Varieties of Religious Experience: A study in Human Nature. London, New York, Bombay: Longmans, Green & Co.

Jayatilleke, Kulatissa N. (1963), Early Buddhist Theory of Knowledge. London: Allen & Unwin.

Katz, Nathan (1982), Buddhist Images of Human Perfection: The Arahant of the Sutta Piṭaka Compared with the Bodhisattva and the Mahāsiddha. Delhi: Motilal Banarsidass.

Kelly, John L. (2011), "The Buddha's Teaching to Lay People." In: Buddhist Studies Review; 28, Issue 1, 2011: 3–77.

Keown, Damien; Prebish, Charles S. (Ed.) (2007), Encyclopedia of Buddhism. London, New York: Routledge.

Kiblinger, Kristin B. (2005), Buddhist Inclusivism: Attitudes towards Religious Others. Aldershot, England, Burlington, VT: Ashgate.

Kinsley, David; Narayanan, Vasudha, (2005) "Devotion" In: Jones, Lindsay (Ed.): Encyclopedia of Religion. Vol. 4: Dacian riders - Esther. Detroit: Thomson Gale (Encyclopedia of Religion; 4): 2316–2322.

Klaus, Konrad (2007), Zu der formelhaften Einleitung der buddhistischen Suttras. In: Klaus, Konrad (Ed.): Indica et Tibetica. Festschrift für Michael Hahn zum 65. Geburtstag von Freunden und Schülern überreicht. Wien: Arbeitskreis für tibetische und buddhistische Studien Universität Wien (Wiener Studien zur Tibetologie und Buddhismuskunde; 66): 309–322.

Klaus, Konrad (2010), Zu den buddhistischen literarischen Fachbegriffen *sutta* und *suttanta*. In: Schlingloff, Dieter; Franco, Eli; Zin, Monika (Ed.): From Turfan to Ajanta. Festschrift for Dieter Schlingloff on the occasion of his eightieth birthday. Bhairahawa, Rupandehi: Lumbini International Research Institute.

Kloppenborg, Ria (1983), The Earliest Buddhist Ritual of Ordination. In: Hoens, Dirk Jan; Kloppenborg, Ria (Ed.): Selected studies on ritual in the Indian religions. Essays to D.J. Hoens. Leiden: E.J. Brill: 158–168.

Lamotte, Étienne (1984), Mahayana Buddhism. In: Bechert, Heinz; Gombrich, Richard F. (Ed.): The World of Buddhism. Buddhist Monks and Nuns in Society and Culture. London: Thames & Hudson.

Lang, Karen C. (2007), Pāli Canon. In: Keown, Damien; Prebish, Charles S. (Ed.): Encyclopedia of Buddhism. London, New York: Routledge: 583–586.

Langer, Rita (2013), Sermon Studies and Buddhism: A Case Study of Sri Lankan Preaching. Tokyo: The International Inst. for Buddhist Studies of the International College for Postgraduate Buddhist Studies (Studia Philologica Buddhica Monograph series; 30).

Law, Bimala Churn (1932–1933), Nirvana and Buddhist Laymen. In: Annals of the Bhandarkar Oriental Research Institute; 14, 1932–1933: 80–86.

Lopez, Donald S. (Ed.) (1995), Curators of the Buddha. The study of Buddhism under colonialism. Chicago, Ill: University of Chicago Press.

Lord, Albert B. (1960), The Singer of Tales. Cambridge, Mass.: Harvard University Press.

Lusby, F. Stanley (2005), Laity. In: Jones, Lindsay (Ed.): Encyclopedia of Religion. Volume 8: Ka'bah - Marx, Karl. Detroit: Thomson Gale: 5286–5291.

Mahony, William (2005), Article: "Upanisads". In: Jones, Lindsay (Ed.): Encyclopedia of Religion. Volume 14: Transcendental meditation - Zwingli, Huldrych. Detroit: Thomson Gale: 9480–9484.

Manné, Berenice J. (1992), Debates and Case Histories in the Pali Canon. Diss. phil. Utrecht: University of Utrecht.

Manné, Berenice J. (1993), On a Departure Formula and its Translation. In: Buddhist Studies Review; 10, Issue 1, 1993: 29–43.

Masefield, Peter (1986), Divine Revelation in Pali Buddhism. Colombo: Sri Lanka Institute of Traditional Studies.

McDermott, James P. (1984), Scripture as the Word of the Buddha. In: Numen; 31, Issue 1, 1984: 22–39.

McMahan, David L. (1998), Orality, Writing, and Authority in South Asian Buddhism. Visionary Literature and the Struggle for Legitimacy in the Mahāyāna. In: History of Religions; 37, 3, 1998: 249–274.

Norman, Kenneth R. (1983), Pali Literature. Including the Canonical Literature in Prakrit and Sanskrit of all the Hinayana Schools of Buddhism. Wiesbaden: Harrassowitz (A history of Indian literature; Vol. VII, Fasc. 2).

Norman, Kenneth R. (2006), A Philological Approach to Buddhism 2. Lancaster: The Pali Text Society.

Oldenberg, Hermann (1983), Buddha. Sein Leben, seine Lehre, seine Gemeinde. Stuttgart: Magnus.

Olson, Carl (2011), Religious Studies: The Key Concepts. Abingdon: New York; Routledge.

Ong, Walter J. (2009), Orality and Literacy. Reprinted. London: Routledge.

Patton, Laurie L. (1996), Myth as Argument. Berlin, Chicago: de Gruyter (Religionsgeschichtliche Versuche und Vorarbeiten; 41).

Platvoet, Johannes G.; Molendijk, Arie (Ed.) (1999): The Pragmatics of Defining Religion. Contexts, Concepts and Contests. Leiden: Brill (Studies in the history of religions; 84).

Premasiri, P. D. (Ed.) (2001), Buddhist Studies:. Essay in Honour of Professor Lily de Silva. Peradeniya: University of Peradeniya.

Ratanasara, Havanpola (1979), 'Reaching Out' as an Expression of 'Going Forth'. In: Carter, John R. (Ed.): Religiousness in Sri Lanka. Colombo: Marga Institute: 101–127.

Ray, Reginald A. (1999), Buddhist Saints in India. New York, NY: Oxford University Press.

Rhys Davids, Thomas W. (1896), The History and Literature of Buddhism. Pilkhana: Bhartiya Publishing House.

Ritter, Adolf M.; Barth, Hans-Martin; Wintzer, Friedrich (1990), Article "Laie". In: Balz, Horst R.; Cameron, James K.; Härle, Wilfried (Ed.): Theologische Realenzyklopädie. Band 20: Kreuzzüge – Leo XIII. Berlin, New York: de Gruyter: 378–399.

Rubin, David (1995), Memory in Oral Traditions. The Cognitive Psychology of Epic, Ballads, and Counting-out Rhymes. New York, NY: Oxford University Press.

Roth, Gustav; Bechert, Heinz; Bretfeld, Sven; Kieffer-Pülz, Petra (Ed.) (1997), Untersuchungen zur buddhistischen Literatur. Göttingen: Vandenhoeck & Ruprecht (Sanskrit-Wörterbuch der buddhistischen Texte aus den Turfan-Funden. Beihefte; 8).

Saibaba, V.V.S. (2005), Faith and Devotion in Theravada Buddhism. New Delhi: D. K. Printword (Emerging Perception in Buddhist Studies; 20).

Samuels, Jeffrey (1999), Views of Householders and Lay Disciples in the Sutta Pitaka. A Reconsideration of the Lay/Monastic Opposition. In: Religion; 29, 1999: 231–241.

Sarao, K.T.S. (2008), Review Article: Greater Magadha. Studies in the Culture of Early India, by Johannes Bronkhorst. In: Orientalistische Literaturzeitung; 103, 2, 2008: 250–254.

Schäfer, Fritz (2002), Der Buddha sprach nicht nur für Mönche und Nonnen. Die ganze Lehre erstmals nur nach seinen Reden für Nichtasketen. 2., vollständig überarbeitete Auflage. Heidelberg-Leimen: Kristkeitz.

Sen Majumdar, Gayatri (2009), Early Buddhism and Laity. Kolkata: Maha Bodhi Book Agency.

Silk, Jonathan A. (1989), A Note on the Opening Formula of Buddhist Sutras. In: Journal of International Association of Buddhist Studies; 12, Issue 1, 1989: 158–163.

Skilling, Peter (2009), Redaction, Recitation and Writing. Transmission of the Buddha's teaching in India in the early period. In: Berkwitz, Stephen C. (Ed.): Buddhist Manuscript Cultures. London: Routledge: 53–73.

Slaje, Walter (2005), Article: „Upaniṣaden“. In: Betz, Hans-Dieter (Ed.): Die Religion in Geschichte und Gegenwart. Handwörterbuch für Theologie und Religionswissenschaft. Volume 6: Sh-Z. Tübingen: Mohr Siebeck: 814–815.

Schmithausen, L. (1981), "On Some Aspects of Descriptions or Theories of 'Liberating Insight' and 'Enlightenment' in Early Buddhism." In: Bruhn, K.; Wezler, A. (Ed.): Studien zum Jainismus und Buddhismus. Gedenkschrift für Ludwig Alsdolf. Wiesbaden: Franz Steiner: 199–250.

Stark, Rodney; Finke, Roger (2000), Acts of Faith. Explaining the Human Side of Religion. Berkeley, Los Angeles, London: University of California Press.

Stoesz, Willis (1978), Buddha as Teacher. In: Journal of American Oriental Society; 46, 2, 1978: 139–158.

Swearer, Donald K. (2009), The Buddhist World of Southeast Asia. Chiang Mai: Silkworm Books.

Taves, Ann (2009), Religious Experience Reconsidered. A Building Block Approach to the Study of Religion and Other Special Things. Princeton, NJ: Princeton University Press.

Todd, Elizabeth (1985), The Value of Confession and Forgiveness According to Jung. In: Journal of Religion and Health; 24, 1, 1985: 39–48.

Tubb, Gary A.; Boose, Emery R. (2007), Scholastic Sanskrit. A Handbook for Students. New York: American Inst. of Buddhist Studies at Columbia University (Treasury of the Indic sciences series).

Tworuschka, Udo (1998), Article: „Mönchtum". In: Cancik, Hubert (Ed.): Handbuch religionswissenschaftlicher Grundbegriffe. Volume 4: Kultbild - Rolle. Stuttgart: Kohlhammer: 147–148.

Vansina, Jan (1997), Oral Tradition as History. London: James Currey.

Vetter, Tilman (1994), "Mahāyāna and the Prajñāpāramitā." In: Asiatische Studien. 48, 4, 1994: 1241–1281.

Wach, Joachim (1972), Types of Religious Experience. Christian and Non-Christian. Chicago: University of Chicago Press.

Walters, Jonathan S. (2007), Article: "Moral Discipline". In: Keown, Damien; Prebish, Charles S. (Ed.): Encyclopedia of Buddhism. London, New York: Routledge: 535–537.

Waterhouse, Helen (1997), Buddhism in Bath: Adaptation and Authority. Leeds: University of Leeds Department of Theology and Religious Studies (Monograph Series; 6).

Weber, Max (1958), The Religion of India. The Sociology of Hinduism and Buddhism. Glencoe, IL.: Free Press.

Weber, Max (1992), Economy and Religion. 2 Volumes Berkley: University of California Press.

Wijayaratna, Môhan (1990), Buddhist Monastic Life. Cambridge: Cambridge University Press.

Williams, Paul (2005), Buddhism. Critical Concepts in Religious Studies. London, New York: Routledge.

Witzel, Michael (1988), The Case of the Shattered Head. In: Studien zur Indologie und Iranistik; 13/14, 1988: 363–415.

Wulff, David (1999), Pschychologists Define Religion. Patterns and prospects of a century-long request. In: Platvoet, Johannes G.; Molendijk, Arie (Ed.): The pragmatics of defining religion. Contexts, Concepts and Contests. Leiden: Brill: 207–244.

Wynne, Alexander (2004), The Oral Transmission of Early Buddhist Literature. In: Journal of International Association of Buddhist Studies; 27, Issue 1, 2004: 97–127.

Indices

1 Pāli-Texts

DN I 109, 38–110, 13 81
DN I 110, 10–17 82
DN I 176, 7–12 77
DN I 176, 12–13 77
DN I 176, 13–15 101
DN I 210, 1–7 102
DN I 234, 5–9 103
DN I 46, 27–28 72
DN I 53, 4–6 100
DN I 85, 12 77
DN I 85, 14–15 77
DN I 85, 15–19 108
DN I 85, 8–12 77
DN I 87, 15–88, 2 90
DN I 88, 32–34–89, 1–9 93
DN II 317, 8–11 97
DN II 71, 28–29 72
DN III 292, 6–7 73
DN III 35, 13–14 117
DN III 35, 3–7 117
DN III 35, 8–12 118
DN III 55, 5–8 106
DN III 57, 15–18 119
MN I 236, 1–13 108
MN I 318, 11–12 114
MN I 318, 17–18 139
MN I 318, 23–24 139
MN I 318, 29–31 139
MN I 318, 5–6 139
MN I 319, 2–4 139
MN I 32, 33–34 73
MN I 352, 35–36–353, 1–8 103
MN I 367, 30–36–368, 1–9 107
MN I 378, 27–31 101
MN I 379, 16–18 156
MN I 379, 18–32 156
MN I 379, 3–4 156
MN I 379, 4–15 156
MN I 386, 3–32 158
MN I 387, 2–4 158
MN I 488, 27–34 102
MN I 493, 24–28 104
MN I 523, 34–36–524, 1–4 104
MN I 524, 6–7 120
MN II 111, 35–112, 1–7 79
MN II 144, 23–31 94
MN II 170, 30–32–171, 1–7 ... 138
MN II 176, 25–34–177, 1–11 ... 101
MN III 6, 10–29–7, 1–3 105
MN III 152, 19–22 74

2 Names of Scholars

Agostini, Giulio, 5, 6
Ahir, D.C., 3, 7
Allon, Mark, 16–18, 43
Anālayo, Bikkhu, 17–18, 43, 56, 75, 111
Bluck, Robert, 4–5, 204
Bodhi, Bhikkhu, 4
Brekke, Torkel, 147–148
Conze, Edward, 1, 174–175
Dutt, Nalinaksha, 2, 3, 15
Eliot, Sir Charles, 37
Foley, John M., 19, 48, 52–53
Freiberger, Oliver, 3, 6–9, 10, 14, 16, 39–40, 98
Gombrich, Richard, 1, 16, 31–32
Griffiths, Paul J., 51–54
Harrison, Paul, 114
Havelock, Eric, 22–23

Hinüber, Oskar von, 16, 18, 70
James, William, 26
Kelly, John, 8
Law, Bimala, 2
Lord, Albert, 16, 21, 42–43, 69, 125
Majumdar, Gayatri, 7
Manné, Berenice J., 59–63, 66, 72, 76, 90, 95, 154–155, 167
Masefield, Peter, 83, 112–115
Oldenberg, Hermann, 18, 182
Ong, Walter, 21–23, 31, 51, 97
Parry, Milman, 22, 42, 52
Patton, Laurie, 49–50
Rawlinson, Andrew, 112
Rhys Davids, Thomas W., 19–20, 48
Ray, Reginald, 3, 9, 51, 63
Taves, Ann, 26–30, 44, 80, 123, 129, 140, 145–147, 153, 171, 192, 196, 198–199, 207, 210
Weber, Max, 15, 132
Witzel, Michael, 65–66

3 Proper Names in Pāli-Discourse

Ajātasattu, King, 77, 100, 108, 117, 170
Ambaṭṭha, 59, 66, 93, 163
Anuruddha, 74
Ānanda, 56–57, 60, 68, 72, 75–76, 102–105, 120, 170, 175
Assaji, 98, 140
Bhaggava, Paribbājaka, 117–118, 124
Bimbisāra, King, 161, 171
Brahmāyu, 94–95, 111, 121, 135, 164–165
Dasama, 170–171
Ghoṭamukha, 170–171, 182
Gopakamoggallāna, 75–76, 176
Jīvaka Komārabhacca, 116, 122, 135
Kaccāna, Mahā, 60, 96, 108
Kaccāna, Abhiya, 74
Kassapa, Acela, 101, 174
Kassapa, Kumāra, 97
Kevaḍḍha, 176
Kūṭadanta, 35, 66, 111, 121–122
Magandiya, 163
Mallikā, Queen, 79, 161, 173
Maṇḍiya and Jāliya, 59, 123–124
Moggallāna, 73, 98, 119, 140, 148
Nāṭaputta, 38, 155, 157–158, 163, 188
Nigrodha, Paribbājaka, 119, 124
Oṭṭhaddha Licchavi, 173–174
Pañcakaṅga, 74, 174–175
Pasenadi, King, 74, 79, 155, 159, 161–162, 167, 170, 175
Pokkharasādi, 35, 59, 77, 81–82, 84, 92–95, 111, 135, 169
Sāriputta, 42, 73, 98, 111, 140, 148, 154, 158–159, 173, 175–176
Sigāla, 35, 62
Soṇadaṇḍa, 59, 95, 122–123, 164
Soṇadaṇḍa, Brahmin, 95, 164–165
Sunakkhatta Licchavi, 91–92, 140, 174
Udena, 170
Upāli, 101, 111, 155–158, 162–163, 169, 188
Vassakāra, 76
Vesavaṇṇa, 176
Yasa, 148

4 Subject Index

añjali, 162
ānupubbikathā, 81–84, 86, 111–112, 115–116, 121–122, 126, 133, 136, 154, 157–158, 187, 197
anusāsanīyapāṭihāriya, 85, 176
Arahat, 12, 67, 70, 83, 90–92, 96, 131–132, 134, 140, 183, 190
atheistic religion, 31, 153, 166
Banares, 148, 186
Bṛhaddevatā, 49–50
Buddhaghosa, 21, 50, 57
buddhavacana, 14
charisma, 128, 132, 149, 166
Christianity, 30, 33, 36–37, 39, 88
composite ascription, 27–28, 30, 45, 145, 177, 184, 187, 196
conversion, 12, 30–32, 45, 54, 89, 145–152, 166, 172, 177, 179–180, 185, 187, 190, 197, 200, 206
dakkhiṇā, 171, 184, 209
dhammacakkhu, 67, 71–72, 82–87, 94, 110–117, 121, 125, 136, 140, 142, 154, 158, 163, 169, 187, 197–198, 201
Dhammapadaṭṭhakathā, 36, 67, 83
Dhutaṅga, 38
Early Buddhism, 7, 12, 31, 101
ehibhikkhu-upasampadā, 151
epic, 22–24, 44, 53
religious experience (theory), 14, 25–32, 44, 89, 112, 127–129, 133, 140, 143, 145, 147–149, 159, 166, 178–179, 182, 196, 198–199, 201, 207
formulaic language, 16, 23–25, 32, 44, 47–48, 50, 54, 69, 116, 195, 206
goal deemed special, 184–185, 190–191, 200
homiletics, 86–87, 205–206
Inclusivism, 207, 209–210
Jainism, 91, 155
jhāna, 4, 31
Kosala, 159, 161, 170
Mahāpadesa, 19, 48
mission, 23–25, 44, 47–52, 62, 65–69, 70–72, 78, 89, 135, 142, 189
mnemonic, 17–20, 43, 48, 53, 75, 99
Navaṅgasatthusāsana, 48
nirodhasamāpatti, 31
oral tradition, 13–17, 19, 26, 44, 47, 49, 51–54, 57, 61, 67, 87, 128, 192, 195–197, 206
oral transmission, 13, 16–18, 21–22, 58, 64, 128, 208
Paratoghosa, 177
Paritta, 114
philology, 14, 19
puñña, 37
Religionswissenschaft, 12–14, 207
saddhā, 128, 191, 204
sammādiṭṭhi, 213
sammāsambuddha, 24
Sīhanāda, 154
simple ascription, 28, 30, 44–45, 127, 145, 177, 187, 196, 199
Sotāpanna, 67, 83, 86, 112, 114–116
stock phrase/formula, 12, 16, 22–25, 30–31, 35, 42–44, 53–56, 65, 70–73, 75–79, 81–84, 99, 102, 106, 109–110, 111–119, 125–128, 133–137, 142–147, 162–165, 177–179, 182, 195–199

theistic religion, 31, 112, 114, 166, 196
Theravada Buddhism, 1, 50, 196, 205, 207
things deemed special, 28, 44–45, 80, 208
Three Jewels, 5–6, 33–36, 45, 71, 76–77, 80–81, 86, 96, 108, 111, 116, 133, 136–137, 142–143, 145, 147, 150, 152–153, 159, 169–170, 178–182, 185–186, 191–193, 197–199, 200–202, 206–211
Vedic, Veda, 18, 33, 35, 38, 49–50, 65, 67, 87, 114, 131, 154
Vesāli, 170–171
Vinaya, 9–10, 18–19, 40, 64, 112, 150, 210
Visuddhimagga, 51, 70

Deutsche Zusammenfassung

1 Fragestellung, Methode und Gegenstand der Arbeit

Laienanhänger[542] oder die nicht-mönchischen Buddhisten[543] *„upāsaka“ (m.) „upāsikā“* (f.) bilden die Mehrheit in einer buddhistischen Gesellschaft. Sie zeichnen sich dadurch aus, dass sie ihren Glauben an die sog. „Drei Juwelen“ ausdrücken: Buddha (Samaṇa Gotama), Dhamma (seine Lehre) und Sangha (seine Gemeinde). Im Allgemeinen werden sie als Gegenstück zu mönchischen Anhängern in einer Institution betrachtet, die im Vergleich dazu eine untergeordnete Rolle als Unterstützer spielen. Das Image der Laienanhänger im Pāli-Kanon, bzw. in Nikaya-Diskursen, wird jedoch manchmal im Kontrast dazu so präsentiert, dass die Menschen mit dem Buddha die Lehre auch lernen und praktizieren. Wissenschaftler haben diese Frage erforscht; ihre Arbeiten führen zu den unterschiedlichsten Ergebnissen. Freiberger kam zu dem Schluss, dass aufgrund der uneinheitlichen Begrifflichkeit in den Texten die so dargestellte Laienanhängerschaft nicht genau abgegrenzt werden könne.[544] Allerdings hält die Autorin die unterschiedlichen Bilder für Erscheinungsformen derjenigen Individuen, die als sogenannte Laienanhänger bezeichnet werden. Zur Abgrenzung muss man sich mit den folgenden Fragen zur buddhistischen Laienanhängerschaft befassen: Welches Konzept verbindet als Prinzip diese Menschen ? Wie und aus welchem Teil des Kanons sollte die Anhängerschaft grundlegend beobachtet werden ?

Diese Arbeit zielt deswegen darauf ab, die Laienanhängerschaft aus dem Erscheinungsbild zu untersuchen, wie es sich im Nikaya-Diskurs wiederspiegelt. Ziel ist es zunächst, herauszufinden, wie das Heilsziel erreicht

542 Der Begriff wird nach Oliver Freiberger in seinem Werk „Der Orden in der Lehre“ (2000) benutzt.

543 In der englischen Schrift wird das Wort Laie oder „laity“ auf Englisch durchgehend vermieden, weil es christliche Meinungen konnotiert, die im Kontext des Pāli-Kanons nicht enthalten sind. Zur Vermeidung christlicher Begriffe macht die Autorin eindeutig einen Unterschied mit der Benennung zwischen mönchischen und nicht-mönchischen Anhängern, um zu zeigen, dass die beiden grundsätzlich Anhänger des Buddha sind.

544 Freiberger, Ein Vinaya für Hausbewohner?, S. 242.

werden kann, ein nicht-mönchischer Anhänger im Buddhismus zu werden. Auf Grund der original im Kontext einer mündlichen Kultur konzipierten Textgestalt sollte der Diskurs mit Hilfe einer passenden Methodik in Übereinstimmung mit charakteristischen Eigenschaften der Mündlichkeit untersucht werden.

Die Arbeit besteht deswegen aus zwei Teilen: an den ersten Teil, die philologische Analyse des Textes, der den Prozess der Begegnung zwischen Buddha und Hörer beschreibt, schließt sich im zweiten Teil dessen Interpretation an, um die Entstehung religiöser Gemeinschaft zu verstehen.

Unter Beachtung der typisch philologischen Charakteristik des Pāli-Diskurses untersucht die Autorin insbesondere die Diskurse in den Dīgha- und Majjhima-nikāyas. Entsprechend der Arbeit schildert fast jeder Diskurs eine Geschichte, in der erzählt wird, wie der Buddha zunächst eine Person oder Personengruppe belehrt hat, in welcher der Hörer zum ersten Mal mit dem Ruf des Buddha von ihrem Anfang an konfrontiert wird; nach dem Ende des Gespräches oder der Predigt enthält diese in der Standardformel sodann die Zufriedenheit des Hörers und das daraus resultierende Glaubensbekenntnis an die „Drei Juwelen"; und wie der Buddha seinen Nachfolger, sowohl Mönche als auch Laienanhänger, weiter angewiesen hat. Deshalb erachtet die Autorin dieser Darstellung, die die Hauptbotschaft eines mündlichen Textes enthält, dass eine Theorie der religiösen Erfahrung dabei anwendbar sein sollte, um dieses Erscheinungsbild zu verstehen, in dem das Ziel, der Pfad zum Ziel, und die Variationen des Pfads in Bezug auf die Entfaltung analysiert werden können. In der Anwendung dieser Theorie spiegelt sich mithin der mentale Prozess hinter der Standardformel und der Religiosität. Durch den Fokus auf die Entwicklung und das Werden des Nachfolgers wird das Konzept der buddhistischen Laienanhänger entwickelt. Auf diese Weise kann dieser Verlauf des buddhistischen Glaubens nach der von Taves entwickelten Methode verglichen werden.

	Begegnung und Erkenntnis		**Religiöse Erfahrung**		**Religiöser Ausdruck**
Taves	Einige Dinge als speziell eingeschätzt	→	Erfahrung als speziell eingeschätzt	→	Glaube und Religiosität
Diese Studie	Buddhas Predigten	→	(Nicht beschrieben)	→	Zufriedenheit / Glaubensbekenntnis

Die obige Tabelle zeigt, dass die Entwicklung des Glaubens und der Prozess der Bekehrung mit Hilfe der Theorie von Taves untersucht werden können. Gemäß den Diskursen ist die Geschichte der Mission Buddhas und seiner Predigten vergleichbar mit den Themen, die die Hörer als besonders einschätzen. Beim Hören der Predigten, wie der Text mit den zwei unterschiedlichen Typen von Standardformeln impliziert, erreicht der Zuhörer Befriedigung mit deren Inhalt oder glaubt dem Buddha, so dass er den Glauben an die „Drei Juwelen" erklärt und den Buddha um Erlaubnis bittet, dessen Anhänger zu werden. In dieser Hinsicht ist es wichtig, Fragen an jedes Wort in den Formelsätzen zu stellen, welche Bedeutung, Absicht oder Gedanken hinter dem Gesagten steht, die aus dem Kontext repräsentiert und impliziert werden.

2 Ergebnisse der Arbeit

Die Ergebnisse der Arbeit werden in drei Teilen berichtet: Erstens das Ergebnis der philologischen Frage nach der Struktur und mündlichen Stilistik in den Diskursen, zweitens die religiöse Erfahrung in Erwiderung auf das Gesagte des Buddha, und drittens die folgenden Tätigkeiten nach der religiösen Erfahrung.

2.1 Ergebnis der philologischen Studie zu dem Pāli-Diskurs

Die standardisierten Schlussphrasen, wie sie sich in den Diskursen in Dīgha- und Majjhima-nikāya finden lassen, folgen drei Typen:

Typ I:[545]

(1) *Idam avoca [Bhagavā],*[546] *attamanā [te bhikkhū]*[547] *[Bhagavato] bhāsitaṃ abhinandun-ti*

545 Die Phrase (2) ist eine Nebenform der Phrase (1). Siehe für diese und die folgenden „stock phrases" die Übersetzungen in Appendix III.

546 An dieser Stelle in den Parenthesen steht das Wort mit anderen Namen der Prediger, zum Beispiel eines Oberjüngers, in anderen Diskursen.

547 An dieser Stelle in den Parenthesen steht das Wort mit anderen Namen der Hörer, zum Beispiel eines Mannes oder eines Volks, in anderen Diskursen.

ODER

(2) Itiha te ubho mahānāgā aññamaññassa subhāsitaṃ samanumodiṃsûti

Der Typ drückt Zufriedenheit mit dem Inhalt der Predigt aus, die positive Gefühle als Reaktion auf die gegebene Antwort ausdrückt; sie erfüllt zugleich das Interesse des Zuhörers oder beseitigt seine Zweifel. Nach dieser Interpretation kann es so verstanden werden, dass der Hörer buddhistisch geworden ist oder dem Buddha bekannt haben soll, und auf diese Weise etwas von seiner Lehre erkannt hat. Das Gespräch oder die Predigt des Buddha wird seinem Verständnis gerecht, das sich irgendwie oder einigermaßen positiv auf das buddhistische Verständnis des Hörers auswirkt.

Typ II: Die formelle Erklärung des Glaubens an den Buddhismus besteht aus drei Teilen: (3) der Bewunderung von Buddhas Predigt, (4) der Erklärung, zu den „Drei Juwelen“ Zuflucht zu nehmen, und der Bitte, (5) *upāsaka* „nicht-mönchischer Anhänger“ oder (6) *bhikkhu*[548] „mönchischer Anhänger“ zu werden:

(3) Seyyathā pi bhante nikkujjitaṃ vā ukkujjeyya paṭicchannaṃ vā vivareyya mūḷhassa vā maggaṃ ācikkheyya andhakāre vā tela-pajjotaṃ dhāreyya: “cakkhumanto rūpāni dakkhintî” ti evam eva Bhagavatā aneka-pariyāyena dhammo pakāsito.

(4) Esâhaṃ bhante Bhagavantaṃ saraṇaṃ gacchāmi dhammañ ca bhikkhu-saṅghañ ca.

(5) Upāsakaṃ maṃ bhagavā dhāretu ajjatagge pāṇupetaṃ saraṇaṃ gataṃ.

ODER

(6) Labheyyāhaṃ bhante bhagavato santike pabbajjaṃ, labheyyaṃ upasampadan-ti.

Diese Formelsprache ist generell in einem Diskurs, in dem der Hörer dem Buddha zumeist zum ersten Mal begegnet und ihn dabei einigermaßen, beispielsweise mit einer Frage, herausfordert. Manchmal wird

548 Dabei gibt es keine *bhikkhunī* „Nonne“ sowie *upāsikā* „Laienanhängerin,“ die in einem Nikāya-Diskurs mit den Schlussphrasen erzählt wird.

die Herausforderung wegen des Unterschieds in dem religiösen Glauben des Hörers ausgegeben, welche der Buddha mit Antworten aufgrund seines Standpunktes besiegt. Zum Ende erklärt der Hörer folgendermaßen den buddhistischen Glauben nach den stereotypischen Formelsätzen. Deswegen können zwei Weisen unterschieden werden: Einerseits können die Phrasen nach der Tradition als Ankündigung des Glaubens angesehen werden, welche die Konversion des Hörers zum buddhistischen Glauben zeigen. Andererseits können die Phrasen symbolisch den Dissenz in der Debatte mit dem Buddha repräsentieren, besonders wenn der Hörer kein mönchischer Nachfolger des Buddha wird und in seinem religiösen Status bleibt.

Typ III: Das Erreichen einer Heilserfahrung besteht aus (7) dem Hören der *Ānupubbikathā*-Predigt und (8) der Erfahrung der *dhammacakkhu*. Die formalisierten Schlussphrasen dieses Typs bezeichnen eine außergewöhnliche Erfahrung beim Hören der Predigt, die gelegentlich Seite an Seite in Verbindung mit dem Typ II der Schlussphrasen auftaucht.

(7) Ekamantaṃ nisinnassa kho [brāhmaṇassa Pokkharasādissa] Bhagavā ānupubbikathaṃ kathesi seyyathīdaṃ dānakathaṃ sīlakathaṃ saggakathaṃ kāmānaṃ ādinavaṃ okāraṃ saṃkilesaṃ nekkhamme ānisaṃsaṃ pakāsesi. Yadā bhagavā aññāsi [brāhmaṇaṃ Pokkharasādiṃ] kallacittaṃ mudu-cittaṃ vinīvaraṇa-cittaṃ udagga-cittaṃ pasanna-cittaṃ atha yā buddhānaṃ sāmukkaṃsikā dhammadesanā taṃ pakāsesi: dukkhaṃ samudayaṃ nirodhaṃ maggaṃ. Seyyathā pi nāma suddhaṃ vatthaṃ apagata-kāḷakaṃ sammad eva rajanaṃ patigaṇheyya.

(8) Evameva kho [brāhmaṇassa Pokkharasādissa] tasmiṃ yeva āsane virajaṃ vītamalaṃ Dhamma-cakkhuṃ udapādi: "yaṃ kiñci samudaya-dhammaṃ sabban taṃ nirodha-dhamman" ti. Atha kho [brāhmaṇo Pokkharasādi] diṭṭha-dhammo patta-dhammo vidita-dhammo pariyogaḷha-dhammo tiṇṇa-vikiccho vigata-kathaṃkatho vesārajjappatto aparapaccayo satthu sāsane.

Wegen des Zusatzes vom Typ II können diese Formelsätze als Ergänzung zu der Erklärung des buddhistischen Glaubens verstanden werden, die besonders das Ergebnis des Predigthörens charakterisieren. Die erwähnte Erfahrung, die *Dhammacakkhu* genannt werden kann, ist ungenau und noch umstritten, wie die Beschreibung in (8) heißt.[549] Dieser Punkt aber wird in dieser Arbeit nicht für wichtig gehalten, weil die gemeinte Erfahrung nicht auf diesen Kontext angewiesen ist. Nach der literalen Bedeutung der Formeln und dem Kontext soll diese Beschreibung der Erfahrung symbolisch als das vollständige Verständnis in der grundlegenden Lehre aus der von Buddha gegebenen *Ānupubbikathā*-Predigt interpretiert werden. Wegen dieser vollständigen Lehren hat der Hörer seinen Glauben vertiefen lassen, dass er einen unerschütterlichen Glauben an Buddha und seine Lehre hat. Diese Erfahrung ist nach der Tradition „Sotāpanna-Erreichen," mit dem der Mensch völlig buddhistisch das Heilsziel erreicht hat. Die Formel in diesem Typ impliziert die Wichtigkeit des Predigt-Hörens, die als Erziehung interpretiert werden kann, mit der ein Mensch sich in seinen Glauben an die Lehre vertiefen kann.

2.2 Entwicklung des Glaubens und Erfahrung

In den Diskursen wird die Entwicklung des Glaubens gezeigt, in der der Ruf des Buddha aus seinem Erleuchtetsein, seinem Wissen und seiner Art der Vermittlung beschrieben wird, sowie aus der physiognomischen Kenntnis über das *purisalakkhaṇa*, die 32 Merkmale auf dem Körper eines „Großen Mannes." In Übereinstimmung mit der in den Diskursen erwähnten Volkstradition werden manchen von ihnen besonders aufgeregt und angezogen, den Buddha zu besuchen. Der Glaube, wie er in den Diskursen abgeschlossen wird, findet seinen Ausdruck im Gebrauch der acht formalisierten Schlussphrasen, der auf vier unterschiedliche Äußerungsformen als Antworten auf die Predigten des Buddha in den Pāli-Diskursen hinweist:

Erste Ebene, die in den Formeln (3), (4), (6), (7) und (8) entwickelt wird: der Zuhörer erkennt den Inhalt der Predigt an und lässt sich davon beeindrucken, erklärt seine Zuflucht zu den „Drei Juwelen" und bittet um Anhängerschaft, die das „offizielle" Verfahren darstellt, um Laienhänger zu werden. In diesem Prozess erreichen sie *dhammacakkhu*, mit der der

549 Zwei Streitpunkte zwischen Masefield (1986), der diese Beschreibung für eine wichtige religiöse Erfahrung aus der Predigt des Buddha hält, und den Verteidigern, zum Beispiel Harrison (1987) und Hallisay (1988).

Zuhörer die buddhistische Lehre vollkommen versteht und unerschütterlichen Glauben an die Religion hat.

Zweite Ebene, die in den Formeln (3), (4) und (5) oder (6) auftaucht: der Zuhörer erkennt den Inhalt der Predigt an und lässt sich davon beeindrucken, erklärt die „Drei Juwelen" als seine Zuflucht und bittet um (5) nicht-mönchische oder (6) mönchische Anhängerschaft.

Dritte Ebene, in der die Formel (1) erwähnt wird: der Zuhörer erkennt und akzeptiert den Inhalt der Predigt, jedoch nicht die Zuflucht zu den „Drei Juwelen" und er bittet nicht um Anhängerschaft.

Vierte Ebene, in der keine Formel präsentiert wird: der Zuhörer erklärt nichts und hat keinen Glauben an den Buddha oder seine Lehre.

Aus der Kategorisierung des Glaubens in diese vier Ebenen ergibt sich, dass der Anhänger des Buddha oder der Buddhist nach der Tradition eine Person ist, die in gewissem Maß den Glauben hat, den er vor einem Zeugen zum Ausdruck gebracht hat. Diese Ausdrucksform ist in den standardisierten Formeln (3), (4), (5) und (6) stereotyp. Auf diese Weise können Bedeutung und Konsequenzen der standardisierten Formeln im Verhältnis zur gehörten Predigt einige Hinweise liefern über die religiöse Erfahrung, aus der gemäß dem Nikaya-Diskurs „der Buddhist" offiziell entsteht. Der Prozess dieser Entwicklung, die in den standardisierten Formeln enthalten ist, kann in zwei Schritten verstanden werden:

Erstens repräsentiert die Bewunderung in der Formel (3), dass der Zuhörer die in der Predigt übermittelte Botschaft verstanden hat, d.h. dass er zumindest teilweise die Bedeutung dieser Botschaft realisiert und bewertet hat. Die Botschaft repräsentiert das Dhamma, welches der Buddha mit Absicht in der Welt durch Gespräche oder Predigten verbreitet hat. Dies bedeutet, dass der Zuhörer eingesehen hat, wie sachlich, vernünftig und wahr diese Botschaft ist. Durch das Wissen über die Bedeutung und den Wert dieser Botschaft hat er diese mit anderen Lehren verglichen, die er gelernt hatte. In dieser Weise hat der Zuhörer realisiert, dass die Botschaft des Buddha wertvoll, weil erleuchtend für ihn ist; diese Erkenntnis findet ihren Ausdruck in der stereotypischen Standardformel.

Zweitens repräsentiert die Erklärung, zu den „Drei Juwelen" Zuflucht zu nehmen (4), das Gefühl der Verehrung für den Buddha, das Dhamma und den Sangha. Diese Formel ist der stereotype Ausdruck der Verehrung für den Buddhismus in späterer Zeit, als diese Institutionen zur Metapher geworden waren in den „Drei Juwelen". Dennoch, in Verbindung mit dem vorstehenden Kontext, hätte der Zuhörer dem Dhamma und dem Buddha Ehrerbietung gewähren sollen, die für ihn präsent waren. Diese Ehrerbietung hätte entstehen sollen aus der Bewertung des Dhamma, in dem der Zuhörer seine Bedeutung erkannt hatte. In dieser Beziehung stellt sich der Zuhörer vor, in welchem Ausmaß der Buddha mit seiner Predigt erleuchtet, allwissend und tiefgründig ist. In einigen Diskursen, in denen ein Oberjünger predigt, ist die Bedeutung von Sangha im Vergleich zu Buddha und Dhamma dadurch offensichtlich, dass der Mönch deshalb der Ehrerbietung wert sei, weil er ein Nachfolger des Buddha ist und deshalb der Übermittlung des Dhamma an die kommenden Generationen fähig ist.

2.3 Religiosität nach der Erfahrung in Bezug auf die Gemeinschaft

Aus der Erkenntnis ergibt sich das Vertrauen auf seine Lehre und seinen Pfad, dass diese Dinge zum echten Ziel leiten müssen. Dieses führt zu der Rückkehr zu dem Buddha und seiner Lehre, wobei die Anhänger für das als „speziell" eingeschätzte Ding im Kontakt zueinander stehen müssen, und demzufolge zu der Gemeinde, die durch die Herrschaft des Buddha und die sozial akzeptierten, religiösen Prägungen organisiert wird. Die hier behandelte Religiosität besteht aus drei Bestandteilen: erstens der Erklärung, zu Buddhas Anhängerschaft zu gehören; zweitens dem Ausdruck des Glaubens an den Buddha und drittens der Ergebenheit, die aus Spenden an die Gemeinschaft des Sangha besteht und aus der religiösen Erziehung.

Die Erklärung, zur Anhängerschaft des Buddha gehören zu wollen, bedeutet die „Bekehrung" zum Buddhismus als Folge der Erkenntnis, dass die Bedeutung des Dhamma und die Überlegenheit des Buddha erkannt und geglaubt wurden. Durch die Erklärung zur Anhängerschaft ist der Zuhörer ein Anhänger geworden, der eine in gewissem Maße aus der Predigt verstandene Kenntnis über die Lehre des Buddha zu erweitern hat, vergleichbar einem mönchischen Anhänger. Aus dieser Art der Bekehrung ergibt sich, dass diese Laienhänger lediglich die Bedeutung der Predigt und die Überlegenheit des Buddha erkannt haben, weil einige von den Erklärenden noch in früheren religiösen Gemeinschaften verbleiben. Die Erklärung bedeutet dabei, dass diese Menschen die Möglichkeit oder Absicht haben, sich selbst in Zukunft auf dem Heilsweg weiter zu entwickeln, weil sie für die Doktrin des Buddha offen sind und weiteren Gesprächen mit dem Buddha oder einem Mönch freudig entgegensehen.

In Bezug auf den Orden stellt sich heraus, dass die Laienanhänger sich der mönchischen Gemeinschaft aus der Erfahrung mit der Predigt dadurch unterwerfen, dass der Orden sowohl die Entwicklung der Lehre materiell unterstützt als auch durch Lernen und Praktizierung der Lehre ihre persönlichen, spirituellen Kenntnisse erweitert. Ohne durch klösterliche Regeln kontrolliert zu werden, haben diese Laienanhänger die Freiheit, ihr eigenes religiöses Leben zu führen. In dieser Freiheit können die Leute flexibler nach ihrem Interesse, ihrer Zeit oder Absicht etc., durch einige Aktivitäten die Lehre lernen und diese praktizieren, oder zu der Gemeinschaft eine Beziehung entwickeln. Sie können gelegentlich die mönchische Gemeinschaft besuchen, um nach Erläuterungen und Anweisungen hinsichtlich des Lernens oder der Praxis der Lehre zu fragen.

Wegen der Bekanntschaft und des Eindrucks durch den Orden sehen die Laienanhänger in der Mönchsgemeinde ein verdienstvolles Feld, das der Welt großen Nutzen bringt, ohne die Vorstellung von religiösem Verdienst, das durch Spenden der nicht-mönchischen Anhänger an die monastischen Anhänger entsteht. Das Gefühl der Einheit wird dadurch angezeigt, dass die nicht-mönchischen Anhänger für die Gemeinschaft des Sangha in seinen Gedanken, seinem Weg und dem Ziel eines spirituellen Lebens empfinden. Unter diesem Aspekt können die Laienanhänger als Zugehörige zur Gemeinschaft gerechnet werden, die beabsichtigen, sich eines Tages dem Heilsweg anzuschließen und damit das Heilsziel zu erreichen, das der Buddha seinen Anhängern gewiesen hat.

Die Arbeit deutet den Erfolg der religiösen, emischen Theorie bei der Analyse der Beziehungen religiöser Menschen innerhalb der Gesellschaft an, wie sie in den Texten repräsentiert wird; diese Texte stellen die religiösen Strukturen an sich dar. Das Ergebnis spiegelt die Tatsache über Religion, dass diese eine Form von sozialer Organisation darstellt, die gemeinsam auf einem speziellen Glauben der Menschen an ein Objekt, an eine Person oder eine Lehre basiert und zu Vorzugsbehandlungen dieses speziellen Glaubens führt. Der Sangha in dieser Beziehung bezeichnet deshalb eine Versammlung von Leuten, die die gleiche Ideologie des Lehrers und damit seine Lehre teilen, die identischen spirituellen Ziele und den gleichen Weg dorthin. Die Arbeit hat außerdem einen Beitrag geleistet zur Kenntnis über die Laienanhänger in den Dīgha- und Majjhima-nikāyas. Diese Studie hat gezeigt, dass die Laien in den Schriften existieren, allerdings präsentiert dieses Konzept die Laien ausschließlich in der einzigartigen Weise der mündlichen Überlieferung. Forscher sollten sich dieses Aspekts bewusst sein und verstärkt Studien zur Mündlichkeit der buddhistischen Schriften erarbeiten.

Im Verhältnis zur mündlichen Tradition, durch die die Diskurse entwickelt worden sind, zielt das durch die Themen und die formalistische Sprache gewonnene Konzept der Laienanhänger darauf ab, die Bedeutung der Predigt und der Homiletik als Weg zur spirituellen Entwicklung des Einzelnen im Buddhismus zu begünstigen. Insbesondere zeigt es, dass der Predigt die Bedeutung zukommt, die Anhänger von normalen Menschen, die keine Anhänger des Buddha sind, zu den Anhängern des Buddha zu wandeln, welche die Bedeutung der „Drei Juwelen" anerkennen, sowie Anhänger des Buddha zu denen, die als „Heilige" einen unerschütterlichen Glauben an Buddha und seine Lehre haben. Diese Folge kann als Vermittlung aus der Tradierung der Pāli-Tradition angesehen werden, dass die Spiritualität im Buddhismus aus der Rezeption der Lehre bzw. dem Lernen der Schriften entwickelt werden kann. Dies ist vielleicht ein besonderer Aspekt, der in dem Text der mündlichen Tradition betont wird, dass sich die vollständigen Lehren des Buddha durch Hören vertiefen lassen. In ähnlicher Weise kann eine Quasi-Antwort auf die Erscheinung des Buddhismus gegeben werden, nach den Perspektiven z.B. der Moral oder der Meditation, oder von einem lehrenden oder praktizierenden Mönch. Daraus ergibt sich die Antwort, dass Buddhismus nachdrücklich von den grundlegenden Regeln, oder von der Meditation geprägt wird.

Aus der Forschungserfahrung mit diesem Thema möchte die Autorin zwei Vorschläge machen, erstens zur Methodologie der Analyse des buddhistischen Texts und zweitens zum Phänomen des Inklusivismus. Hinsichtlich der Methodologie hat die Studie gezeigt, dass eine Theorie der religiösen Erfahrung, wie von Ann Taves entwickelt, anwendbar ist auf die Erforschung des Buddhismus, der als eine rationale Religion betrachtet wird, weil das Phänomen Buddhismus analysiert werden kann als verschiedene Beziehungen in unterschiedlichsten Ebenen der sozialen

Organisation. Diese komplexen Verbindungen können mithin in jedem Kontext untersucht werden, d.h. in den Schriften selbst oder in einem sozialen und kulturellen Kontext. Hinsichtlich der inklusivistischen Tendenz, insbesondere derjenigen zum Animismus, kann die Theorie der religiösen Erfahrung angewendet werden auf lokale Kulte in Beziehung zu den „Drei Juwelen", die als überlegen zu jedem anderen Wesen dargestellt werden und die angebetet werden wegen ihres Versprechens von Leben und Glückseligkeit. In dieser Beziehung erkennen die Buddhisten die Bedeutung und die Überlegenheit der „Drei Juwelen" an; allerdings können sie nicht korrekt wissen, in welcher Weise die Juwelen für sie bedeutungsvoll sind. Dies zeigt die Wichtigkeit der religiösen Erziehung für den Buddhismus, der die Menschen auf den Pfad führt, den der Buddha gewiesen hat.

RELIGIONSWISSENSCHAFT

Herausgegeben von Horst Bürkle, Manfred Hutter, Johannes Laube (†) und Hans-Joachim Klimkeit (†)

Band 1 Ketut Waspada: Harmonie als Problem des Dialogs. Zur Bedeutung einer zentralen religiösen Kategorie in der Begegnung des Christentums mit dem Hinduismus auf Bali. 1988.

Band 2 Xinping Zhuo: Theorien über Religion im heutigen China und ihre Bezugnahme zu Religionstheorien des Westens. 1988.

Band 3 Christoph Bochinger: Ganzheit und Gemeinschaft. Zum Verhältnis von theologischer und anthropologischer Fragestellung im Werk Bruno Gutmanns. 1987.

Band 4 Thomas Puttanil: A Comparative Study of the Theological Methodology of Irenaeus of Lyon and Sankaracharya. 1990.

Band 5 Philippe Dinzolele Nzambi: Proverbes bibliques et proverbes kongo. Étude comparative de Proverbia 25-29 et de quelques proverbes kongo. 1992.

Band 6 Horst Bürkle (Hrsg.): Grundwerte menschlichen Verhaltens in den Religionen. 1993.

Band 7 Soegeng Hardiyanto: Zwischen Phantasie und Wirklichkeit. Der Islam im Spiegel des deutschen Denkens im 19. Jahrhundert. 1992.

Band 8 Bernd Sebastian Jürgens: B.R. Ambedkar - Religionsphilosophie eines Unberührbaren. 1994.

Band 9 Christoph Kleine: Hōnens Buddhismus des Reinen Landes: Reform, Reformation oder Häresie? 1996.

Band 10 Dieter Zeller (Hrsg.): Religion im Wandel der Kosmologien. 1999.

Band 11 Manfred Hutter (Hrsg.): Buddhisten und Hindus im deutschsprachigen Raum. Akten des Zweiten Grazer Religionswissenschaftlichen Symposiums (2.-3. März 2000). 2001.

Band 12 Hans-Bernd Zöllner: Buddhadasa Bhikkhu (1906–1993). Buddhismus im *Garten der Befreiung*. 2006.

Band 13 Franz Winter: Das frühchristliche Mönchtum und der Buddhismus. Religionsgeschichtliche Studien. 2008.

Band 14 Christiane Schulze: „Frieden durch Religion" – ein japanisches Modell. Das interreligiöse Friedensprogramm der Risshō Kōsei-kai (1957–1991). 2008.

Band 15 Manfred Hutter (Hrsg.): Religionsinterne Kritik und religiöser Pluralismus im gegenwärtigen Südostasien. 2008.

Band 16 Karl-Heinz Golzio: Die Ausbreitung des Buddhismus in Süd- und Südostasien. Eine quantitative Untersuchung auf der Basis epigraphischer Quellen. 2010.

Band 17 Gabriele Reifenrath: „I´m a Hindu and I´m a Swaminarayan". Religion und Identität am Beispiel von Swaminarayan-Frauen in Großbritannien. 2010.

Band 18 Lauren Drover: Christen in Thailand. Am Beispiel der Karen und der Akha. 2012.

Band 19 Kenneth Fleming: Buddhist-Christian Encounter in Contemporary Thailand. 2014.

Band 20 Sompornnuch Tansrisook: *Non-Monastic Buddhist* in Pāli-Discourse. Religious Experience and Religiosity in Relation to the Monastic Order. 2014.

www.peterlang.com